COGNITIVE FUNCTIONING AND SOCIAL STRUCTURE OVER THE LIFE COURSE

COGNITIVE FUNCTIONING AND SOCIAL STRUCTURE OVER THE LIFE COURSE

Edited By
Carmi Schooler
National Institute of Mental Health
Bethesda, Maryland

and

K. Warner Schaie
Pennsylvania State University
University Park, PA

1947

With the Assistance of Paula Darby Lipman

Ablex Publishing Corporation
Norwood, New Jersey

Library of Congress Cataloging-in-Publication Data

Cognitive functioning and social structure over the life course.
    Bibliography: p.
    Includes index.
    1. Cognition. 2. Human information processing. 3. Developmental psychology. I. Schooler, Carmi. II. Schaie, K. Warner (Klaus Warner), 1928–00.
BF311.C5516   1987   153   86-32056
ISBN 0-89391-410-X

Ablex Publishing Corporation
355 Chestnut Street
Norwood, N.J. 07648

Contents

Acknowledgments

This book is the result of the inspiration of Matilda White Riley of the National Institute of Aging, who saw a need and took the steps to fulfill it. She, together with Paul Baltes of the Max-Planck Institute (Berlin), convened the first of the series of conferences upon which this book is based and has subsequently borne a major responsibility for the continuance of the series.

We would also like to thank Paula Darby Lipman for her invaluable assistance in all of the stages of this book and the conferences upon which it is based. She, together with Pearl Slafkes, did much of the work on the subject index. Pearl Slafkes, Zita Givens, Virginia Marbley, Margaret Renfors and Ann Shuey, assisted in various other aspects of manuscript preparation. Without all of this excellent assistance, preparing this book would have been a much more onerous and much less pleasant task.

About the Authors

1. What are theories of adult intellectual development theories of?

Robert J. Sternberg is IBM Professor of Psychology and Education in the Department of Psychology at Yale University, where he is also Director of Graduate Studies. His main interests are in human intelligence and the psychology of love. Sternberg is currently developing a new test of intelligence based upon his triarchic theory of intelligence, and has previously developed an intellectual skills training program based on this same theory. *Cynthia Berg* is a Doctoral Candidate in the Department of Psychology at Yale University. Her research interests include cognitive and intellectual development across the life span, with an emphasis on everyday problem solving, people's intuitive ideas about intelligence, and adult spatial cognition and aging.

2. Psychological effects of complex environments during the life span: A review and theory

Carmi Schooler, Senior Investigator, Laboratory of Socio-Environmental Studies, National Institute of Mental Health, pursues a wide-ranging series of research projects on the social-structural and cultural determinants of psychological functioning across the life-span.

3. Applications of psychometric intelligence to the prediction of everyday competence in the elderly

K. Warner Schaie is Professor of Human Development and Psychology at the Pennsylvania State University where he also directs the Gerontology Center. His research interests are in cognitive development in adulthood and research methodology for the study of life-span problems in developmental psychology in the context of the broader environment.

4. Age-related differences in visual information processing: qualitative or quantitative?

Geoffrey Loftus received his undergraduate degree from Brown University in 1967 and his Ph.D. from Stanford University in 1971, both in Experimental Psychology. He was a Post Doctoral Fellow with George Sperling at New York University from 1971–72. Since 1972, he has been full time on the University of Washington faculty where he is currently a full professor. His research has been in the areas of human perception, memory and information processing. He has also worked on methodology and measurement in the social sciences.

5. On the nature of expertise

Robert Glaser is founder and director of the Learning Research and Development Center at the University of Pittsburgh, where he is University Professor of Psychology and Education. His current research focuses on the acquisition of knowledge and skill in subject-matter learning, expertise in scientific and technical fields, and the use of computers in instruction and research.

6. Theory-guided analysis of mechanisms of development and aging through testing-the-limits and research on expertise

Reinhold Kliegl, Ph.D., is a research scientist at the Max Planck Institute for Human Development and Education, Berlin. His research focuses on the formation of expert knowledge and on cognitive adaptivity and development in adulthood and old age. Paul B. Baltes, Ph.D., is Co-director of the Max Planck Institute for Human Development and Education, Berlin, and professor of psychology at the Free University of Berlin. His specialization is in life-span developmental psychology and the study of plasticity and constraints in cognitive development.

7. On the growth of knowledge and the decentralization of *g* in adult intellectual development

William J. Hoyer is Professor of Psychology at Syracuse University. He received his Ph.D. in experimental psychology and life-span developmental psychology from West Virginia University in 1972. His primary area of research is cognitive behavior in adulthood and old age, with emphasis on the investigation of age-related changes in visual attention, cognitive capacity, and decision-making. He has authored over fifty research articles in the area of cognitive aging.

8. Age, experience and compensation

Timothy A. Salthouse is Professor of Psychology in the School of Psychology at Georgia Institute of Technology. His major research interests are the reasons for age-related effects in cognitive functioning, and the contribution of experience in minimizing the consequences of those effects.

9. Longevity, social structure and cognitive aging

Ronald P. Abeles is Deputy Associate Director of the Behavioral Sciences Research program at the National Institute on Aging. After receiving his doctoral degree in social psychology from Harvard University, he was a postdoctoral fellow in psychology and political science at Yale University, an assistant professor in the Department of Psychology, Boston University, and on the staff of the Social Science Research Council. While at the American Institutes for Research, he conducted research on the interrelationships of work and personality and on the consequences of temporal patternings of life events for individuals' socioeconomic outcomes. *Matilda White Riley* is Associate Director of the Behavioral Sciences Research program at the National Institute on Aging and professor emeritus of sociology, Rutgers University and Bowdoin College. She was President of the American Sociological Association in 1986. She has worked extensively in the fields of research methodology, mass communications, and the sociology of age and aging. Her publications include *Sociological Traditions from Generation to Generation* (with R.K. Merton; Ablex, 1980), *Aging from Birth to Death: Interdisciplinary Perspectives* (AAAS Selected Symposium 30; Westview, 1979), and *Aging and Society* (3 volumes; Russell Sage Foundation, 1968–1972).

10. Continuity of learning-generalization through the life span: The effect of job on men's intellectual process in the United States and Poland

At the time that Joanne Miller, Kazimierz M. Slomczynski, and Melvin L. Kohn wrote "Continuity of Learning-Generalization," all three were members of the Laboratory of Socio-environmental Studies of the National Institute of Mental Health. *Joanne Miller* is now associate professor of sociology at City University of New York—Queens College. She is conducting research on the structure and legitimation of authority relations in work organizations. *Kazimierz Slomczynski* is at present a fellow at Osaka University, on leave from his position as associate professor of sociology at the University of Warsaw. He is conducting comparative research on social structure and personality in Poland and Japan. *Melvin Kohn* is a professor of sociology at Johns Hopkins University; his principal current interest is cross-national comparative research, focusing on the study of social stratification and the inter-generational transmission of values.

11. Learning and life-course accomplishments

Herbert J. Walberg was awarded a Ph.D. in educational psychology by the University of Chicago in 1964, and held research appointments at that university, Educational Testing Service, and the University of

Wisconsin and taught at Rutgers and Harvard University. Now Research Professor of Education at the University of Illinois at Chicago, his main research interest is the educational promotion of human development.

12. A developmental epidemiological perspective on social adaptation and cognitive function

Sheppard G. Kellam is Professor and Chairman of the Department of Mental Hygiene at The Johns Hopkins School of Hygiene and Public Health with joint appointments in Psychiatry and Behavioral Sciences. Over many years he has been involved in research on developmental epidemiology and psychopathology, and with designing and implementing preventive trials directed at risk behaviors of children, most recently in Baltimore.

13. Sociocultural determination of mental aging

David R. Heise, Professor of Sociology at Indiana University, Bloomington, developed Affect Control Theory to understand the emotional bases of social interaction. Additionally, he has published articles and books on personality and socialization, and he is a past editor of *Sociological Methodology* and of *Sociological Methods and Research.*

Foreword:

Carmi Schooler and Warner K. Schaie

In August 1983, Matilda White Riley of the National Institute on Aging and Paul B. Baltes of the Max-Planck Institute (Berlin) convened a planning group to consider new directions for research on intellectual and cognitive processes in middle and later life. One emergent theme was the need for conceptualization of and research on the influence of social structural factors on intellectual functioning during the different phases of adulthood. While cognitive psychologists had developed elaborate models of intellectual functioning, they had only begun to offer explanations for interindividual differences in functioning as people grow older. The participants of the interdisciplinary planning group suggested that some aspects of social structure may provide important clues towards understanding systematic sources of interindividual differences.

Consequently, a two-day workshop was held in September, 1984 at the National Institutes of Health in Bethesda, Maryland, co-sponsored by the National Institute on Aging and the Max-Planck Institute (Berlin). The goal of this workshop was to focus on the interplay between changes in intellectual functioning and the changing social roles which people hold at different phases of their lives. The workshop was conceived as an interdisciplinary attempt to: 1) specify the dynamic linkages between social structure and the changing nature and processes of intellectual functioning as people move through the life course, 2) enlarge the concept of intellectual functioning as it pertains to the special conditions of middle and later life.

Prior to this workshop, cognitive scientists, life-span psychologists, and sociologists had generally not examined the relationship between social structural factors and cognitive development over the life course, but had instead focused more narrowly on research problems seen as important by fellow workers within their respective fields. The conference goal, then, was to begin the process of breaking down the disciplinary barriers that had impeded the study of how cognitive functioning is affected over the life course by social structure.

Careful attention was paid to the selection of participants to include only those who were known from their previous work to be sympathetic to an interdisciplinary approach, and whose substantive work was considered to be at the leading edge of their respective fields. For this volume, thirteen chapters have been selected from the papers presented at that conference. They are presented in three groups that approach the basic theme from different perspectives. Part One includes four chapters that provide theoretical and empirical approaches to the study of cognitive functioning within the context of the everyday environment. These are followed by the four chapters of Part Two that provide empirical and theoretical material summarizing current research on experience and expertise as components of intellectual functioning in middle and latter life. The five chapters in Part Three specify how social structure impacts on individual development over the life course.

While all of the chapters reflect the forefront of research in their respective fields, each has implications that reach beyond its immediate area of concern toward a more broadbased investigation of the relationship of social structure to cognitive functioning over the life course. In the Afterword we draw out some of the common substantive and theoretical themes. Based on these themes we suggest possible next steps to be taken toward a deeper understanding of how individuals' ways of thinking are affected by their successive positions in the social structure as they pass through the various phases of their lives. Answers to these questions are necessary to successfully deal with the social and psychological concomitants of the dramatic increase in longevity that is now taking place.

Part I
COGNITIVE
FUNCTIONING

Chapter One

What Are Theories of Adult Intellectual Development Theories of?

Robert J. Sternberg
Cynthia A. Berg

In recent years, there have been two fundamental and active debates regarding the nature of adult intellectual development. The first debate concerns changes in *levels* of intelligence with age. The second concerns changes in the *nature* of intelligence with age. The major claim of this chapter is that neither of these debates has been entirely well-conceived. The first debate, over levels of intelligence, assumes that what is meant by intelligence remains static across adult age levels. If the meaning of intelligence is dynamic, however, over adult intellectual development, then it is not possible globally to compare intelligence across age levels. We shall claim that limited comparisons are possible, but only of those aspects of intelligence that are indeed the same across the age span. The second debate, over the nature of intelligence, has represented a confused state of affairs in which different answers to different questions have been taken to be different answers to the same questions. When the confusion is resolved, the second debate proves to be highly relevant to resolving the first.

We wish to acknowledge at the outset that chronological age may not be an ideal variable to index changes in levels of intelligence and

We would like to thank K. Warner Schaie and Carmi Schooler for their comments on an earlier draft of this paper.

Preparation of this report was supported in part by Contract N0001483K0013 from the Office of Naval Research and Army Research Institute. An earlier version of the report was presented at a conference sponsored by the National Institute on Aging, Bethesda, Maryland, September 1984.

Request for reprints should be sent to Robert J. Sternberg, Department of Psychology, Yale University, Box 11A Yale Station, New Haven, Connecticut 06520.

changes in the nature of intelligence. Chronological age represents many influences on development other than simply maturational influences. For instance, the social and historical influences that affect an entire cohort (e.g., Baltes, Reese, & Lipsitt, 1980; Schaie, 1979) are associated with chronological age. Constructs such as functional age, biological age, psychological age, and distance from death have been offered as more appropriate variables for indexing changes that occur with time (Birren & Cunningham, 1985; Lieberman & Coplan, 1969). It is arguable, however, whether these alternative measures have proven more useful, thus far, than chronological age for indexing the age of the individual (Neugarten, 1977; Schaie & Hertzog, 1985). Recognizing these limitations of chronological age, we shall use it as the variable of interest in discussing changes in levels of intelligence and changes in the nature of intelligence, as it has predominated as the index for psychological changes that occur with time in life-span research.

LEVELS OF INTELLIGENCE

Consider first the question of levels of intelligence. Here, the question is whether in typical instances, a person's intelligence increases, remains the same, or decreases over age. The modern debate probably most directly traces back to work by Horn and Cattell (1966, 1967), in which it was claimed that whereas crystallized ability seems to increase throughout the life span, although at a decreasing rate in later years, fluid ability seems first to increase and later to decrease. In the Horn–Cattell conceptualization, crystallized ability is best measured by tests requiring knowledge of the cultural milieu in which one lives, for example, vocabulary and general information, whereas fluid ability is best measured by tests requiring mental manipulation of abstract symbols, for example, figural analogies and number series completions.

Schaie (1974) questioned what he called the "myth of intellectual decline," according to which some or all intellectual functions start to decline relatively early in adulthood. Schaie noted that cross-sectional studies tended to support the notion of relatively earlier intellectual decline, on the average, than did longitudinal studies. In his own work, Schaie combined cross-sectional and longitudinal methods, and interpreted his results as suggestive of less intellectual decline than was suggested by the Horn–Cattell formulation.

Horn and Donaldson (1976) attempted to refute Schaie's (1974) view, and also the view that what appeared to be a gradual intellectual decline in adulthood is in fact a decline appearing just before death (Jarvik, Eisdorfer, & Blum, 1973; Riegel & Riegel, 1972). The main thrust of Horn and Donaldson's argument was that the major evidence arguing against early intellectual decline in many (if not all) individuals was based upon "positive sampling bias and wishful thinking in the conduct and interpretation of research" (p. 701).

A reply by Baltes and Schaie (1976) seemed to defuse the debate and to call into question whether there was much substantive basis for the debate in the first place. These authors argued that Horn and Donaldson had seriously misrepresented the earlier positions taken by Schaie and Baltes, in that these authors did not totally reject the notion of some decline.

Their reply would certainly seem to defuse what had been a heated debate: All parties agree that some decline sometimes occurs, and the substantive question that no one has yet resolved is that of the exact circumstances that lead to increase, stability, or decline. These circumstances, according to Baltes and Schaie (see also Baltes, Dittmann-Kohli, & Dixon, 1984; Scheidt & Schaie, 1978; Willis & Schaie, 1986), will vary according to person, task, and situation of measurement.

Issues in psychology have a way of fading in irresolution rather than of cleanly disappearing following resolution. We suspect that the issue of the relation between age and levels of intelligence may be one such issue. Horn and his colleagues never really questioned whether there would be variability in the developmental course of different abilities as a function of person, task, or situational variables. The theory they advanced was one of what happens, on the average, for specified sets of tasks and situations. The position of Horn is that one kind of ability, fluid ability, declines with age, whereas another kind of ability, crystallized ability, does not decline with age. The early position of Schaie (1979) was that whereas there are declines in fluid ability, they are later and of a smaller magnitude than Horn had suggested. Even if one allows for plasticity (trainability of intelligence), multidimensionality (multiple aspects of intelligence), multidirectionality (multiple paths along which intelligence can develop), and interindividual variability (individual differences in intelligence and change in intelligence over age), which we suspect Horn would, the question of whether fluid abilities decline, on the average, remains.

The answer is theoretically important, in that it potentially resolves the question of whether the developmental function of levels of intelligence is or is not monotonically increasing. The answer is also practically important, in that it may have implications for issues such as retirement age, ability of older persons to fulfill certain job and personal responsibilities, and ability of older persons to make important decisions in their everyday lives (e.g., Stagner, 1985; Willis & Schaie, 1986). We therefore believe it important that the issue of levels of intelligence not be written off or ignored.

In order to determine whether levels of intelligence decrease in old age, one must first determine what intelligence is during adulthood, and particularly, whether it is the same thing that it is at younger ages. To clarify this point, we would like to introduce a distinction made in the psychometric literature between observed and latent variables (Schaie & Hertzog, 1985). Observed variables are those variables that can actually be measured and assessed through observation or testing. For example, scores on measures of intelligence, such as the Number Subtest (consisting of questions regarding simple arithmetic calculations) on the Thurstones' Test of Primary Mental Abilities (Thurstone & Thurstone, 1949) are observable variables. Latent variables are abstract concepts that are theoretically defined and only imperfectly revealed through observed variables. For instance, intelligence itself is a latent variable in that no one measure of mental functioning perfectly measures intelligence. Intelligence is typically not considered to be a unitary construct and can be thought to consist of several other latent variables. For example, intelligence has often been thought to consist of the latent variables verbal and nonverbal intelligence (see Botwinick, 1977; Cattell, 1971; Wechsler, 1958). The selection of latent variables that comprise intelligence is largely determined by one's theory of intelligence and has ranged from few latent constructs (e.g., Cattell, 1971; Spearman, 1927) to several (Gardner, 1983; Guilford, 1967; Horn, 1982; Thurstone, 1938).

The issue that we are addressing is that the latent variables that comprise intelligence may not be the same for adults of various ages or may not be of equal importance at various adult ages. If intelligence does not comprise the same latent variables at different ages during adulthood, then attempts to compare levels of intelligence in adulthood may be misguided. A less extreme possibility is that intelligence will comprise the same latent variables in adulthood, yet the observed variables necessary to measure the latent variables will differ with adult age. We consider these possibilities in the next section and consider their implication for the "levels" debate.

THE NATURE OF INTELLIGENCE

Consider next the question of the nature of intelligence over the adult life span. The first issue is whether or not intelligence comprises the same latent variables at various points during adult intellectual development. If the same latent variables are found to constitute intelligence at various adult ages, a second issue still remains, namely, if the same observable variables accurately measure these latent variables at various points during the adult life span. Until quite recently, the first issue has received little attention in comparison to the second issue. For example, psychometric conceptions of intelligence—such as Cattell and Horn's conception of fluid and crystallized abilities—typically assume that intelligence consists of the same latent mental abilities throughout the adult life span. A great deal of research has addressed the issue of age-related differences in how well certain observable tasks measure abilities such as fluid and crystallized abilities, an area of research concerned with measurement equivalence (see, e.g., Baltes & Nesselroade, 1970; Cohen, 1957; Schaie & Hertzog, 1985). However, the issue of measurement equivalence is primarily of interest when the first issue regarding changes in the latent structure of intellectual development has been adequately addressed.

New theoretical models of adult intellectual development such as the neofunctionalist position articulated by Baltes and his colleagues (see Baltes, et al., 1984; Dittmann-Kohli & Baltes, in press) and the reconceptualization of adult cognitive development proposed by Cavanaugh, Kramer, Sinnott, Camp, and Markley (1985), sugggest that intelligence may comprise slightly different latent variables over the adult life span, or at least that the weights of the latent variables that comprise intelligence may differ in their contribution to intelligence during adulthood. These models adopt a contextual view of intelligence, emphasizing the role of intelligence in adults' adaptation to their everyday environments. Baltes et al. (1984) and Cavanaugh et al. (1985), for instance, assert that everyday types of abilities are more characteristic of adult intellectual life and thus may more accurately reflect what intelligence consists of in later life than would more traditional cognitive abilities. Post-formal operational models (e.g., Commons, Richards, & Armon, 1983; Kramer, 1983; Labouvie-Vief, 1982; Pascual-Leone, 1983) of adult intellectual development have also examined the qualitative changes that may occur in the nature of intelligence with age, concentrating on the new cognitive structures that might emerge in adult intellectual life. These post-formal operational models attempt to explain how reasoning develops beyond the point, in early adolescence, at which the child can reason formally. Many post-formal operational models point to the increasingly complex social environment in adulthood as an instigator of structural change (see Cavanaugh et al., 1985).

Currently, however, these new theoretical models, which address the potentially changing nature of adult intellectual development, do not provide empirically based methods for determining how the subconstructs that contribute to intelligence might change over the adult life span. For instance, the approaches of Baltes et al. (1984) and Cavanaugh et al. (1985) do not specify empirically why everyday intellectual skills capture the nature of intelligence increasingly with age, nor do they delineate those everyday cognitive abilities that are indicative of intelligence. Post-formal operational models of adult intelligence have yet to identify the new nature of adult cognitive thought (e.g., relativistic, dialectical, etc.) and consequently have yet to demonstrate, unequivocally, a new stage of structural change in adult intellectual development.

We believe that in order fully to understand intelligence and how its nature changes over the life span, it is necessary to understand intelligence in terms of two kinds of theories of intelligence: explicit theories and implicit theories. Consider each of these two kinds of theories in turn.

Explicit theories of intelligence are constructed by behavioral scientists, and are tested on data collected from people performing tasks presumed to measure intelligent functioning. Often the construction of these theories is influenced by, as well as tested on, these data. Psychometric and information-processing theories of intelligence are examples of explicit theories of intelligence. Usually, a selected battery of psychometric tests or cognitive tasks is administered to individuals who vary in age over the life span, and then sources of stability and change over this span are investigated. A typical finding, for example, is that adults decrease in their speed of performance as they grow older, at least beyond a certain age (e.g., Cerella, Poon, & Williams, 1980; Salthouse, 1985). What findings such as these mean for adult intellectual development continues to be a matter of debate.

A problem with both psychometric and information-processing approaches, as well as with other approaches, is that if the latent constructs that are tapped through intellectual tasks administered to subjects are not equally appropriate as constructs constituting intelligence across the life span, then neither the psychometric approach, the information-processing approach, nor any other explicit approach will tell us how *intelligence* changes in level across the life span. In this case, observable measures of intelligence derived from such explicit approaches to intelligence would be unable to tell us about changes in level, because intelligence has changed in kind. A less serious problem would arise if it were found that the latent constructs that constitute intelligence are similar at different ages in adulthood, although the observable measures differ in their ability to index these latent variables. This latter problem has typically been addressed by assuming the equal relevance of the latent variables, thereby addressing only issues of measurement equivalence (Baltes & Nesselroade, 1970; Schaie & Hertzog, 1985).

One might argue that psychometric methods such as factor analysis do, indeed, allow one to detect changes in the nature of intelligence: After all, factorial structure may differ across age levels. But the changes in factor structure are nevertheless based on psychometric theories that assert the equal relevance of a given set of factors (latent variables) for measuring intelligence over the adult life span. It may be, however, that not only the factorial structure, but the factors themselves should differ over the life span, because intelligence as a construct has a different character at different points in adult intellectual development. Thus, some kind of guidance is needed regarding just how intelligence differs at various ages. Implicit theories can be helpful in determining what kinds of constructs are relevant for measuring intelligence at different age levels.

Implicit theories of intelligence are common-cultural notions of the nature of intelligence. They are people's conceptions of what intelligence is. Why should such conceptions be important? First, they are important because intelligence is, to some extent, a cultural invention. Neisser (1979), for example, asserts that an individual's intelligence is the degree to which that individual corresponds to his or her culture's prototype of an exceptionally intelligent person. Second, implicit theories are important because they form the basis for the type of informal assessments of people's intelligence that we make in our everyday lives. Many more assessments of intelligence are based on implicit theories (i.e., at job interviews and at social engagements) than are based on explicit theories (i.e., evaluations on the basis of intelligence tests). Goodnow (1984, 1986) posits that intelligence is less a quality that people possess a certain amount of and more a quality that is attributed to individuals through observations of their behaviors. Implicit theories of intelligence are thus important in delineating the culture's prototype of an intelligent person and in determining the basis upon which people make attributions of intelligence.

On the one hand, there are certain mental structures and processes that are a function of the way people are put together. What people say intelligence is has little to do with what structures and processes of thought reside, in some sense, in the head. On the other hand, what people say intelligence is does have quite a bit to do with the relevance of these structures and processes to the notion of intelligence at different points in the life span. Society dictates, through the implicit theories of its members, what constitutes intelligent behavior at different points in the life span.

Implicit theories give us a sense of the developmental tasks that are appropriate for evaluating an individual's intelligence at different points in the life span. It is possible, of course, that these tasks will cease to change after some arbitrary age, such as 16. Indeed, this is what the creators of the Stanford-Binet and other similar intelligence tests seem to have believed. But their belief was based on *their* implicit theories of intelligence over the life span. These implicit theories may be unrepresentative of society's, or at least contemporary society's. On this view, what is intelligent at a given point along the life span may change not only as a function of age, but also as a function of cohort.

Expectations for people change over time. As a result, so do our notions of intelligence.

Many theorists have acknowledged that the tasks involved in adapting to the environment change over age and are largely a function of the way society has structured social roles. The notion that life tasks change with adult development has been evidenced in theories such as Levinson's (1978) stage theory of the common social events that encompass adult development; Havighurst's (1972) concept of developmental tasks that are determined through social and psychological components; and Neugarten's (1977) idea of the life periods of adult development (socially defined periods of infancy, childhood, youth, young adulthood, middle age, young-old age, and old-old age). What is expected of a person of a given age in one society may differ from what is expected of a person at another age in that society as well as differ from what is expected of a person of the same age in another society or culture (e.g., Gutmann, 1977). Thus, what is considered to be "intelligent" behavior may vary as well from age to age within a culture and from culture to culture within an age level. In the extreme case, we do not evaluate the intelligence of a 6-month-old in terms of the same developmental tasks used to evaluate the intelligence of a 6-year-old. Similarly, we do not use the same tasks to evaluate the respective intelligences of a 6-year-old and a 60-year-old. Implicit theories, then, suggest the shift in emphasis among the latent constructs that comprise intelligence throughout intellectual development.

In sum, explicit theories have, in the past, been focused on the constancies in the nature of intelligence over the life span, although they may tell us something as well about the inconstancies. They have typically assumed constancies in the latent structure of intelligence in adult intellectual development. Implicit theories have, thus far, been focused on the inconstancies in the nature of intelligence over the life span, although they may tell us something about the constancies as well. They typically point out the dynamic nature of the constructs that comprise intelligence over the life span. The two kinds of theories do not have the same "epistemological" status: Explicit theories are invented and then tested through empirical data. Implicit theories are discovered through empirical data. The two kinds of data are different: For explicit theories, the relevant data are usually performances on cognitive tasks that are posited from theory to measure intelligence; for implicit theories, the relevant data are usually questionnaires that measure, directly or indirectly, what people conceive intelligence to be. Both kinds of theories are useful, in conjunction, to gain a full sense of just what constitutes intelligence at various points in the life span. We shall consider next the explicit theory and implicit theories that drive our own view of intelligence.

Table 1. Main Aspects of Intelligence According to Explicit (Triarchic) Theory

I. Componential Subtheory
    A. Metacomponents
        1. Recognizing existence of a problem
        2. Defining nature of the problem
        3. Selecting lower-order components to solve problem
        4. Selecting strategy into which to combine components
        5. Selecting a mental representation upon which strategy acts
        6. Allocating mental resources
        7. Solution monitoring
        8. Utilizing external feedback
    B. Performance Components (partial list)
        1. Encoding stimuli
        2. Inferring relations between stimuli
        3. Mapping higher-order relations between relations
        4. Applying old relations to new stimulus domains
        5. Comparing stimuli
        6. Justifying selected solutions
        7. Responding to stimuli
    C. Knowledge-Acquisition Components
        1. Selective encoding of information
        2. Selective combination of information
        3. Selective comparison of new to old information
II. Experiential Subtheory
    A. Dealing with relative novelty
    B. Automatizing information processing
III. Contextual Subtheory
    A. Adaptation to environment
    B. Shaping of environment
    C. Selection of environment

Explicit Theory

We have proposed a triarchic theory of adult intellectual development that begins its theory construction with the examination of the nature of intelligence both within and across age levels. The triarchic theory states that intelligence can be understood in terms of three aspects (Berg & Sternberg, 1985; Sternberg, 1984, 1985): its relation to the internal (mental) world of the individual; its relation to the experience of the individual; and its relation to the external world (environment) of the individual. We attempt only to summarize our conclusions here. A summary of the main aspects of the triarchic theory is shown in Table 1.

The relation of intelligence to the internal world of the individual is dealt with by a "componential subtheory" of intelligence. The componential subtheory posits executive processes—metacomponents—that control nonexecutive processes—performance components and knowledge-acquisition components—that execute the instructions of the metacomponents. A review of the literature on information processing by individuals of different ages reveals that, on the average, there can be little doubt that there are nearly universal declines in speed and some declines in accuracy of processing in old age. Although we would not argue with life-span psychologists regarding the plasticity of abilities (e.g., Baltes & Willis, 1982) and the existence of individual differences in amounts of change (Schaie, 1979), a vast amount of data (e.g., Berg & Sternberg, 1985; Cerella, et al., 1980; Hoyer, 1985; Reese & Rodeheaver, 1985; Salthouse, 1982, 1985) suggests that there are indeed some componential declines, on average, with age. Assessments of componential abilities of adults performing tasks that reflect their everyday competence are needed to determine whether these componential deficits are general across information-processing tasks and ability domains that encompass intellectual functioning. Research suggests that when the abilities under examination are of a more everyday nature and are abilities that are well-practiced, such as chess playing (Charness, 1981a, 1981b), bridge playing (Charness, 1983), and typing ability (Salthouse, 1984), the typical componential deficits of older adults are far less pronounced.

The relation of intelligence to the experience of the individual is dealt with by an "experiential subtheory" of intelligence. The experiential subtheory posits that the components of intelligence operate at different levels of experience with a task or situation, and that the two levels most relevant for assessing intelligence are those that occur when the components are operating in a relatively novel fashion or are in the process of becoming automatized (both with regard to rate and to asymptote). Intelligence, then, is not best demonstrated when routine utilization of one's processing components occurs. Otherwise, the individual who can solve problems presented in one format efficiently, but who has difficulty when the problem is presented somewhat differently, would be considered quite intelligent. We argue that it is the individual who can adjust to a change in problem situations and who can eventually automate the component processes of task solution who is most intelligent.

The data on novelty are fairly straightforward: Older adults are less well able to deal with novel kinds of tasks and situations than are younger adults (e.g., Botwinick, 1977; Horn & Cattell, 1967; Kausler & Puckett, 1980). This inability to deal with novelty may derive from a variety of sources, but it seems not to be attributable simply to a lack of interest in learning new things on the part of older persons (Camp, Rodrigue, & Olson, 1984). Cognitive intervention research has revealed that performance on tests of fluid intelligence can be improved with practice and training (Baltes & Willis, 1982; Denney, 1979). This research indicates that older individuals can become better at dealing with novel tasks.

The data on automatization are more mixed: Older adults may or may not automatize more slowly than do younger adults, but they most probably reach a lower asymptote of automatization than do younger adults (e.g., Madden & Nebes, 1980; Plude et al., 1983). Thus, again, we interpret the evidence as indicating some decline in older age of experiential functioning as defined by this subtheory. Any conclusions drawn regarding age-related differences in experiential functioning, however, must be qualified by the fact that there has been virtually no control for degree of novelty or automatization of a task or situation as a function of the task or situation confronted by the subjects being tested. It should not be assumed, as it often seems to have been, that a given task or situation is equally novel or automatized for subjects of different ages. In fact, many of the tests that have been used to measure age differences in the ability to deal with novelty and automatization—primarily markers of fluid intelligence—are perceived by older individuals to be less familiar, more difficult, more effortful, and more highly speeded measures than they are perceived to be by younger adults (Cornelius, 1984).

The relation of intelligence to the external world of the individual is dealt with by a contextual subtheory of intelligence, according to which intelligence is viewed as the ability to apply the components of intelligence, at different levels of experience, in adjusting to a change in the environment. Producing an optimal fit between oneself and the environment involves one of the following three processes, among others: (a) adjusting oneself to the environment; (b) shaping the existing environment to be more compatible with one's own behavioral repertoire; (c) selecting another environment more suitable to oneself. Because environments change and the context of one's life also changes with increasing age, there is no single answer to the question of whether the components of intelligence as they function in real-world environments decrease with age: It depends on the context.

If the environment for older people were exactly the same as it is for younger people, then contextual performance would almost certainly decline, given the declines in componential functioning that seem to be the rule rather than the exception. However, as individuals age, environments change in a variety of ways. For instance, for many individuals, as they grow older, environments become increasingly less complex, and this change in the environment seems to have detrimental effects on cognitive functioning (e.g., Gribbin, Schaie, & Parham, 1980; Schooler, Chapter 2 of this volume). If the older adult selects and then shapes his or her environments carefully and indeed has the option to perform such selection and shaping, then declines in actual real-world performance may be minimized by capitalization on those abilities that have remained most intact, and by utilization of accumulated knowledge that younger adults may not have. For example, Salthouse (Chapter 8 of this volume) has found that older typists compensate for their decreased motor capacities through efficient planning strategies (i.e., reading further ahead in the text and planning for what will come next), thereby maintaining high typing speeds. Instances of adjusting to the environment through shaping and selecting indicate that older individuals do so with regard to their work environments. For instance, some older individuals do select out of work environments that are physically demanding (Powell, 1973) and that require quick sensori-motor performance (Barrett, Mihal, Panek, Sterns, & Alexander, 1977). Clearly traditional intellectual assessments are inadequate in assessing one's ability to adapt to, shape, and select environments.

How, then, does the triarchic theory deal with the interface between aging and intelligence? First, the mental components of intelligence are asserted to remain relevant to intellectual functioning, regardless of the age of the individual. Thus, the potential "mental hardware" of intelligence does not change as a function of age. Second, the need to consider the functioning of these components in relatively novel tasks and situations, and the rates and asymptotes of automatization also remain constant, although the level of novelty and automatization for particular tasks and situations may, in fact, change with age. Thus, a given task will not necessarily measure the ability to deal with novelty, or to automatize information processing, for individuals of different ages. Third, the need to consider how the components operate at different levels of experience in the environment remains the same across age. However, what constitutes intelligent adaptation, selection, or shaping may change with age. Buying a large house, for example, may be very intelligent for a young couple with a growing family, but not for an older couple whose children have all gone away. Hence, the vehicles with which it is appropriate to measure the components of intelligence may change—perhaps drastically—as individuals grow older. The tests that are appropriate for younger individuals may be inappropriate for older ones.

Consider, for example, quantitative word problems of the kind found on many intelligence tests. For individuals in school or recently out of school, such problems might be contextually appropriate. But for individuals who have not had to deal with such problems in half a century, they may be wildly inappropriate. Moreover, they will clearly be much more novel for the older individuals than for the younger ones. The point, quite simply, is that although the mental hardware of intelligence may not change with age, its age-appropriate instantiations do, and hence the vehicles for measuring intelligence ought to change as well to reflect tasks that are contextually appropriate for older individuals.

On this point of view, then, does intelligence decrease in older age? The answer, as Baltes and his colleagues have noted, is that it depends. If one considers traditional psychometric and information-processing assessments of intelligence, then almost certainly, one will witness a decline, on the average, in intelligence with age. The average decline is a genuine one, and not solely a function of the particular theory one prefers or of the experimental design one happens to use. If one views intelligence as it is used in context, as the triarchic theory does, decline is far from inevitable. Older adults may enter new environments as their internal abilities falter. These new environments may alter the abilities required of the older adult. It is possible for older adults to create, or have created for them, environments in which their intelligence as utilized in the real world decreases, remains the same, or actually increases relative to what it was in earlier adulthood. The older adult may adapt to his or her environment in later life better than he or she adapted to the environment characterizing earlier life.

Specific details for determining adaptive behaviors that can be considered intelligent at various points in adult development are needed. Implicit theories can provide such details and can convey a sense of the changes in behavioral content that are relevant to understanding intelligence at different ages. They fill in some of the content of the contextual subtheory of the triarchic theory.

Implicit Theories

We have conducted three studies investigating people's implicit theories of intelligence at different points in adult intellectual development. Participants in the first study were adults in the New Haven area who were recruited through a random sampling of the New Haven area telephone directory. Participants in the second and third studies were adults in the New Haven area recruited through their local churches. In the first study, 152 individuals of various adult ages ranging from 17 to 83 years were asked to list behaviors characteristic of exceptionally intelligent and exceptionally unintelligent individuals of either 30, 50, or 70 years of age. In the second study, 22 individuals ranging in age from 24 to 84 were asked to rate the importance of the behaviors obtained in the first study to defining intelligent and unintelligent individuals of 30, 50, and 70 years of age. In the third study, 69 individuals ranging in age from 26 to 85 were asked to rate how likely it would be for individuals of average intelligence and for individuals of exceptional intelligence at 30, 50, and 70 years of age to be engaged in a subset of behaviors from the second study.

The main findings from these studies were that people have distinctive implicit theories of intelligence that relate to individuals in young, middle, and late adulthood, and that the importance of the characteristics underlying these theories varied in an age-related way (Berg & Sternberg, unpublished). The most salient of these differences was the heavier weight placed on everyday intellectual abilities at 50 and 70 years of age relative to 30 years of age, particularly by individuals of middle age and older age.

In order to convey a sense of the main similarities and differences across the age levels, it may be useful for the reader simply to inspect the factors that were obtained in the third study for the prototypically intelligent individual at 30, 50, and 70 years of age, as well as some behaviors representative of each factor. Table 2 shows a listing of these factors and some representative behaviors (all having loadings on the factors of .6 or greater). The factors were obtained by factor analyzing difference scores for the prototypical exceptionally intelligent individual minus the prototypical average-intelligent individual for all subjects. The three factors obtained for the ratings of what characterizes intelligence at 30 years of age were (a) novelty in problem solving, (b) crystallized intelligence, and (c) everyday competence; for the ratings of what characterizes intelligence at 50 years of age the factors were (a) novelty in problem solving, (b) everyday competence, and (c) social competence; for the ratings of what characterizes intelligence at 70 years of age the factors were (a) composite fluid and crystallized intelligence, (b) everyday competence, and (c) cognitive investment. The two things worth noting are that the factors accord well with the triarchic theory of intelligence, as well as with other explicit theories, and that there is a shift toward more emphasis on intelligence in its everyday contexts at the higher age levels (as evidenced by this factor accounting for more variance for older prototypes than younger prototypes).

Although implicit theories of intelligence do not fully define what intelligence is, we believe they are important for helping us delimit the scope for theories of intelligence. Our results thus indicate the need for explicit theories of adult intellectual development that take into account changing life demands as the individual grows older (as in the contextual subtheory of the triarchic theory). Moreover, implicit theories suggest that traditional intellectual assessments are probably inadequate in assessing the types of intelligent behavior that we have identified through people's implicit theories of intelligence, such as "successfully adapting to one's everyday environment." Thus, the tasks and measures through which it is appropriate to assess the ability of an individual's mental components to operate on novelty and to become automated differ with increasing adult age.

In sum, explicit and implicit theoretical approaches to studying the

Table 2. Main Aspects of Intelligence According to Implicit Theories

30-Year-Old

I. Novelty in Problem Solving
- A. Is interested in gaining knowledge and learning new things
- B. Displays curiosity
- C. Challenges what is presented to him or her in the media
- D. Is able to learn and reason with new kinds of concepts
- E. Is able to analyze new topics in new and original ways

II. Crystallized Intelligence
- A. Is experienced in his or her field
- B. Is competent in career choice
- C. Is able to draw conclusions from information given
- D. Displays clarity of speech
- E. Displays the knowledge to speak intelligently

III. Everyday Competence
- A. Displays good common sense
- B. Adjusts to life situations
- C. Is able to adapt to disastrous life situations
- D. Is interested in his or her family and home life
- E. Is able to adapt well to the environment

50-Year-Old

I. Novelty in Problem Solving
- A. Is able to analyze topics in new and original ways
- B. Is able to perceive and store new information
- C. Is able to learn and reason with new kinds of concepts
- D. Challenges what is presented to him or her in the media
- E. Displays curiosity

II. Everyday Competence
- A. Adjusts to life situations
- B. Is perceptive about people and things
- C. Is able to adapt to disastrous life situations
- D. Is able to adapt well to the environment
- E. Is aware of events beyond his or her area of expertise

III. Social Competence
- A. Acts in a mature manner
- B. Has high moral values
- C. Is interested in his or her family and home life
- D. Displays good common sense
- E. Is experienced in his or her field

70-Year-Old

I. Composite Fluid and Crystallized Intelligence
- A. Displays a good vocabulary
- B. Reads widely
- C. Is able to understand feedback and act upon it
- D. Is able to sift out relevant from irrelevant information
- E. Is able to draw conclusions from information given

II. Everyday Competence
- A. Displays wisdom in actions and thoughts
- B. Is perceptive about people and things

(continued)

Table 2. (Continued)

      C. Thinks before acting or speaking
      D. Is able to adapt to disastrous life situations
      E. Is aware of what is going on around him or her
III. Cognitive Investment
      A. Displays curiosity
      B. Is competent in career choice
      C. Appreciates young and old individuals
      D. Is interested in his or her family and home life

Note. Factor names are our own. Behaviors listed are samples of full lists of behaviors with factor loadings of .6 or greater. Behaviors are listed in order of decreasing loadings. The percentages of variance accounted for by each factor are as follows: For the 30-year-old prototype, Factor 1 accounts for 26.5%, Factor 2 accounts for 16.7%, and Factor 3 accounts for 16.1% of the variance in the data. For the 50-year-old prototype, Factor 1 accounts for 25.5%, Factor 2 accounts for 21.1%, and Factor 3 accounts for 13.5% of the variance in the data. For the 70-year-old prototype, Factor 1 accounts for 27.9%, Factor 2 accounts for 17.5%, and Factor 3 accounts for 10.9% of the variance in the data.

nature of adult intelligence need to be viewed as complementary. Implicit theories identify the changing perceived nature of intelligence throughout adult development and suggest the relevant content through which the operation of the mental components of intelligence, as outlined in an explicit theory, can be assessed. Implicit theories preliminarily identify the latent constructs that comprise intelligence and suggest ways that these latent constructs change in importance over the life span. The implicit theories discovered here suggest that novelty in problem solving, crystallized intelligence, and everyday competence constitute the core constructs of intelligence in adulthood. The implicit theories we observed also provide evidence to suggest that everyday competence is perceived as becoming more important in middle and late adulthood than in younger adulthood. These implicit theories provide some support for the contextual subtheory of our explicit theory in that the contexts to which individuals must adapt may change in adulthood in a fairly regular fashion. (Implicit theories could also differ with regard to other subject characteristics, such as race of ratee, occupation of ratee, socioeconomic status of ratee, etc.) The explicit theory then further details the specific components and subprocesses involved in executing the contextually relevant intelligent behavior. Our explicit theory takes the latent constructs identified through implicit theories to be relevant for assessing intelligence and makes them operational so that assessments can be made. The triarchic theory of adult intellectual development is concerned with identifying how the observed measures necessary to measure the latent variables will differ with age.

Relations of Our Theoretical Viewpoint to Other Viewpoints

We see both our theory of the nature of intelligence and our views regarding changes in levels of intelligence as in partial agreement with positions advocated by others. Consider the interface between our position and those of others.

First, in the fluid-crystallized theory of adult intelligence, the fluid ability discussed by Horn and Cattell (1966, 1967) maps closely into what we refer to as componential functioning of a relatively novel kind. The crystallized ability discussed by Horn and Cattell maps closely into what we refer to as componential functioning of a relatively automated kind. Whereas we separate three kinds of information-processing components that give rise to fluid and crystallized ability, Horn and Cattell do not. But the conclusions remain the same: The components of intelligence, as applied to fairly abstract and academic tasks, show a decline in functioning in later life. The products of these components may well not show a decline, because the products result from the functioning of the components at an earlier point in life. Thus, whereas an older individual might be less able than a younger adult to acquire new vocabulary efficiently, the older adult may nevertheless have the better vocabulary, as the result of experiences earlier in life. Where the theory of fluid-crystallized ability differs from the combined explicit and implicit theory advanced here is in the concern for the potentially changing nature of intelligence throughout the adult life span. As we indicated previously, the fluid-crystallized ability theory really assumes that the latent constructs that comprise intelligence remain the same over the adult life span. The combined explicit and implicit theory proposed here begins its theory construction with an empirical examination of the latent constructs thought to comprise intelligence through the examination of people's implicit theories of intelligence.

Baltes et al. (1984) make an internal-external distinction similar to the one we make, and seem to be in essential agreement with us: A decline in internally oriented abilities is typically demonstrated, but declines in externally oriented abilities are far less clear. Moreover, even internally oriented abilities show plasticity, multidimensionality, multidirectionality, and interindividual variability, which weakens any general conclusions that can be drawn. In addition, there is considerable overlap between the notion of selective optimization with compensation as proposed by Baltes and colleagues and our notion of the fit between a person and his or her environment. We agree with the viewpoint of adult intellectual development characterized as a process of individual adaptation to the contexts of life at the same time that we believe it important to recognize some generalized declines in internally oriented abilities. If we wish to avoid deteriorated performance by older individuals, we suspect that the means to this goal, on the average, are instructing individuals how to select and shape their environments. Certainly, conventional testing can reveal individual differences in changes in ability, and training can improve the internally oriented abilities of some individuals, to a greater or lesser extent. We doubt that either of these solutions will prove as viable or as helpful in the long term as will environmental selection and shaping. What our approach seems to add to conceptions such as those of Baltes and his colleagues is a way empirically to derive what is involved in successful adaptation to the variety of environments and contexts we encounter in everyday life that may require our intelligent functioning.

We would argue that the three theories considered here—fluid-crystallized abilities (Horn–Cattell), the neofunctionalist view (Baltes and colleagues), and the triarchic theory (Sternberg and Berg)—share elements in common, dealing with different issues regarding the nature of intelligence across the life span. The fluid-crystallized ability theory deals with factorial structure, the neofunctionalist theory with sources of variability in the developmental course of intelligence over the life span, and the triarchic theory with the relation of information processing, experience, and the environment to intelligence.

To conclude, we have addressed two questions pertaining to change in intelligence over the life span. The first deals with changing levels of intelligence, the second with the changing nature of intelligence. We have argued that resolution of the issue of whether or not there are changes in the levels of intelligence with age cannot be accomplished until some agreement is reached regarding the actual nature of intelligence over the adult life span. By examining people's implicit theories of adult intelligence, we found that people perceive the nature of intelligence to change in emphasis over the adult life span, with more everyday cognitive abilities becoming of increasing importance with age. Thus, resolution of the issue of changes in the levels of intelligence with age must encompass the fact that intelligence is not one thing, but rather has multiple aspects, aspects that may shift in importance as a function of age, environment, and life contexts. Some of these aspects show decline with age; others do not. The question of whether there is a decline in intelligence with age is an important and legitimate one to ask, so long as one is willing to accept as an answer, "It depends." Test-relevant abilities do decline, on the average, but life-relevant abilities may or may not, depending on the course and contexts of one's life.

REFERENCES

Baltes, P.B., Dittmann-Kohli, F., & Dixon, R.A. (1984). New perspectives on the development of intelligence in adulthood: Toward a dual-process conception and a model of selective optimization with compensation. In P.B. Baltes & O.G. Brim, Jr. (Eds.), *Life-span development and behavior* (Vol. 6, pp. 33–76). New York: Academic Press.

Baltes, P.B., & Nesselroade, J.R. (1970). Multivariate longitudinal and cross-sectional sequences for analyzing ontogenetic and generational change: A methodological note. *Developmental Psychology, 1,* 162–168.

Baltes, P.B., Reese, H.W., & Lipsitt, L.P. (1980). Life-span developmental psychology. *Annual Review of Psychology, 31,* 65–110.

Baltes, P.B., & Schaie, K.W. (1976). On the plasticity of intelligence in adulthood and old age: Where Horn and Donaldson fail. *American Psychologist, 31,* 720–725.

Baltes. P.B., & Willis, S.L. (1982). Plasticity and enhancement of intellectual functioning in old age: Penn State's Adult Development and Enrichment Project (ADEPT). In F.I.M. Craik & S.E. Trehub (Eds.), *Aging and cognitive processes* (pp. 353–389). New York: Plenum.

Barrett, G.V., Mihal, W.L., Panek, P.E., Sterns, H.L., & Alexander, R.A. (1977). Information-processing skills predictive of accident involvement for younger and older commercial drivers. *Industrial Gerontology, 4,* 173–182.

Berg, C.A., & Sternberg, R.J. (unpublished). *Implicit theories of intelligence over the adult life span.* Manuscript submitted for publication.

Berg, C.A., & Sternberg, R.J. (1985). A triarchic theory of intellectual development during adulthood. *Developmental Review, 5,* 334–370.

Birren, J.E., & Cunningham, W. (1985). Research on the psychology of aging: Principles, concepts, and theory. In J.E. Birren & K.W. Schaie (Eds.), *Handbook of the psychology of aging* (2nd ed., pp. 3–34). New York: Van Nostrand Reinhold.

Botwinick, J. (1977). Intellectual abilities. In J.E. Birren & K.W. Schaie (Eds.), *Handbook of the psychology of aging* (pp. 580–605). New York: Van Nostrand Reinhold.

Camp, C.J., Rodrigue, J.R., & Olson, K.R. (1984). Curiosity in young, middle-aged, and older adults. *Educational Gerontology, 10,* 387–400.

Cattell, R. (1971). *Abilities: Their structure, growth, and action.* New York: Houghton Mifflin.

Cavanaugh, J., Kramer, D.A., Sinnott, J.D., Camp, C.J., & Markley, R.P. (1985). On missing links and such: Interfaces between cognitive research and everyday problem solving. *Human Development, 28,* 146–168.

Cerella, J., Poon, L.W., & Williams, D.M. (1980). Age and the complexity hypothesis. In L.W. Poon (Ed.), *Aging in the 1980s: Psychological Issues* (pp. 332–340). Washington, DC: American Psychological Association.

Charness, N. (1981a). Aging and skilled problem solving. *Journal of Experimental Psychology: General, 110,* 21–38.

Charness, N. (1981b). Search in chess: Age and skill differences. *Journal of Experimental Psychology: Human Perception and Performance, 7,* 467–476.

Charness, N. (1983). Age, skill and bridge bidding: A chronometric analysis. *Journal of Verbal Learning and Verbal Behavior, 22,* 406–416.

Cohen, J. (1957). The factorial structure of the WAIS between early adulthood and old age. *Journal of Consulting Psychology, 21,* 283–290.

Commons, M.L., Richards, F., & Armon, C. (Eds.). (1983). *Beyond formal operations: Late adolescent and adult cognitive development.* New York: Praeger.

Cornelius, S.W. (1984). Classic pattern of intellectual aging: Test familiarity, difficulty, and performance. *Journal of Gerontology, 39,* 201–206.

Denney, N.W. (1979). Problem solving in later adulthood: Intervention research. In P.B. Baltes & O.G. Brim, Jr. (Eds.). *Life-span development and behavior* (Vol. 2, pp. 37–66). New York: Academic Press.

Dittmann-Kohli, F., & Baltes, P.B. (in press). Towards an action-theoretical and pragmatic conception of intelligence during adulthood and old age. In C.N. Alexander & E. Langer (Eds.) *Beyond formal operations: Alternative endpoints to human development.* New York: Cambridge University Press.

Gardner, H. (1983). *Frames of mind.* New York: Basic Books.

Goodnow, J.J. (1984). On being judged "intelligent." *International Journal of Psychology, 19,* 91–106.

Goodnow, J.J. (1986). Some lifelong everyday forms of intelligent behavior: Organizing and reorganizing. In R.J. Sternberg & R. Wagner (Eds.), *Practical intelligence: Origins of competence in the everyday world.* (pp. 143–162). Cambridge, England: Cambridge University Press.

Gribbin, K., Schaie, K.W., & Parham, I.A. (1980). Complexity of life style and maintenance of intellectual abilities. *Journal of Social Issues, 36,* 47–61.

Guilford, J.P. (1967). *The nature of human intelligence.* New York: McGraw-Hill.

Gutmann, D. (1977). The cross-cultural perspective: Notes toward a comparative psychology of aging. In J.E. Birren & K.W. Schaie (Eds.), *Handbook of the psychology of aging* (pp. 302–326). New York: Van Nostrand Reinhold.

Havighurst, R. (1972). *Developmental tasks and education.* New York: David McKay.

Horn, J.L. (1982). The aging of human abilities. In B.B. Wolman (Ed.), *Handbook of developmental psychology* (pp. 847–870). Englewood Cliffs, NJ: Prentice-Hall.

Horn, J.L., & Cattell, R.B. (1966). Refinement and test of the theory of fluid and crystallized general intelligences. *Journal of Educational Psychology, 58,* 253–270.

Horn, J.L., & Cattell, R.B. (1967). Age differences in fluid and crystallized intelligence. *Acta Psychologica, 26,* 107–129.

Horn, J.L., & Donaldson, G. (1976). On the myth of intellectual decline in adulthood. *American Psychologist, 31,* 701–719.

Hoyer, W.J. (1985). Aging and the development of expert cognition. In T.M. Shlechter & M.P. Toglia (Eds.), *New directions in cognitive science* (pp. 69–87). Norwood, NJ: Ablex.

Jarvik, L.F., Eisdorfer, C., & Blum, J.E. (1973). *Intellectual functioning in adults.* New York: Springer.

Kausler, D.H., & Puckett, J.M. (1980). Frequency judgments and correlated cognitive abilities in young and elderly adults. *Journal of Gerontology, 35,* 376–382.

Kramer, D.A. (1983). Post-formal operations? A need for further conceptualization. *Human Development, 26,* 91–105.

Labouvie-Vief, G. (1982). Dynamic development and mature autonomy: A theoretical prologue. *Human Development, 25,* 161–191.

Levinson, D.J. (1978). *The seasons of a man's life.* New York: Ballantine.

Lieberman, M.A., & Coplan, A.S. (1969). Distance from death as a variable in the study of aging. *Developmental Psychology, 2,* 71–84.

Madden, D.J., & Nebes, R.D. (1980). Aging and the development of automaticity in visual search. *Developmental Psychology, 16,* 377–384.

Neisser, U. (1979). The concept of intelligence. In R.J. Sternberg & D.K. Detterman (Eds.), *Human intelligence: Perspectives on its theory and measurement* (pp. 179–189). Norwood, NJ: Ablex.

Neugarten, B.L. (1977). Personality and aging. In J.E. Birren & K.W. Schaie (Eds.), *Handbook of the psychology of aging* (pp. 626–649). New York: Van Nostrand Reinhold.

Pascual-Leone, J. (1983). Growing into maturity: Toward a metasubjective theory of adulthood stages. In P.B. Baltes & O.G. Brim, Jr. (Eds.), *Life-span development and behavior* (Vol. 5, pp. 118–156). New York: Academic Press.

Plude, D.J., Kaye, D.B., Hoyer, W.J., Post, T.A., Saynisch, M.J., & Hahn, M.V. (1983). Aging and visual search under consistent and varied mapping. *Developmental Psychology, 19,* 508–512.

Powell, P. (1973). Age and occupational change among coal-miners. *Occupational Psychology, 47,* 37–49.

Reese, H.W., & Rodeheaver, D. (1985). Problem solving and complex decision making. In J.E. Birren & K.W. Schaie (Eds.), *Handbook of the psychology of aging* (2nd ed., pp. 474–499). New York: Van Nostrand Reinhold.

Riegel, K.F., & Riegel, R.M. (1972). Development, drop, and death. *Developmental Psychology, 6,* 306–319.

Salthouse, T.A. (1982). *Adult cognition.* New York: Springer-Verlag.

Salthouse, T.A. (1985). Speed of behavior and its implications for cognition. In J.E. Birren & K.W. Schaie (Eds.), *Handbook of the psychology of aging* (2nd ed., pp. 400–426). New York: Van Nostrand Reinhold.

Schaie, K.W. (1974). Translations in gerontology—from lab to life. *American Psychologist, 29,* 802–807.

Schaie, K.W. (1979). The Primary Mental Abilities in adulthood: An exploration in the development of psychometric intelligence. In P.B. Baltes & O.G. Brim, Jr. (Eds.), *Life-span development and behavior* (Vol. 2, pp. 67–115). New York: Academic Press.

Schaie, K.W. & Hertzog, C. (1985). Measurement in the psychology of adulthood and aging. In J.E. Birren & K.W. Schaie (Eds.), *Handbook of the psychology of aging* (2nd ed., pp. 61–92). New York: Van Nostrand Reinhold.

Scheidt, R.J., & Schaie, K.W. (1978). A taxonomy of situations for the elderly populations: Generating situational criteria. *Journal of Gerontology, 33,* 848–857.

Spearman, C. (1927). *The abilities of man.* New York: Macmillan.

Stagner, R. (1985). Aging in industry. In J.E. Birren & K.W. Schaie (Eds.), *Handbook of the psychology of aging* (2nd ed., pp. 789–817). New York: Van Nostrand Reinhold.

Sternberg, R.J. (1984). Toward a triarchic theory of human intelligence. *Behavioral and Brain Sciences, 7,* 269–315.

Sternberg, R.J. (1985). *Beyond IQ: A triarchic theory of human intelligence.* New York: Cambridge University Press.

Thurstone, L.L. (1938). *Primary mental abilities.* Chicago: University of Chicago Press.

Thurstone, L.L., & Thurstone, T.G. (1949). *SRA Primary Mental Abilities.* Chicago: Science Research Associates.

Wechsler, D. (1958). *The measurement and appraisal of adult intelligence* (5th ed.). Baltimore: Williams & Wilkins.

Willis, S.L. & Schaie, K.W. (1986). Practical intelligence in later adulthood. In R.J. Sternberg & R.K. Wagner (Eds.), *Practical intelligence: Origins of competence in the everyday World* (pp. 236–268). New York: Cambridge University Press.

Chapter Two

Psychological Effects of Complex Environments During the Life Span: A Review and Theory

Carmi Schooler

This chapter reviews findings supporting a theory about the psychological effects of environmental complexity. The theory is suggested by the results of a survey research program on work and adult personality.[1] It is supported not only by findings about the psychological effects of complex environments during the work years, but also by evidence from a wide variety of other sources, including research about environmental effects on children and the aged, as well as animal and social psychological experiments.

According to the theory, the complexity of an individual's environment is defined by its stimulus and demand characteristics. The more diverse the stimuli, the greater the number of decisions required, the greater the number of considerations to be taken into account in making these decisions, and the more ill defined and apparently contradictory

This chapter is gratefully dedicated to the memory of a pioneer scholar in the attempt to understand the interaction of people and their environments, my teacher and uncle— Isidor Chein (1936, 1972; Chein, Gerard, Lee, & Rosenfeld, 1964; *Brown v. Board of Education,* 1954; Cook, 1982).

Since this chapter was written by the author as part of his duty as a U.S. Government worker, it is not copyrighted.

[1] This chapter is a revised and updated version of Schooler (1984). From its inception over 20 years ago, my research on work and personality has been a collaborative effort with Melvin Kohn. He, Nina Schooler, Jonathan Schooler, James Demetre, and Elliot Lebow have provided extensive and extremely useful critiques of both the substance and form of the present review.

I would also like to thank the many fellow workers throughout the National Institutes of Health who provided extremely useful bibliographic leads and informal overviews of various research topics.

the contingencies, the more complex the environment. To the degree that the pattern of reinforcement within such an environment rewards cognitive effort, individuals should be motivated to develop their intellectual capacities and to generalize the resulting cognitive processes to other situations. The aspect of cognitive functioning that would seem to be particularly likely to be affected in this way is intellectual flexibility—the ability to utilize an assortment of approaches and vantage points in confronting cognitive problems in a nonstereotypic way.

Nonintellective aspects of psychological functioning may also be affected by environmental complexity. To the extent that complex environments reward initiative and independent judgment, such environments should foster a generalized orientation favoring self-directedness rather than conformity to external authority. On the other hand, values, orientations, and behaviors that are adaptive in complex environments may be maladaptive in simpler ones. Simple environments may not provide sufficient rewards to insure the development or continuance of relatively high levels of cognitive functioning and self-directedness. Consequently, continued exposure to relatively simple environments may result in a decrement in cognitive functioning, particularly intellectual flexibility, and a change to values, orientations, and behaviors in keeping with the level of environmental demand. If, as seems plausible, such adaptation can occur, at least to some extent, at any age, changes in environmental complexity should produce changes in intellectual functioning and related values and orientations at any point in the individual's life course: midlife, childhood, old age.

The theory is rough-hewn in the sense that its parameters are not quantified and many of its key terms are inexactly defined. Being "a hypothesis which has undergone verification, and which is applicable to a large number of related phenomena" it does, however, fit *Webster's* definition of a scientific theory (1961). At a minimum, it serves the heuristic purpose of tying together findings from all stages of the life span and from levels of analysis ranging from the biochemical to the sociological.

The first section of the chapter summarizes the evidence from the research program on work and personality about the effects of environmental complexity on psychological plasticity during the mid-period in the life span between childhood and old age. The next two sections review the accumulating evidence that changes in environmental complexity also result in psychological plasticity in these early and late stages of the human life span. Later sections discuss relevant animal and social psychological experiments.

MIDLIFE: THE PSYCHOLOGICAL EFFECTS OF
OCCUPATIONAL CONDITIONS

The research program on the psychological effects of occupations (Kohn
& Schooler, 1969, 1983) is the source of much of the evidence about
the psychological effects of environmental complexity during midlife.
The original purpose of that research was to test the hypothesis that
differences between middle-class and working-class parents' values for
their children and their child-rearing practices arise in substantial part
from differences in their work experience (Kohn, 1963). The key difference was hypothesized to be the relatively greater degree of occupational self-direction—the use of initiative, thought, and independent
judgment—required by higher-status occupations. Because the requirement for such self-direction can be seen as a particularly complex
environmental demand, and because their work is an important part
of most adults' environments, the study also provides evidence about
the effects of environmental complexity on adult psychological functioning.

Measures of many facets of individual psychological functioning other
than parental values were included in the survey questionnaire, thus
permitting examination of a wide range of potential effects of environmental complexity. These additional facets include measures of
intellectual flexibility, values for self, self-conceptions, and social orientations. Because occupational conditions determining the level of
occupational self-direction were only some of the dimensions of occupational experience that might have psychological effects, questions
about the gamut of potentially effective occupational conditions were
included in the survey. As a result, jobs could be described in terms
of their locations on the various dimensions on which occupations
could be differentiated and such dimensions of work (e.g., substantive
complexity, hierarchical position, time pressure), rather than specific
named occupations (e.g., lawyer, furniture upholsterer, chicken sexer),
became the units of analysis.

Of the more than 50 occupational dimensions, including position in
the organizational structure, opportunity for occupational self-direction,
and pressures and uncertainties of the job, the measures that most
clearly reflect environmental conditions meeting the theoretical definition of environmental complexity proposed above are those of occupational self-direction. These are routinization, closeness of supervision, and most important of all, the substantive complexity of work—
the degree to which performance of the work demands thought and
independent judgment. Because the worker must make many decisions
taking into account ill-defined or apparently conflicting contingencies,
substantively complex work fits the definition of environmental com-

plexity. Substantive complexity is measured through a detailed inquiry about precisely what people do when working with data, with things, and with people.

Among the psychological variables relevant to the hypothesized effects of environmental complexity are measures of the degree to which values both for one's children and for one's self reflect self-direction rather than conformity to external standards. Orientations relevant to the hypothesis that environmental complexity leads to a self-directed rather than a conformist orientation include authoritarian conservatism, fatalism, idea-conformity, and self-deprecation (Kohn & Schooler, 1969, 1983). For the index of intellectual flexibility, the psychological variable hypothesized to be most affected by environmental complexity, a wide variety of indicators was sampled. These included men's solutions to seemingly simple but highly revealing cognitive problems involving well-known issues, their handling of perceptual tests, their propensity to agree when asked agree-disagree questions, and the impression they made on the interviewer during a long session that required a great deal of thought and reflection. None of these indicators is assumed to be completely valid; but all are assumed to reflect, in some substantial degree, men's flexibility in attempting to cope with the demands of a complex situation.[2] For both psychological and occupational functioning, principal component factor analysis was used to develop the multiple-indicator-based measures derived from the initial cross-sectional data. The data on psychological and occupational functioning came from interviews conducted in 1964 with a sample of 3,101 men, representative of all men employed in civilian occupations throughout the United States (Kohn & Schooler, 1969).

The results of the initial analyses were consonant with the hypotheses that occupational self-direction results in intellectual flexibility and a self-directed orientation and value system (Kohn & Schooler, 1969), but they left unanswered the question of whether occupational conditions actually affect psychological functioning. The relationships found

---

[2] The actual questions are (a) the Goodenough estimate of a man's intelligence (see Witkin, Dyk, Faterson, Goodenough, & Karp, 1962), based on a detailed evaluation of the Draw-a-Person Test; (b) the Witkin et al. (1962) appraisal of the sophistication of body concept in the Draw-a-Person Test; (c) a summary score for his performance on a portion of the Embedded Figures Test (see Witkin et al., 1962); (d) the interviewer's appraisal of the man's intelligence; (e) the frequency with which the man agreed when asked the many agree-disagree questions included in the interview; (f) a rating of the adequacy of his answer to the relatively simple cognitive problem: "What are all the arguments you can think of for and against allowing cigarette commercials on TV"; and (g) a rating of the adequacy of his answer to another relatively simple cognitive problem: "Suppose you wanted to open a hamburger stand and there were two locations available. What questions would you consider in deciding which of the two locations offers a better business activity?"

between occupational conditions and psychological functioning could have resulted entirely from processes of selective recruitment, selective retention, and men's efforts to mold their jobs to fit their needs, values, and capacities.

In an attempt to determine the nature of the causal relationship between occupational conditions and psychological functioning, an econometric technique called two-stage least squares (Blalock, 1971; Goldberger, 1964) was used to test a causal model which posited reciprocal effects between substantive complexity of work and psychological functioning (Kohn & Schooler, 1973). These analyses established a prima facie case that substantively complex work has a decidedly greater impact on intellectual flexibility and self-directed orientations than the reverse.

Even with the use of two-stage least squares, cross-sectional data cannot provide definitive evidence of causality; only longitudinal data, measuring real change in real people, can be definitive. Moreover, while the interviews provided retrospective information about the substantive complexity of past jobs, they could not provide information about men's psychological functioning at the times they held those jobs. Thus there was no way of taking into account earlier levels of psychological functioning in assessing the effects of current occupational conditions on psychological functioning.

The longitudinal data necessary to assess the reciprocal effects of occupational conditions and psychological functioning more adequately were gathered through a 10-year follow-up survey of a representative portion (687 men) of the original sample (for details see Kohn & Schooler, 1978, 1981, 1982). In analyzing these longitudinal data, linear structural equation analysis (Jöreskog, 1973; Jöreskog & Sörbom, 1976a, 1976b) was used to deal with the related problems of measurement error and the estimation and statistical testing of complex causal models involving reciprocal effects.[3] The prototypic longitudinal analysis (Kohn & Schooler, 1978) showed that the effect on intellectual flexibility of

---

[3] The problem of separating unreliability of measurement from real change is a critical one for causal analyses, particularly those involving longitudinal data and reciprocal effects. This is so because the magnitude of the effect of the independent variable will be underestimated in direct proportion to the amount of error in its measurement (Blalock, 1972; Heise, 1975). This is problematic for longitudinal analysis because the estimates of the stability of a variable are affected by the amount of error in the initial measure. In the analysis of reciprocal effects the problem is further exacerbated because each variable in a pair is an independent variable vis-à-vis the other.

The essence of the linear structural equation method of purging measurement error is the use of multiple indicators to make measurement models for each concept, inferring from the covariation of the indicators the degree to which each reflects the underlying concept that they all are hypothesized to reflect and the degree to which each reflects anything else, which for measurement purposes is considered to be error.

the substantive complexity of the work done, a key source of environmental complexity on the job, is real and noteworthy—on the order of one fourth as great as the effect of men's earlier levels of intellectual flexibility on their present intellectual flexibility.[4,5]

The causal model was expanded (Kohn & Schooler, 1982) to consider simultaneously several structural imperatives of the job and three major dimensions of personality—intellectual flexibility, a self-directed orientation to self and society, and a sense of distress. This analysis pointed to the importance for personality of the substantive complexity of work, the job condition most directly related to the complexity of environmental demands. Job conditions that facilitate occupational self-direction, particularly substantive complexity, increase men's intellectual flexibility and promote a self-directed orientation to self and society; jobs that limit occupational self-direction decrease men's intellectual flexibility and promote a conformist orientation to self and society.[6] To the extent that the necessity for using initiative, thought, and independent judgment represent complex environmental demands, these findings provide strong empirical support for the hypothesis that environmental complexity on the job increases adult intellectual flexibility

[4] The size of the path, which is .18, might not in ordinary circumstances be considered especially striking; but a continuing effect of this magnitude on so stable a phenomenon as intellectual flexibility is impressive, for the cumulative impact is much greater than the immediate effect at any one time. Continuing effects, even small-to-moderate ones, on highly stable phenomena become magnified in importance.

[5] The principal component analysis used initally, and the linear structure equation measurement model which was later developed to purge measurement error, revealed the existence of two dimensions, one perceptual, the other ideational. Because of the high stability of the perceptual component and our greater theoretical interest in the ideational component, nearly all of the causal analyses were carried out with the ideational measure. Analyses using perceptual flexibility, do indicate, though, that the effect of substantively complex work on intellectual flexibility was as strong for perceptual flexibility as for ideational flexibility (Kohn & Schooler, 1981).

[6] Not only do occupational conditions indicative of environmental complexity affect intellectual flexibility and self-directed orientations, but reciprocal effects of intellectual flexibility and self-directed orientations on job conditions also occur (Kohn & Schooler, 1983; chapters 5 and 6). These effects of psychological functioning on job conditions, however, are not contemporaneous, but rather, lagged, occurring gradually over time. Thus, self-directed orientation results over time in being less closely supervised, having greater income, and doing physically lighter work—in short, in more advantageous jobs. More important for the concerns of this chapter is the important impact of ideational flexibility on the substantive flexibility of the job. It is noteworthy that this effect is lagged rather than contemporaneous. The implication is that the structure of most jobs does not permit any considerable variation in the substantive complexity of the work. Job conditions are not readily modified to suit the needs or capacities of the individual worker. Over a long enough time, though, many men either modify their jobs or move on to jobs more consonant with their intellectual functioning. Thus, the long-term effects of ideational flexibility on substantive complexity are considerable, even though the contemporaneous effects appear to be negligible.

and generates a self-directed orientation to self and society. These results consistently imply that the principal process by which a job affects personality is one of straightforward generalization from the lessons of the job to life off the job, rather than such less direct processes as compensation and reaction formation. In doing so, they provide clear evidence that complex environmental demands directly affect the psychological functioning of employed American men by increasing their intellectual flexibility and promoting self-directed values and orientations.

Other studies in the same research program strongly suggest that environmentally complex work conditions have similar effects on other populations. J. Miller, Schooler, Kohn, and K.A. Miller (1979) found that occupational self-direction is related to ideational flexibility and self-directed orientations in the same way in employed women as in employed men. Although longitudinal data were not available, linear structural equation analyses indicated that working in a substantively complex job increases women's intellectual flexibility, while working in a routinized job decreases it. Replications in Poland (J. Miller, Slomczynski, & Kohn, chapter 10 of this volume; Slomczynski, Miller, & Kohn, 1981) and Japan (Naoi & Schooler, 1985), also using cross-sectional data, indicate that substantively complex work has the same effects on men in those countries as in the U.S.

Besides replication in different populations, there have been other forms of extension of the hypotheses about the psychological effects of substantively complex work. Substantively complex housework has been shown to affect women the same way as substantively complex work done for pay (Schooler, Kohn, J. Miller, & K.A. Miller, 1983; Schooler, J. Miller, K.A. Miller, & Richtand, 1984). The demonstration of a strong positive effect of the substantive complexity of their work on the intellectuality of both men's and women's leisure-time activity (K.A. Miller & Kohn, 1983) is powerful evidence that people generalize from job experience, not only to their psychological functioning off the job, but to the actual activities they perform in their leisure time. Yet another type of generalization is implied by the finding (Schooler, 1976) that men from ethnic groups with a recent and pervasive history of serfdom tend to show the intellectual inflexibility and conformist orientation of men working under the environmental conditions characteristic of serfdom. This tendency suggests that the restrictive social and occupational conditions that prevailed within European societies may have affected those societies' cultures in a manner analogous to the way in which the lack of occupational self-direction affects an individual's cognitions, values, and orientations.

In toto the results of this program of research on the psychological effects of occupational conditions are in accord with the hypothesized effects of environmental complexity.[7] As the theory posits, the greater the diversity and complexity of the stimuli and decisions individuals face on the job, the greater the resulting increase in their intellectual flexibility and the more self-directed their orientation.

CHILDHOOD

There is considerable evidence that exposure to a complex environment during childhood has effects on both adult and childhood psychological functioning similar to the effects of environmentally complex occupational conditions during the middle of the life span. In one analysis, data gathered for the Kohn and Schooler occupational study (1969, 1983) were used to examine the effects on adult psychological functioning of complexity of childhood environment (Schooler, 1972). Complexity and multifacetedness of childhood environment were linked to being young, having a well-educated father, and being brought up in an urban setting, in a liberal religion, and in a region of the country far from the South. Being raised in a complex environment was shown to result in a relatively high level of intellectual functioning, a rejection of external constraints on behavior, and a subjectivism stressing concern for the quality of one's inner life. These results had been hypothesized on the basis of a limited version (cf. Schooler, 1972, pp. 299–300) of the present theory that focused on the psychological effects of a complex multifaceted childhood environment on adult functioning. Comparable results have also been found in Japan (Schooler & Smith, 1978; Smith & Schooler, 1978).

Spaeth (1976) examines the effects of childhood environmental complexity on adult functioning from another sociological perspective. His interest is how social-structurally based differences in environmental complexity affect the socioeconomic achievement process. Complexity is defined in terms of the variety of stimuli in a person's surroundings. Spaeth sees such stimulation as encouraging intellectual growth and cites many studies indicating that parental behavior designed to increase the variety of stimuli to which children are exposed is correlated with family socioeconomic status. Using empirically based, but admittedly approximate, estimates of the correlations between environmental complexity and IQ and between these two variables and socioeconomic status, he presents a path-analytic model indicating that "the cognitive socialization which parents provide for a child totally mediates the

---

[7] For a review of research by other investigators supporting these conclusions, see Kohn and Schooler (1983, chapter 12). Kohn and Schooler's formulations and empirical findings have also been used by several sociologists in their theorizing about the psychological effects of social environments (Coser, 1975; Gabennesch, 1972).

effects of parental SES [socioeconomic status] on IQ" (Spaeth, 1976, p. 114). Examining the effects of environmental complexity throughout the life cycle, he concludes that because the more cognitively complex a person's earlier environments, the higher that person's subsequent socioeconomic status, cognitive complexity is an important mechanism in the status-attainment process.

The two studies discussed here have focused on the effect of the complexity of childhood environment on adult psychological functioning. Other studies have examined the effects of complex environments on children's cognitive functioning from shortly after birth through high school.

Effects of environmental complexity on infant cognitive functioning are shown by Scarr-Salapatek and Williams (1973). They demonstrate in a controlled experiment that low-birthweight infants born to impoverished mothers benefit substantially from a program that greatly increases the complexity of their environments. In the hospital, the experimental subjects were exposed to "visual, tactile and kinesthetic stimulation that approximated good home conditions for normal newborns" (Scarr-Salapatek & Williams, 1973, p. 97). Afterward, there were home visits by social workers, which included demonstrations of games that "would promote . . . hand-eye coordination, reaching, grasping, vocalizing, sitting up, self-feeding, and the like" (p. 98). The control-group received no home visits and the standard minimally stimulating hospital care for low-birthweight infants. At 1 year the average IQ of the experimental group was nearly 10 points higher than that of the control group. The experimental group's mean score of 95 actually brought them "to nearly normal levels of development" (p. 99).

A series of studies on the effects of early home environment on infant and childhood cognitive development (Gottfried, 1984), using the Home Observation for Measurement of the Environment (HOME) Inventory, found strong and consistent relationships between environmental complexity and cognitive development. Furthermore, the "results invariantly showed that home environmental variables related to cognitive development, independent of SES . . . [partialling out] correlations with maternal intelligence . . . revealed that the relationship between home environment and children's cognitive development is not spuriously due to their relationship with mothers' intelligence" (Gottfried, 1984, p. 334).

Yarrow, Rubenstein, and Pedersen (1975) carried out a careful observational study of the relationship between the psychological functioning and the environments of five-month-old infants. They found that the variety of social and inanimate stimulation is positively related to mental and psychomotor status and cognitive motivational functioning. They note, however, that this relationship may not be entirely due to the effect of the environment on the infant, because the level of functioning of the infants may affect the complexity of their environments. Although they raise this possibility of what they call bidirectional effects, they do not test it.

The possibility that children's characteristics may affect their environment is tested in Williams's (1976) study of the relationship between ability and household environment in school children. The study uses linear structural equation analysis both to develop pyschometrically sophisticated environmental measures and to test models that include reciprocal effects between children's abilities and their environments. The most potent of the family environmental measures is a stimulus dimension "defined by items measuring the extent to which parents specifically structured opportunities for their children to interact with things and people in their environment" (Williams, 1976, p. 88). Despite the author's concern about "the somewhat fallible data," some effects are quite substantial, pointing to the possibility that

> The environment best suited to intellectual development . . . is one containing things and people of quality and quantity. The frequently documented importance of appropriate adult models and a wide variety of learning situations is documented again here in the substantial effects of the stimulus dimensions of family environments. (p. 91)

Evidence that manipulating the complexity of preschool children's environments can affect their intellectual functioning can be found in the evaluations of the Head Start programs (The Consortium on Developmental Continuity, 1977; The Consortium for Longitudinal Studies, 1979; Mann, Harrell, & Hurt, 1977). In these programs the children "are encouraged to solve problems, initiate activities, explore, experiment, question, and gain mastery through learning by doing" (Brown & Grotberg, 1980, p. 338). The results of the most comprehensive evaluative analyses "were both statistically significant and robust: the increase in IQ scores at age 6 shown by children who had participated in preschool programs was attributable to the pre-school experience, independent of the effects of sex, initial IQ score, and the various measures of family background" (The Consortium for Longitudinal Studies, 1979, p. 12). The experience also affected the way the children evaluated themselves. Children who attended preschool were more likely than control children to give achievement-related reasons for being proud of themselves. Although longitudinal follow-up studies found significant treatment/control differences in children 9 through 12 years old, "in projects with children aged 13 years and above, there were no treatment/control differences on IQ" (The Consortium for Longitudinal Studies, 1979, p. 12). This unfortunate decay in the effects of Head Start as children continue their education in the environments usually provided by their school systems is consistent with the hypothesis that intellectual functioning is negatively affected when environments become less complex and demanding.

Post–Head-Start attempts to manipulate environmental complexity in order to improve the intellectual functioning of children at high risk for poor performance have emphasized early intervention and meta-learning (learning how to learn) (Detterman & Sternberg, 1982). Ramey, MacPhee, and Yeates (1982) report a controlled study in which the experimental infants were exposed, from the age of 3 months onward, to a wide variety of age-appropriate stimuli in a manner intended to promote language and concept-attainment skills. At 3 years a more structured educational curriculum was implemented, designed to provide a good deal of variety while giving systematic exposure to such areas as science and math. At 5 years of age the experimental group had about an 8-point advantage in IQ. There were also striking differences between the experimental and control group in the correlation between mother and child IQ. The correlation in the control group was not different from the expected correlation of .5. In the experimental group the mother-child IQ correlation was .14, suggesting that the experimental procedure had somehow changed the processes through which intellectual functioning is transmitted across generations. More dramatic IQ differences between experimental and control children have been reported by a somewhat similar early-intervention program (Garber & Heber, 1982), but see Sommer and Sommer (1983) for a cautionary note.

Evidence consonant with the possibiity that exposure to environmental complexity during high school can affect intellectual functioning is found in a study by Rosenbaum (1975, 1976). Analyses of the school records of a socially homogeneous school with a highly stratified track system indicated that tracking has a marked influence on changes in IQ scores between 8th and 10th grades even when the effects of initial IQ, sex, and social class are controlled. The more complex and demanding the curriculum the greater the IQ gain; the simpler and less demanding the curriculum the greater the IQ loss.

K.A. Miller, Kohn, and Schooler (1985, 1986) have examined the processes by which students' educational experiences affect their psychological functioning. To do this they used linear structural equations analysis on data from interviews conducted in 1974 with a subsample of the children of the respondents in the Kohn and Schooler study of work and personality (1983). The results suggest that educational self-direction, in particular the substantive complexity of schoolwork, has a decided impact on students' intellectual flexibility. Even in competition with the powerful genetic and environmental effects of parental intellectual functioning and social class, measures of which were also included in the model, complex academic environments increase a student's intellectual flexibility. Further analyses indicate that substantively complex schoolwork also increases the self-directedness of students' orientations.

All in all, the studies reviewed in this section confirm that environmental complexity has the predicted effect of improving intellectual functioning throughout childhood. The studies with relevant data also suggest that exposure to complex environments leads to a self-directed orientation and that both the orientational and intellectual results of childhood environmental complexity can be carried into adulthood.

RESEARCH WITH THE ELDERLY

At the other end of the age range, recent years have seen a great increase in research on the plasticity of intellectual functioning among older adults. Much of the impetus for this research has come from the argument about the inevitability of intellectual decline in old age. However, even those who tend to see such decline as physiologically based, pervasive, and relatively inevitable admit the possibility that environmental and cultural factors can affect the process (Arenberg & Robertson-Tchabo, 1980; Donaldson, 1981; Horn, 1978).

Those who tend to downplay the inevitability of the effects of age on intellectual functioning are more likely to stress the effect of environmental factors upon both level of performance and change across age (Schaie, 1984). Summarizing his analyses of intelligence changes in adulthood, Schaie (1980) concludes that "interindividual differences with regard to health and living conditions exert an influence on the development of intelligence . . . so significant, that one can hardly speak of a general process of intellectual development in adulthood" (p. 373). Among the living conditions that Schaie sees as important is environmental complexity.

A longitudinal study by Owens (1966; see also Cunningham & Owens, 1983) links IQ changes in adulthood to specific life experiences. The subjects, 96 entrants to Iowa State University, were tested with the Army Alpha test in 1919, 1950, and again in 1961. Variables reflecting the complexity of the individuals' life experiences during the intervals between the intitial and subsequent measures of IQ, such as amount of further education, field of college specialization, rural-to-urban migration, numbers of hobbies and recreational activities, and earned income proved important correlates of temporal shifts in test score. "The demonstration that patterns of living moderate the relationships of age to mental ability implies that cognitive decline, like cognitive development, is conditioned to some extent on the nature and intensity of environmental stimulation" (Owens, 1966, p. 325). Results consonant with these conclusions also emerged from a second longitudinal study of complexity of life-style and intellectual functioning (Gribbin, Schaie, & Parham, 1980).

Several experiments have demonstrated also that environmental manipulations can affect the intellectual functioning of older adults. Plemons, Willis, and Baltes (1978; see also Willis & Baltes, 1981) have shown that cognitive training of older adults can affect fluid intelligence (i.e., abilities thought to be independent of acculturation and relatively dependent on the physiological state of the individual; see Cattell, 1963). A further series of experiments on the modifiability of fluid intelligence is reported by Baltes and Willis (1982). These studies focus on the enhancement of a specifically targeted aspect of fluid intelligence (i.e., induction, attention, figural relations) through the manipulation of test familarity or through educational training in ability-specific problem-solving skills. Although there are some differences among abilities, the results indicate that not only are the targeted abilities substantially modifiable, but that the degree of enhancement is not a function of age.

Other experimental studies probed the environmental determinants of memory improvement in late adulthood (Langer, Rodin, Beck, Weinman, & Spitzer, 1979). The experimental manipulation involved increasing the cognitive demand of the environment and then varying the motivation of respondents to attend to and remember these environmental factors. In one study, motivation was manipulated by varying the degree of reciprocal self-disclosure offered by interviewers. In a second study, motivation to practice recommended cognitive activities was altered by varying whether positive outcomes were contingent on attending to and remembering these activities. In both studies, experimental subjects showed a significant improvement on standard short-term memory tests. They also improved on ratings of alertness, mental activity, and social adjustment, relative to controls. "Thus, restructuring the environment to make it more demanding, and then motivating elderly people to increase their cognitive activity, leads to improvements in memory that are generalizable" (Rodin & Langer, 1980, p. 25).

Finally, suggestive evidence about the interrelationships among aging, complex environments, and psychological functioning is provided by J. Miller, Slomcynski, and Kohn's (see chapter 10 of this volume) analysis of the effects of substantively complex work on intellectual flexibility in different age cohorts in both the United States and Poland. They found that in both countries the degree to which substantively complex work increases intellectual flexibility remains the same across the life span. What differs is the substantive complexity of the work done. In both countries older workers do less substantively complex work. Thus, leaving aside the possible effects of retirement, part of the intellectual decrement reported in the elderly may result from the reduced complexity of their work environments. Whether or not this is the case, the evidence from both the experimental and longitudinal survey studies reviewed in this section strongly suggests that complex environments continue to affect humans in their later years in ways similar to the ways their environments affected them earlier. The degree of this similarity is a question we will return to later.

ANIMAL STUDIES

Evidence about the effects of complex environments is not limited to humans. Research, much of it with rats, indicates that complex environments have similar cognitive effects on animals. Since the effects of environmental complexity may well differ from species to species, and since the degree of environmental restriction to which the animals are experimentally subjected generally far exceeds that which normally occurs with humans, such similarities do not necessarily provide support for a theory about the effects of environmental complexity on humans. Still, the experimentally demonstrated effects of environmental complexity on rat behavior are quite similar to those we are concerned with demonstrating in humans. The biological and biochemical effects of environmental complexity are also quite suggestive.

The relative effects of complex and simple environments on rats have been studied from a variety of perspectives (for a critical review of much of this research see Henderson, 1980). Joseph and Gallagher (1980) examined the effects of environmental restriction on maze learning, overresponsiveness, and exploratory behavior. Their experiments demonstrate that rats reared in a restricted environment have poor maze-learning ability. In addition, such rats develop a limited behavioral repertoire characterized by a generalized tendency to overrespond, a propensity toward perseverance in repetitious patterns of limited and circumscribed responding and the absence of habituation to repeated contact with novel stimuli.

The biological and biochemical effects of environmental complexity have been studied in a long series of experiments by Rosenzweig and his collaborators (Rosenzweig, Bennett, & Diamond, 1968, 1972a, 1972b; Wallace, 1974). They find evidence that maze training increases not only cognitive performance but also brain weight. The number of glial cells also increases, as does the size of the synaptic junctions. A biochemical change resulting from maze training, the increase in the proportion of RNA to DNA, is seen as suggestive of higher metabolic activity. There is also altered activity of acetylcholinesterase. Further-more, although the occipital cortex is the most affected area of the brain, these changes are not just the results of visual activity since similar changes occur in blinded rats.

Bennett, Rosenzweig, Morimoto, and Hebert (1979) report that the biological and biochemical effects of maze training occur not only when such training takes place at 30 days (approximately 1 week after weaning) but also at 70 days (well beyond sexual maturity). The two ages were also similar in the magnitude of the effects and their pattern of dis-tribution among regions of the cortex. Bennett et al. (1979) also find that the social stimulation of housing 12 animals in a group is as effective in producing cerebral changes as giving individuals maze training. The presence of others of their species not only may increase the complexity of the rats' environment, but may also facilitate their learning how to deal with the inanimate characteristics of that envi-ronment. Socially based learning of appropriate environmental manip-ulations has been demonstrated in the imitative learning not only of chimpanzees (Goodall, 1964) but also of cats (Herbert & Harsh, 1944). It is also worth noting that rats reared in relatively complex seminatural outdoor environments have even heavier cortices than those exposed to maze training (Wallace, 1974).

Finally, there is substantial evidence that the behavioral effects of early environmental deprivation are reversible. Bernstein (1979) tested deprived rats with a difficult discrimination problem. He found that if the time in an enriched environment is equal to the time of early deprivation, exposure to an enriched environment is not sufficient to compensate for the effects of early restriction. If the length of such exposure, however, is extended beyond the time of early deprivation, the effects of early restriction are reversible.

Research with rats also provides evidence of a loss of biopsychological adaptivity as the animals age. A review of this topic by Coper, Janicke, and Schulze (in press) provides evidence of such loss in thermoregu-lation, motor activity, and learning. Although the research on the first topic is not directly relevant to the present chapter, the research on the latter two topics is. A relevant series of experiments on motor activity involves performance on the rotarod test. In this test rats are placed on a rotating rod on which they have to run for a 2-minute period in a direction opposite to that of the rotation, the speed of rotation being increased on successive days. The results indicate that, aside from decreasing coordination, the attention and endurance nec-essary for solving a complex task also diminish in old animals. Relevant learning experiments include those on passive avoidance learning that measure the animal's ability to learn and remember to avoid a noxious stimulus after one exposure. The results indicate that there is an age-related deficit in learning to avoid such stimuli that stems from an impairment of the ability to store or retrieve from memory brief events that occur in the relatively recent past. Other experiments focused on another form of learning. In these, the rats were tested on the speed with which they were able to switch from a fixed ratio of immediate reinforcement to a situation in which a 10-second delay in lever pressing was required. Under normal conditions all age groups learned the fixed ratio task with the same efficiency. However, the older rats lost efficiency under hypoxia. More importantly, the older rats had more difficulty adapting to the delayed reinforcement procedure than did the young rats—a difference that was made even greater under reduced oxygen levels. Thus, although the ability to adapt clearly remains among the older rats, the ability to adapt to altered environmental conditions, particularly when such adaptation involves behavioral flexibility in difficult circumstances, would seem to be diminished.

All in all, the research on animals serves as a source of clues about the possible physiological effects of complex environments on humans. In addition, such research provides some evidence of reduced flexibility of response to environmental change in older animals, especially in physically demanding circumstances. A similar tendency may well exist for humans (see chapter 4 in this volume, by Loftus, Truax, & Nelson, and chapter 6, by Kliegl & Baltes). What is most remarkable, however, is the way the behavioral findings for animals parallel those for humans: No matter at what stage of the life cycle, exposure to the demands of complex environments generally improves cognitive functioning.

RELEVANT EXPERIMENTAL SOCIAL PSYCHOLOGICAL STUDIES

Although not directly dealing with the effects of environmental complexity in increasing the level of intellectual functioning and self-directed orientation, several sets of social psychological experiments are relevant to the proposed theory. They are relevant not only because their findings are congruent with the theory, but also because of the light they shed on the mechanisms through which environmental complexity has its effects.

Among the experiments providing an example of how generalization from particular environmental conditions affects psychological functioning in other situations are those of Breer and Locke (1965). They used college students as subjects in an investigation of task experiences as sources of attitudes. They found that participating in tasks in which certain forms of social organization (e.g., working individually vs. working as a group) are more likely to be successful than are other forms, affected not only situationally specific orientations, but also abstract beliefs, values, and preferences. Breer and Locke's conclusions about the ways in which the characteristics of tasks that individuals perform have generalized effects on their psychological functioning are equally applicable to the theory of environmental complexity presented here. They note that

> In any task situation certain patterns of behavior will have greater in-strumental reward value than others. By virtue of the reinforcing quality of task outcomes, these particular forms of behavior will have a better chance of being emitted than any others. At the same time individuals working on the task can be expected to respond cognitively (through apprehending the instrumental nature of these acts), cathectically (by developing a positive attachment to this kind of behavior) and evaluatively (by defining such behavior as legitimate and morally desirable) . . . beliefs, preferences, and values developed in one task situation will generalize to all others (depending on similarity). (Breer & Locke, 1965, pp. 15–17)

There have also been a wide range of social-psychologically oriented experimental studies that have dealt with environmental complexity. These studies, most of which have used college students as subjects, have been reviewed by Streufert and Streufert in their book *Behavior in the Complex Environment* (1978). Both the Streuferts' theory and the literature they review are concerned with a somewhat different set of problems from those dealt with here. The Streuferts' major concern is with the determinants of multidimensional thinking processes—the conditions under which persons who process stimulus information tend to place stimuli on several different dimensions. Furthermore, by lim-iting their concern to "laboratory" experiments and specifically ex-cluding developmental and applied points of view, they do not take into consideration any of the studies reviewed here. Despite these differences their approach is generally compatible with ours.

Multidimensional thinking and intellectual flexibility may well be related. The Streuferts themselves link such non–self-directed attitudes as authoritarianism to unidimensional thinking. They certainly see multidimensional thinking as affected by the same sorts of environ-mental conditions as are here hypothesized to result in intellectual flexibility.

> It appears that multidimensionality has value specifically in those situ-ations where it produces useful results, i.e., situations where . . . a large number of stimuli must be taken into account, and where various alter-natives have to be considered while looking at various overlapping groups of stimuli in various ways. On the other hand, unidimensionality would be an advantage where decisions have to be made according to a clear

criterion, where rapidity of action is required. (Streufert & Streufert, 1978, p. 99)

The Streuferts do raise two interrelated problems which are relevant to the present theory: Do not only low but also very high levels of environmental complexity lead to a decrement of multidimensional (or ideationally flexible) thinking? Are there interpersonal differences in how people react to various levels of environmental complexity? Their answer to both of these questions is yes. They accept as their model of the effect of different levels of environmental complexity the inverted U hypothesis (Malmo, 1959).

> Experience with too many unfamiliar events in too short a period of time is likely to produce overload due to too much incongruity. . . . Overload . . . tends to reduce dimensionality of perception. On the other hand, too little incongruity of experience is also a likely producer of unidimensional perceptions. (Streufert & Streufert, 1978, p. 92)

According to the Streuferts, such environmental experiences interacting with genetic dispositions produce individual differences in degree of multidimensional thinking.

The implications of the present theory for the dual questions of the effects of very high levels of environmental complexity and the nature of individual differences are similar to the Streuferts' conclusions. The theory presented here hypothesizes that individuals will exercise their potential for ideationally flexible and self-directed behavior as long as such behavior is rewarded. As we have noted, simple environments may extinguish such behavior. Environments, however, can also become so complex that individuals of a given ability level cannot deal effectively with the problems presented and such overload may result in a decrement in their functioning.[8] Individual differences in effectiveness in dealing with complex environments may result from the interaction of past environmental experience with genetic or other predispositions

---

[8] If the inverted U hypothesis is correct, it would suggest that the levels of environmental complexity involved in the generally positive relationships between complexity and intellectual functioning reported throughout the chapter have generally not been great enough to move people to the side of the U curve where their performance would deteriorate.

One problem with the inverted U hypothesis is that by shifting the point at which the downward slide in performance is said to occur, almost any set of results can be explained. This difficulty does not necessarily invalidate the inverted U hypothesis. It is, however, the case that most statements of the hypothesis are unclear as to whether the point of change in direction is the same for everybody or whether the level at which performance begins to deteriorate differs by population or even by individual (see Schooler & Zahn, 1968).

and, of course, from age.[9] Such differences make ideationally flexible or self-directed behavior more rewarding for one person than another even at similar levels of environmental complexity.

DISCUSSION

Both theoretical and methodological questions can be raised about the theory presented in this chapter. The theoretical criticisms are that the hypotheses are so broadly stated and so generally applied that almost any environmental manipulation can be seen as providing confirmation; that no instances are reported in which environmental manipulations fail to increase intellectual functioning; and that there is no discussion of the types of environmental manipulation that would be predicted to result in a reduction of such functioning. Methodological concerns center on the attribution of causal effects on the basis of structural equation analysis rather than experimental design.

The answers to both types of criticism are interconnected. It is not exactly true that no instances are presented in which changes in environmental complexity decreased human intellectual functioning. The structural equation analyses of the occupational study data (Kohn & Schooler, 1982; 1983, chapter 6) strongly imply that not only do increases in environmental complexity result in increases in intellectual flexibility, but also that decreases in occupational self-directedness result in decreases in intellectual flexibility. Furthermore, an examination of changes in the level of substantive complexity and other indicators of occupational self-direction indicates that the occupational self-direction of a substantial proportion (at least 20%) of the sample was lower in 1974 than 1964. In addition, there are occupational conditions that do not imply environmental complexity and that consequently do not affect intellectual flexibility. For example, hours worked and dirtiness are job conditions that have no independent effects on intellectual flexibility or self-directed orientations, although they do affect other aspects of psychological functioning (e.g., distress). Thus the occupation

---

[9] People may differ in their ability to cope with the stimulus level of complex environments for nonintellective reason such as differences in style of stimulus intensity control (Buchsbaum, 1976) or stimulus-seeking behavior (Zuckerman, 1974), both of which are affected by biological predispositions. Thus Buchsbaum (1974) has demonstrated a genetic component to the style (augmenting vs. reducing) of stimulus intensity control. Sensation seeking has been negatively related to platelet monoamine oxidase (MAO) activity (Murphy, Belmaker, Buchsbaum, Martin, Ciaranello, & Wyatt, 1977; Schooler, Zahn, Murphy, & Buchsbaum, 1978). There is also evidence that, whatever the cause, at least one class of person, schizophrenics, has particular difficulty dealing with complex environments, particularly when the complexity is of a social nature (Schooler & Spohn, 1982).

study provides examples of environmental conditions that on the basis of the environmental complexity theory would not be expected to affect intellectual functioning, and which in fact do not, as well as evidence that changes in occupational conditions resulting in decreases in environmental complexity lead to decreases in intellectual flexibility.

Experimental manipulations intended to restrict environmental complexity in humans are more hard to come by. One kind of reduction of environmental complexity, sensory deprivation, has been experimentally tried with humans. Although the reported results—a "precipitous decline" in the ability to carry out complex cognitive tasks (Suedfeld, 1975)—may come about because of mechanisms other than those suggested here, they are consistent with the presented hypotheses. Nor is it hard to imagine other environmental manipulations that would limit or reduce environmental complexity and thus be predicted to result in a reduction in intellectual functioning. Two such manipulations are simplification of the complexity of jobs (and it has been argued that employers have purposely deskilled jobs in order to gain more control over their employees; see Braverman, 1974, but see also Spenner, 1983) and curricular changes that simplify the demands of schoolwork (and such simplification is among the causes cited for the declining trend in SAT performance; see Walberg, 1983). Although, as we have seen, there have been animal studies involving the experimental constriction of environmental complexity, ethical considerations limit the likelihood of environment-constricting manipulations being tried with human subjects as part of a formal experimental design.

Limitations in the feasibility of the experimental method have led to the search for other ways to investigate the causes of human behavior. Starting with the seminal work of Herbert Simon (1957), methodologists in various social sciences, and now also psychology (cf. Bentler's 1980 *Annual Review of Psychology* article) have pointed to the necessity of using linear structural equation models for examining causal relationships that for ethical, practical, or theoretical reasons are not amenable to experimental investigation. Such use of structural equation analysis admittedly lacks the assurance, which random assignment provides for experimental design, that the apparent effects are not spurious, but specifically result from the variables being manipulated. However, several forms of structural equation analysis permit the modeling of complex causal relationships, such as reciprocal effects, that cannot be tested through experimental manipulation (Joreskog and Sorbom, 1976a, 1976b; for more general discussions of linear structural equation methods in causal modeling see Bentler, 1980; Heise, 1975; Kessler & Greenberg, 1981). In addition, such analyses are particularly amenable to survey and other types of data readily gathered from representative samples. Consequently, the results are frequently not open to the questions about generalizability that plague the vast majority of experimental studies that usually have to be carried out on nonrepresentative samples.

True, it is impossible to prove that a particular model is the only one that might fit the data, but it is possible both to assess the plausibility of the assumptions upon which a particular model is based and to compare models in terms of how well they fit the data they are supposed to describe. All of the models in the program on the effects of occupational conditions on psychological functioning were subjected to both types of test. In fact, the analyses of the key reciprocal relationship between intellectual flexibility and substantive complexity of work was used as a textbook example of how such analyses should be carried out (cf. Kessler & Greenberg, 1981, pp. 31–33, 130). Given that the models were appropriately specified and evaluated, measurement error taken into account and representative samples utilized, the use made of linear structural equation analysis to model the reciprocal causal relationships between environmental conditions and psychological functioning would seem to be justified.

Even for those not fully convinced that linear structural equation analysis is an appropriate way to estimate causal effects, this chapter provides evidence that environmental complexity is related to more effective cognitive functioning across all stages of the life span. This relationship has been found in both sexes, in several nations, and even in species other than man. Although the evidence is not as extensive, the review also indicates that environmental complexity is related to a self-directed rather than conformist orientation. These psychological concomitants of environmental complexity have been found both in research designs using experimental manipulation and in linear structural equation analysis. Although none of the studies is perfect, and few are able to completely exclude alternate explanations, it is rare to find a theory, no matter how rough-hewn, that is congruent with such a range of phenomena—one that stretches not only across populations, but across the research of academic disciplines from biochemistry to sociology. Certainly, from the point of view of psychology, with the exception of the nonlinearity implied by the possibility of an inverted U effect, the hypotheses about the effects of environmental complexity on psychological functioning seem in accord with principles of reinforcement and generalization accepted by most classical learning theorists.

To the extent that individuals exposed to complex environments develop capacities and orientations likely to be rewarded in such environments, they have the advantage of having developed an approach likely to be effective in other complex environments that they encounter. Questions remain of how long such capacities and orientations will endure in the absence of reinforcement. Individuals may well differ in this as well as in the speed with which they acquire such capacities and the ease with which they can generalize them across situations. There may also be individual differences in the optimal level of environmental complexity. The determinants of such individual differences also remain a question.

One such determinant may well be aging. On the other hand, Heise's findings (chapter 13 of this volume) of cross-cultural differences in the view of the aged should warn us against unquestionably accepting the notion that the elderly are invariably frail and weak-minded, while Salthouse's experiments (chapter 8) clearly show that the elderly can often maintain their level of performance even if they have to do so in new ways. Furthermore, Miller et al.'s findings (chapter 10) suggest that under some conditions the intellectual functioning of the elderly may benefit intellectually more from complex environments than do the young. What we have to learn is how environments that foster appropriate levels of cognitive functioning throughout the life span can be developed and maintained.

REFERENCES

Arenberg, D., & Robertson-Tchabo, E.A. (1980). Age differences and age changes in cognitive performance: New "old" perspectives. In R.L. Sprott (Ed.), *Age, learning ability and intelligence* (pp. 139–157). New York: Van Nostrand Reinhold.

Baltes, P.B., & Willis, S. (1982). Plasticity and enhancement of intellectual functioning in old age: Penn State's Adult Development and Enrichment Project (ADEPT). In F.I.M. Craik & S.E. Trehub (Eds.), *Aging and cognitive processes* (pp. 353–389). New York: Plenum.

Bennett, E.L., Rosenzweig, M.R., Morimoto, H., & Hebert, M. (1979). Maze training alters brain weights and cortical RNA/DNA ratios. *Behavioral and Neurological Biology, 26,* 1–22.

Bentler, P.M. (1980). Multivariate analysis with latent variables: Causal modeling. *Annual Review of Psychology, 31,* 419–456.

Bernstein, L. (1979). Hebb's claim of irreversibility in environmentally restricted rats. *American Psychologist, 34,* 802–803.

Blalock, H.M., Jr. (1971). Simultaneous-equation techniques. In H.M. Blalock, Jr. (Ed.), *Causal models in the social sciences* (pp. 153–157). Chicago: Aldine-Atherton.

Blalock, H.M., Jr. (1972). *Social Statistics* (2nd ed.). New York: McGraw-Hill.

Braverman, H. (1974). *Labor and monopoly capital: The degradation of work in the twentieth century.* New York: Monthly Review Press.

Breer, P.E., & Locke, E.A. (1965). *Task experience as a source of attitudes.* Homewood, IL: Dorsey Press.

Brown, B., & Grotberg, E.H. (1980). Head Start: A successful experiment. *Courrier, 30,* 337. (Extract)

Brown v. Board of Education, 347 U.S. 483 (1954).

Buchsbaum, M. (1974). Average evoked response and stimulus intensity in identical and fraternal twins. *Physiological Psychology, 2,* 365–370.

Buchsbaum, M. (1976). Self-regulation of stimulus intensity: Augmenting/reducing and the average evoked response. In G. Schwartz & D. Shapiro (Eds.), *Consciousness and self-regulation* (pp. 101–135). New York: Plenum.

Cattell, R.B. (1963). Theory of fluid and crystallized intelligence: A critical experiment. *Journal of Educational Psychology, 54,* 1–22.

Chein, I. (1936). The problems of heredity and environment. *Journal of Psychology, 2,* 229–244.

Chein, I. (1972). *The science of behavior and the image of man.* New York: Basic Books.

Chein, I., Gerard, D.L., Lee, R.S., & Rosenfeld, E. (1964). *The road to H: Narcotics, delinquency, and social policy.* New York: Basic Books.

The Consortium on Developmental Continuity. (1977). *The persistence of preschool effects* (Final Report Grant No. 18–76–07843; U.S. Department of Health, Education and Welfare, Office of Human Development Services). Washington, DC: U.S. Government Printing Office.

The Consortium for Longitudinal Studies. (1979). *Lasting effects after preschool* (DHEW Publication No. OHDS 80–30179). Washington, DC: U.S. Government Printing Office.

Cook, S.W. (1982). Obituary, Isidor Chein (1912–1981). *American Psychologist, 37,* 445–446.

Coper, H., Janicke, B., & Schulze, G. (in press). Biopsychological research on adaptivity across the life-span of animals. In P.B. Baltes, R.M. Lerner, & D.L. Featherman (Eds.), *Life-span development and behavior* (Vol. 7). New York: Academic Press.

Coser, R.L. (1975). The complexity of roles as a seedbed of individual autonomy. In L.A. Coser (Ed.), *The idea of social structure* (pp. 237–263). New York: Harcourt Brace Jovanovich.

Cunningham, W.R., & Owens, W.A., Jr. (1983. The Iowa State study of the adult development of intellectual abilities. In K.W. Schaie (Ed.), *Longitudinal studies of adult psychological development* (pp. 20–39). New York: Guildford Press.

Detterman, D.K., & Sternberg, R.J. (Eds.) (1982). *How and how much can intelligence be increased.* Norwood, NJ: Ablex.

Donaldson, G. (1981). Letter to the editor. *Journal of Gerontology, 36,* 634–636.

Gabennesch, H. (1972). Authoritarianism as world view. *American Journal of Sociology, 77,* 857–875.

Garber, H., & Heber, R. (1982). Modification of predicted cognitive development in high-risk children through early intervention. In D.K. Detterman & R.J. Sternberg (Eds.), *How and how much can intelligence be increased* (pp. 121–137). Norwood, NJ: Ablex.

Goldberger, A.S. (1964). *Econometric theory.* New York: Wiley.

Goodall, J.M. (1964). Tool-using and aimed throwing in a community of free-living chimpanzees. *Nature, 201,* 1264.

Gottfried, A.W. (Ed.). (1984). *Home environment and early cognitive development.* Orlando, FL: Academic Press.

Gribbin, K., Schaie, K.W., & Parham, I.A. (1980). Complexity of life style and maintenance of intellectual abilities. *Journal of Social Issues, 36*(2), 47–61.

Heise, D.R. (1975). *Causal analysis.* New York: Wiley.

Henderson, N.D. (1980). Effects of early experience upon the behavior of animals: The second twenty-five years of research. In E.C. Simmel (Ed.), *Early behavior: Implications for social development* (pp. 45–77). New York: Academic Press.

Herbert, M.J., & Harsh, C.M. (1944). Observational learning in cats. *Journal of Comparative and Physiological Psychology, 37,* 81–95.

Horn, J.L. (1978). Human ability systems. In P. B. Baltes (Ed.), *Life-span development and behavior* (Vol. 1, pp. 212–256). New York: Academic Press.

Jöreskog, K.G. (1973). A general method for estimating a linear structural equation system. In A.S. Goldberger & O.D. Duncan (Eds.), *Structural equation models in the social sciences* (pp. 85–112). New York: Seminar Press.

Jöreskog, K.G., & Sörbom, D. (1976a). Statistical models and methods for analysis of longitudinal data. In D.J. Aigner & A.S. Goldberger (Eds.), *Latent variables in socioeconomic models* (pp. 285–325). Amsterdam: North-Holland.

Jöreskog, K.G., & Sörbom, D. (1976b). Statistical models and methods for test-retest situations. In D.N.M. deGruijter, L.J.T. van der Kamp, & H.F. Crombag (Eds.), *Advances in psychological and educational measurement* (pp. 135–170). New York: Wiley.

Joseph, R., & Gallagher, R.E. (1980). Gender and early environmental influences on activity, overresponsiveness, and exploration. *Developmental Psychobiology, 13,* 527–544.

Kessler, R.C., & Greenberg, D.F. (1981). *Linear panel analysis: Models of quantitative change.* New York: Academic Press.

Kohn, M.L. (1963). Social class and parent-child relationships: An interpretation. *American Journal of Sociology, 68,* 471–480.

Kohn, M.L., & Schooler, C. (1969). Class, occupation and orientation. *American Sociological Review, 34,* 659–678.

Kohn, M.L., & Schooler, C. (1973). Occupational experience and psychological functioning: An assessment of reciprocal effects. *American Sociological Review, 38,* 97–118.

Kohn, M.L., & Schooler, C. (1978). The reciprocal effects of the substantive complexity of work and intellectual flexibility: A longitudinal assessment. *American Journal of Sociology, 84,* 24–52.

Kohn, M.L., & Schooler, C. (1981). Job conditions and intellectual flexibility: A longitudinal assessment of their reciprocal effects. In D.J. Jackson & E.F. Borgatta (Eds.), *Factor analysis and measurement in sociological research: A multi-dimensional perspective.* (pp. 281–313). London: Sage.

Kohn, M.L., & Schooler, C. (1982). Job conditions and personality: A longitudinal assessment of their reciprocal effects. *American Journal of Sociology, 87,* 1257–1286.

Kohn, M.L., & Schooler, C. (1983). In collaboration with J. Miller, K.A. Miller, C. Schoenbach, & R. Schoenberg. *Work and personality: An inquiry into the impact of social stratification.* Norwood, NJ: Ablex.

Langer, E.J., Rodin, J., Beck, P., Weinman, C., & Spitzer, L. (1979). Environmental determinants of memory improvement in late adulthood. *Journal of Personality and Social Psychology, 37,* 2003–2013.

Malmo, R.B. (1959). Activation: A neuropsychological dimension. *Psychological Review, 66,* 367–396.

Mann, A.J., Harrell, A., & Hurt, M., Jr. (1977). *A review of Head Start research since 1969 and an annotated bibliography* (DHEW Publication No. OHDS 78–31102). Washington, DC: U.S. Government Printing Office.

Miller, J., Schooler, C., Kohn, M.L., & Miller, K.A. (1979). Women and work: The psychological effects of occupational conditions. *American Journal of Sociology, 85,* 66–94.

Miller, K.A., & Kohn, M.L. (1983). The reciprocal effects of job conditions and the intellectuality of leisure-time activities. In M.L. Kohn & C. Schooler (Eds.), *Work and personality: An inquiry into the impact of social stratification* (pp. 217–241). Norwood, NJ: Ablex.

Miller, K.A., Kohn, M.L., & Schooler, C. (1985). Educational self-direction and cognitive functioning of students. *Social Forces, 63,* 923–944.

Miller, K.A., Kohn, M.L., & Schooler, C. (1986). Educational self-direction and personality. *American Sociological Review, 51,* 372–390.

Murphy, D.L., Belmaker, R., Buchsbaum, M.S., Martin, N., Ciaranello, R., & Wyatt, R.

(1977). Biogenic amine-related enzymes and personality variations in normals. *Psychological Medicine, 7,* 149–157.

Naoi, A., & Schooler, C. (1985). Occupational conditions and psychological functioning in Japan. *American Journal of Sociology, 90,* 729–752.

Owens, W.A. (1966). Age and mental abilities: A second adult follow-up. *Journal of Educational Psychology, 57,* 311–325.

Plemons, J.K., Willis, S.L., & Baltes, P.B. (1978). Modifiability of fluid intelligence in aging: A short-term longitudinal approach. *Journal of Gerontology, 33,* 224–231.

Ramey, C.T., MacPhee, D., & Yeates, K.O. (1982). Preventing developmental retardation: A general systems model. In D.K. Detterman & R.J. Sternberg (Eds.), *How and how much can intelligence be increased* (pp. 67–119). Norwood, NJ: Ablex.

Rodin, J., & Langer, E. (1980). Aging labels: The decline of control and fall of self-esteem. *Journal of Social Issues, 36*(2). 12–29.

Rosenbaum, J.E. (1975). The stratification of socialization process. *American Sociological Review, 40,* 48–54.

Rosenbaum, J.E. (1976). *Making inequality: The hidden curriculum of high school tracking.* New York: Wiley.

Rosenzweig, M.R., Bennett, E.L., & Diamond, M.C. (1968). Modifying brain chemistry and anatomy by enrichment or impoverishment of experience. In G. Newton & S. Levine (Eds.), *Early experience and behavior* (pp. 258–298). Springfield, IL: Charles C. Thomas.

Rosenzweig, M.R., Bennett, E.L., & Diamond, M.C. (1972a). Brain changes in response to experience. *Scientific American, 226,* 22–29.

Rosenzweig, M.R., Bennett, E.L., & Diamond, M.C. (1972b). Chemical and anatomical plasticity of brain: Replications and extensions. In J. Gaito (Ed.), *Macromolecules and behavior* (2nd ed., pp. 205–277). New York: Appleton-Century-Crofts.

Scarr-Salapatick, S., & Williams, M.L. (1973). The effects of early stimulation on low birth weight infants. *Child Develoment, 44,* 94–101.

Schaie, K.W. (1980). Age changes in intelligence. In R.L. Sprott (Ed.), *Age, learning ability and intelligence* (pp. 41–77). New York: Van Nostrand Reinhold.

Schaie, K.W. (1984). Midlife influences upon intellectual functioning in old age. *International Journal of Behavioral Develoment, 7,* 463–478.

Schooler, C. (1972). Social antecedents of adult psychological functioning. *American Journal of Sociology, 78,* 299–322.

Schooler, C. (1976). Serfdom's legacy: An ethnic continuum. *American Journal of Sociology, 81,* 1265–1286.

Schooler, C. (1984). Psychological effects of complex environments during the life span: A review and theory. *Intelligence, 8,* 259–281.

Schooler, C., Kohn, M.L., Miller, K.A., & Miller, J. (1983). Housework as work. In M.L. Kohn & C. Schooler (Eds.), *Work and personality: An inquiry into the impact of social stratification* (pp. 242–260). Norwood, NJ: Ablex.

Schooler, C., Miller, J., Miller, K.A., & Richtand, C.N. (1984). Work for the household: Its nature and consequences for husbands and wives. *American Journal of Sociology, 90,* 97–124.

Schooler, C., & Smith, K.C. (1978). ". . . and a Japanese wife." Social structural antecedents of women's role values in Japan. *Sex Roles, 4,* 23–41.

Schooler, C., & Spohn, H.E. (1982). Social dysfunction and treatment failure in schizophrenia, *Schizophrenia Bulletin, 8,* 85–98.

Schooler, C., & Zahn, T. (1968). The effect of closeness of social interaction on task performance and arousal in chronic schizophrenia. *Journal of Nervous and Mental Disease, 147,* 394–401.

Schooler, C., Zahn, T., Murphy, D.L., & Buchsbaum, M.S. (1978). Psychological correlates of monoamine oxidase activity in normals. *Journal of Nervous and Mental Disease, 166,* 177–186.

Simon, H.A. (Ed.). (1957). *Models of man: Social and rational.* New York: Wiley.

Slomczynski, K.M., Miller, J., & Kohn, M.L. (1981). Stratification, work, and values: A Polish–United States comparison. *American Sociological Review, 46,* 720–744.

Smith, K.C., & Schooler, C. (1978). Women as mothers: The effects of social structure and culture on value and behavior. *Journal of Marriage and the Family, 40,* 613–620.

Sommer, R., & Sommer, B.A. (1983). Mystery in Milwaukee: Early intervention, IQ, and psychology textbooks. *American Psychologist, 38,* 982–985.

Spaeth, J.L. (1976). Cognitive complexity: A dimension underlying the socioeconomic achievement process. In W.H. Sewell, R.M. Hauser, & D.L. Featherman (Eds.), *Schooling and achievement in American society* (pp. 103–160). New York: Academic Press.

Spenner, K.I. (1983). Temporal change in the skill level of work. *American Sociological Review, 48,* 824–837.

Streufert, S., & Streufert, S.C. (1978). *Behavior in the complex environment.* New York: Wiley.

Suedfeld, P. (1975). The benefits of boredom: Sensory deprivation reconsidered. *American Scientist, 63,* 60–69.

Walberg, H.J. (1983, Fall). Educational standards: Needs and prospects. *Educational Leadership, 81,* 19–30.

Wallace, P. (1974). Complex environments effects on brain development. *Science, 185,* 1035–1037.

Webster's Second New International Dictionary (Unabridged). (1961). Springfield, MA: G & C Merriam.

Williams, T. (1976). Abilities and environments. In W.H. Sewell, R.M. Hauser, & D.L. Featherman (Eds.), *Schooling and achievement in American society* (pp. 61–101). New York: Academic Press.

Willis, S.L., & Baltes, P.B. (1981). Letter to the editor. *Journal of Gerontology, 36,* 636–638.

Witkin, H.A., Dyk, R.B., Faterson, H.F., Goodenough, D.R., & Karp, S.A. (1961). *Psychological differentiation: Studies of development.* New York: Wiley.

Yarrow, L.J., Rubenstein, J.L., & Pedersen, F.A. (1975). *Infant and environment: Early cognitive and motivational development.* New York: Wiley.

Zuckerman, M. (1974). The sensation seeking motive. In B.A. Maher (Ed.), *Progress in experimental personality research* (pp. 80–148). New York: Academic Press.

Chapter Three

Applications of Psychometric Intelligence to the Prediction of Everyday Competence in the Elderly

K. Warner Schaie

INTRODUCTION

Almost 50 years ago Louis Leon Thurstone began his seminal work of developing a taxonomy and measurement instruments for the assessment of well-specified components of human intelligence. In his early enthusiasm, he spoke of identifying the very "building blocks of the mind" (Thurstone, 1935, p. 135). Thurstone was an eminently practical man, and nothing was farther from his mind than creating synthetic dimensions that would interest only basic researchers. His hope was to identify those basic components, called by him the Primary Mental Abilities (PMA), whose combinations and permutations would characterize the essentials of individual difference variance in the manifold behavioral situations that require the exercise of competence.

Thurstone was successful in identifying dimensions that have consistently accounted for substantial proportions of individual difference variance, and he created model assessment tools with exemplary psychometric characteristics such as high reliability and internal consistency. He was less successful, however, in demonstrating the utility of his psychometric system for the prediction of differential everyday criteria in educational settings. Even more problematic was the fact that summary IQ measures derived from the published PMA batteries were less effective in predicting overall academic performance than was true for more global measures such as the Stanford-Binet Intelligence

Test that had been constructed with the objective of selecting highly correlated test items.

Other assessment systems that follow the Thurstonian tradition, such as the work of Guilford (1967), the extensive development of factor reference kits by the Educational Testing Service (Ekstrom, French, Harmon, & Derman, 1976), and the second-order factor studies associated with the work on fluid and crystallized intelligence (Cattell, 1971) have introduced many technical refinements. It is questionable, however, whether they have proceeded any further than Thurstone in the quest for ecological validity.

Strong concerns have also been raised regarding the potential inadequacy of dealing with products of the mind rather than with the processes that lead to the observed performance. Consequently much recent work in cognitive psychology either has followed Piaget's quest for the accurate description of the origin and transformation of cognitive structures (Flavell, 1963; Piaget, 1972), or has sought to apply information-processing strategies to develop fine-grained portrayals of the components and timing of effortful behavior (Sternberg, 1977). Moreover, the contextual relevance of all the traditional paradigms has been seriously challenged (e.g., Charlesworth, 1979). Attempts to integrate the different approaches to the conceptualization and measurement of intelligence generally suggest that different paradigms may be relevant to alternative facets of the construct that may have differential import for acquisition and display of intelligent behavior. See for example Sternberg's triarchic theory (Sternberg, 1984; Sternberg & Berg, chapter 1 of this volume).

This argument can be extended further by proposing that different paradigms for the study of cognitive behavior may also have greater or lesser relevance for different life stages. To do so, it may be instructive to address the question as to what criteria for intelligent behavior might be most appropriate for adults and the elderly. I will then argue that the work of Thurstone and his followers may deserve renewed attention because their psychometric approaches appear to be particularly appropriate for the assessment and prediction of everyday competence in adults and the elderly. Finally, some steps will be described that I and my associates have taken to relate the wide body of knowledge on the psychometric performance of the elderly to the assessment and predictions of real-life issues affecting that particular target population.

THE CRITERION ISSUE

Early efforts at assessing intellectual competence had little reason to worry about ecological validity issues (Cook & Campbell, 1979; Schaie,

1978). For example, it was unambiguously clear to Binet and Simon (1905) that their work was concerned with identifying objective assessments of public school performance (also see Brooks & Weintraub, 1976). And Wechsler's principal concern was with the utility of intelligence tests for clinical diagnosis (Matarazzo, 1972; Wechsler, 1939). When more basic researchers entered the field of human intelligence, however, the importance of ecological validity receded. These investigators (e.g., Burt, Guilford, Spearman, or Thurstone) were far more concerned about theoretical issues regarding the nature of intellectual structures. They preferred description by means of reasonably pure measures of specific abstract components of intelligence rather than the complex tasks characterizing real life. The distinction between competent performance on abstract measures of intellectual structures such as might be observed in the laboratory and the competencies involved in daily life were therefore bound to emerge.

Most work with children is concerned either with the acquisition of intelligent behavior or with the description and prediction of a single universally relevant criterion (e.g., performance in the public school system). When dealing with adults and the elderly, however, we are no longer concerned with the emergence of intellectual structures, but rather with their maintenance or decline. Likewise, the call for the direct measurement of criterion variables seems naive, because there does not seem to be any single criterion that has the social importance and situational generality that is associated with successful performance in a societally mandated and universally experienced educational system.

If the necessity of multiple criteria for intellectual competence in adults is accepted, it is then possible to distinguish two somewhat different approaches that may each contribute to our understanding of the complexity of adult behavior. The first is in agreement with contexturalism and considers the possibility that different behavioral situations demand alternative combinations of intellectual abilities for their competent mastery. In addition, it should be noted that the situational demands that impinge on an individual's cognitive performance may vary markedly depending on the developmental tasks implicit in a given life stage (Chickering & Havighurst, 1981; Schaie, 1977/1978). The individual's response may also be determined by the perceived attributes of a given situation, and such perceptions, in turn, may differ by life stage (Schaie, Gonda, & Quayhagen, 1982). It is necessary therefore to specify life-stage–specific situational taxonomies and to provide instruments that allow the appraisal of observed and perceived competence in specific situations (see Scheidt & Schaie, 1978; Willis & Schaie, 1986). Although there may be essential skills that are required in some situations, it may nevertheless be possible to respond adaptively to many other situations given different permutations and combinations of cognitive skills.

A second approach, by contrast, proceeds from the assumption that there are classes of everyday activities that are *essential* for adaptive functioning in given life circumstances. It is argued that the inability to perform certain essential tasks of daily living will often lead to the institutionalization or other curtailment of independence for many elderly people. Examples of such critical tasks might be medication compliance, appropriate responses to written or oral requests by public authorities, or payment of utility bills when due. An important characteristic of such activities is their high face validity, in addition to immediate relevance to effective functioning of individuals in their community.

We are here not concerned with the increasingly popular methods of functional assessment (e.g., Pfeiffer, 1975). The criteria we are searching for must instead refer specifically to the exercise of intellectual abilities. Specific situation-relevant competencies for the above examples would be the ability to interpret medicine bottle labels, comprehending the meaning of textual materials, and interpreting materials presented in charts in documents. Although no exhaustive taxonomy of the requisite real-life tasks has thus far been attempted, reasonably representative measurement instruments are available that assess tasks such as those just mentioned (Educational Testing Service, 1977).

Our identification of possible criteria for real-life competence will soon inform us, however, that there are a multitude of behavioral situations and specific everyday behaviors, only few of which circumstances occur with respect to any given individual. Moreover, we are often concerned with the prediction of performance in circumstances that cannot be under our direct scrutiny. Our assessment of individuals for such purposes then must proceed at a greater level of abstraction, one that permits a more parsimonious organization of the underlying structure of intellect. A more basic level is also appropriate for attempts at behavioral intervention, unless work is to remain at a purely symptomatic level (Willis & Schaie, 1983a; Willis, 1985).

WHAT KIND OF "INTELLIGENCE" WILL PREDICT REAL-LIFE COMPETENCE?

Given the kinds of criteria outlined above, it now becomes necessary to ask at what level the structure of intellect might most profitably be sampled in adults and the elderly. My introductory statement indicated a preference for the Thurstonian approach and its derivatives. Let me now suggest further reasons for such a preference.

For some time, a number of students of adult developments have attempted to conceptualize further Piagetian stages that might account for qualitatively different aspects of intellectual functioning beyond young adulthood (e.g., Commons, Richards, & Kuhn, 1982; Riegel, 1973). But there remains a real question whether there are cognitive transformations in adulthood that lead to even near-universal stages. Indeed, it appears that operational definitions of Piagetian stages in adulthood lead to measurement systems that collapse upon intellectual and cognitive style dimensions of existent psychometric measurement frameworks (Hooper, Hooper, & Colbert, 1984; Humphreys, Rich, & Davey, 1985). The basic problem seems to be that the Piagetian approach was conceptualized for the study of the acquisition of cognitive behaviors in childhood. Without extensive reconceptualizations (Schaie, 1977/1978) it remains therefore of limited value in explaining maintenance and decline or reorganization of cognitive structures in adulthood.

Quite different limitations adhere to the utility of switching directly to an information-processing approach as our preferred basic measurement system. Information-processing studies may tell us much about the mind's processes and capabilities in optimally functioning individuals such as college students. Much of the work to date, however, has been concerned with the investigation of response speed under various instructions but with the primary requirement that subjects had reached a uniform criterion level of accuracy. Such an approach may be rather problematic in work with average adults and the elderly. Many subjects, first of all, could never be brought to a reasonably high criterion level. But more important, speed of response may be an irrelevant predictor for real-life tasks in which the range of response speed required for an adaptive response may be quite wide (Sternberg, 1984). As pointed out by others, any real-life situation would involve a rather wide array of componential processes, any one of which would show only low correlation with a specific criterion task (e.g., Egan, 1978, 1981). While we certainly should continue to explore the possibilities of componential analyses with older persons, it seems that the laboratory tasks used in the classical information-processing studies may not be best suited for our purposes.

What is at issue here is that we need predictors that represent the skills required to produce intellectual *products* rather than the *processes* that lead to their acquisition. Second, the basic ability measures to be used must be efficient markers of the ability factors to be assessed to permit test batteries short enough for pragmatic assessment conditions. Third, we need to identify a limited set of factors that is likely to reproduce as much individual difference variance in as many classes of real-life behaviors as is possible. And fourth, we need measures that have been tested on and adapted for the entire spectrum of adults, well into the old-old age range. I would like to suggest that these considerations imply that it should be possible to identify some subset from the broad spectrum of psychometric abilities that is likely to provide the most useful predictors of everyday competence.

PSYCHOMETRIC ABILITIES AS PREDICTORS OF REAL-LIFE COMPETENCE IN THE ELDERLY

Three distinct lines of inquiry will now be mentioned briefly that may be pertinent to the provision of the required assessment system. The first is concerned with identifying a suitable subset of ability measures. In this context, I would only remind the reader that I and my associates have studied the performance of adults and the elderly on the five mental abilities identified by Thurstone (1938) as accounting for the largest amount of individual difference variance in intellectual performance for the past three decades (Schaie, 1979, 1983). In addition to obtaining normative data on age changes and age differences it has also been possible to show that the structural properties of the mental abilities are well maintained across the adult life span (Hertzog & Schaie, 1986). This work has now culminated in the publication of a revision of the Thurstone tests suitable for adults and the elderly with extensive norms and other data on the psychometric characteristics of the updated battery that was named the *Schaie–Thurstone Test of Adult Mental Abilities (STAMAT)* (Schaie, 1985). The STAMAT battery includes the following five variables: (a) *Recognition vocabulary* is the ability to comprehend spoken and written language. (b) *Spatial orientation* is the ability to mentally rotate spatial concepts such as might be involved in translating information provided by maps into driving behavior. (c) *Inductive reasoning* involves the identification of a rule or general principle from specific instances. (d) *Number* assesses the ability to manipulate quantitative information. (e) *Word fluency* involves vocabulary recall and indicates proficiency at active verbal communication. Also used in our current work are other fluid-ability measures that come from the ETS Reference Kit of factors (Ekstrom et al., 1976) or derive from the ADEPT project (Baltes & Willis, 1982). Some of these provide alternative modes of assessing verbal ability and inductive reasoning. Others provide factor markers for some additional ability constructs including *figure relations,* the ability to analyze relationships among visual patterns; *memory span,* the ability to retain numerical symbols and meaningful words in short- and long-term storage; *social knowledge,* the ability to ascertain critical aspects and nuances of social interactions; and *perceptual speed,* the ability to make quick perceptual discriminations and translate these into a motoric response. Further work is in progress to collect normative data on these additional ability markers over the adult age range from the 20s to the 80s.

The second line of inquiry consisted of the development of a situational taxonomy for the elderly. Four major attribute dimensions were identified (social/nonsocial, active/passive, supportive/depriving, common/unusual) and a Q-sort instrument was developed to permit ratings of relative perceived competence in prototypic situations (Scheidt & Schaie, 1978). Stability characteristics of this instrument have been studied over a three-year period (Gilewski & Schaie, 1984), and appropriately sized correlations have been demonstrated with the abilities of inductive reasoning and spatial orientation (Schaie et al., 1982; Willis & Schaie, 1986). The relationship of this instrument to a full ability battery still remains to be investigated.

A third, even more promising line of inquiry is concerned with relating psychometric abilities to an instrument that consists of prototypic items for several classes of everyday activities, the ETS Basic Skills Test (Educational Testing Service, 1977). An initial study based on the ADEPT data showed substantial correlations of psychometric abilities, particularly of fluid-ability markers, with the real-life criterion measure in a group of rural elderly (Willis & Schaie, 1983b). Similar data were collected on a somewhat different ability battery as part of our cognitive training inquiry (Schaie & Willis, 1986; Willis & Schaie, 1983a) on a larger group of urban elderly. In the latter study, substantial correlations were shown between the Basic Skills Test and the latent psychometric constructs of inductive reasoning, verbal ability, and perceptual speed. Normative data on the matrix of relationships between psychometric abilities and real-life tasks have also been collected for a large sample (over 1,300 participants) covering the adult age range from the 20s to the 80s as part of the fifth wave of the Seattle Longitudinal Study, for which data collection has just been completed. The availability of this large data set will now make it possible to examine more closely just how performance on individual everyday tasks may depend on the cognitive dimensions described within the psychometric ability framework.

SUMMARY

It is argued that prediction of competent everyday behavior in adults and the elderly, assuming multiple criteria for both tasks and situations, can best be accomplished by concentrating on ability subsets derived from a Thurstonian structure of intellect model. Piagetian approaches are considered too complex and relevant specifically to the acquisition of cognitive structures. Information-processing paradigms are considered useful for obtaining an understanding of the components of psychometric performance, but seem to be at too detailed a level to be useful for the prediction of the cognitive products involved in everyday competence. Finally, some work was described that begins to investigate the network of relations between psychometric abilities and everyday competence in adults and the elderly.

REFERENCES

Baltes, P.B., & Willis, S.L. (1982). Plasticity and enhancement of intellectual functioning in old age: Penn State's Adult Development and Enrichment Project (ADEPT). In F.I.M. Craik & S.E. Trehub (Eds.), *Aging and cognitive processes* (pp. 353–389). New York: Plenum.

Binet, A., & Simon, T. (1905). Methodes nouvelles pour le diagnostic du niveau intellectual des anormaux. *L'Année Psychologique, 11,* 191.

Brooks, J., & Weintraub, M. (1976). A history of infant intelligence testing. In M. Lewis (Ed.), *Origins of intelligence* (pp. 19–58). New York: Plenum.

Cattell, R.B. (1971). *Abilities: Their structure, growth and action.* Boston: Houghton Mifflin.

Charlesworth, W.R. (1979). An ethological approach to studying human intelligence. *Human Development, 22,* 212–216.

Chickering, A.W., & Havighurst, R.J. (1981). The life cycle. In A.W. Chickering (Ed.), *The modern American college* (pp. 16–50). San Francisco, CA: Jossey-Bass.

Commons, M.I., Richards, F.A., & Kuhn, D. (1982). Systematic and metasystematic reasoning: A case for levels of reasoning beyond Piaget's stage of formal operations. *Child Development, 53,* 1058–1069.

Cook, T.C. & Campbell, D.T. (1979). *Quasi-experimentation: Design analysis issues for field settings.* Chicago: Rand McNally.

Educational Testing Service. (1977). *Basic Skills Assessment Test:Reading.* Princeton, NJ: Author.

Egan, D.E. (1978). *Characterizing spatial ability: Different mental processes reflected in accuracy and latency scores* (Report No. NAMRL-1250). Pensacola, FL: Naval Aerospace Medical Research Laboratory.

Egan, D.E. (1981). An analysis of spatial orientation test performance. *Intelligence, 5,* 85–100.

Ekstrom, R.B., French, J.W., Harmon, H., & Derman, D. (1976). *Kit of factor-referenced cognitive tests* (rev. ed.). Princeton, NJ: Educational Testing Service.

Flavell, J.H. (1963). *The developmental psychology of Jean Piaget.* New York: Van Nostrand Reinhold.

Gilewski, M., & Schaie, K.W. (1984, November). *The relation between memory, psychometric abilities and perceived competence in everyday situations in the elderly.* Paper presented at the meeting of the Gerontological Society of America, San Antonio, TX.

Guilford, J.P. (1967). *The nature of human intelligence.* New York: McGraw-Hill.

Hertzog, C., & Schaie, K.W. (1986). Stability of adult intellectual functioning: I. Analysis of longitudinal covariance structures. *Psychology and Aging, 1,* 159–171.

Hooper, F.H., Hooper, J.O., & Colbert, K.K. (1984). *Personality and memory correlates* of intellectual functioning: Young adulthood to old age (Contributions to Human Development, Vol. 11). New York: Karger.

Humphreys, L.G., Rich, S.A., & Davey, T.C. (1985). A Piagetian test of general intelligence. *Developmental Psychology, 21*, 872–877.

Matarazzo, J.D. (1972). *Wechsler's measurement and appraisal of adult intelligence.* Baltimore: Williams & Wilkins.

Pfeiffer, E. (Ed.). (1975). *Multidimensional functional assessment: The OARS methodology.* Durham, NC: Duke University Center for the Study of Aging and Human Development.

Piaget, J. (1972). Intellectual evolution from adolescence to adulthood. *Human Development, 15*, 1–12.

Riegel, K.F. (1973). Dialectical operations in the final period of cognitive development. *Human Development, 16*, 346–370.

Schaie, K.W. (1977/1978). Toward a stage theory of adult cognitive development. *Aging and Human Development, 8*, 129–138.

Schaie, K.W. (1978). External validity in the assessment of intellectual functioning in adulthood. *Journal of Gerontology, 33*, 695–701.

Schaie, K.W. (1979). The Primary Mental Abilities in adulthood: An exploration in the development of psychometric intelligence. In P.B. Baltes & O.G. Brim, Jr. (Eds.), *Life-span development and behavior* (Vol. 2, pp. 67–115). New York: Academic Press.

Schaie, K.W. (1983). The Seattle Longitudinal Study: A 21-year exploration of psychometric intelligence in adulthood. In K.W. Schaie (Ed.), *Longitudinal studies of adult psychological development* (pp. 64–135). New York: Guilford Press.

Schaie, K.W. (1985). *Manual for the Schaie-Thurstone Test of Adult Mental Abilities (STAMAT).* Palo Alto, CA: Consulting Psychologists Press.

Schaie, K.W., Gonda, J.N., & Quayhagen, M. (1982). The relationship between intellectual performance and perception of everday competence in middle-aged, young-old and old-old adults. In H. Loewe, J.E. Birren, & U. Lehr (Eds.), *Entwicklungspsychologie des mittleren und höheren Lebensalter* (pp. 43–67). Berlin: VEB Deutscher Wissenschaftlicher Verlag.

Schaie, K.W., & Willis, S.L. (1986). Can decline in intellectual functioning in the elderly be reversed? *Developmental Psychology, 22*, 223–232.

Scheidt, R.J., & Schaie, K.W. (1978). A situational taxonomy for the elderly: Generating situational criteria. *Journal of Gerontology, 33*, 848–857.

Sternberg, R.J. (1977). *Intelligence, information processing, and analogical reasoning: The componential analysis of human abilities.* Hillsdale, NJ: Erlbaum.

Sternberg, R.J. (1984). Toward a triarchic theory of human intelligence. *The Behavioral and Brain Sciences, 7*, 269–315.

Thurstone, L.L. (1935). *The vectors of the mind.* Chicago: University of Chicago Press.

Wechsler, D. (1939). *The measurement of adult intelligence.* Baltimore: Williams & Wilkins.

Willis, S.L. (1985). Towards an educational psychology of the adult learner. In J.E. Birren & K.W. Schaie (Eds.), *Handbook of the psychology of aging* (2nd ed.), pp. 818–847. New York: Van Nostrand Reinhold.

Willis, S.L., & Schaie, K.W. (1983a). *Enhancing intellectual performance in well functioning elderly.* Paper presented at the annual meeting of the Gerontological Society of America, San Francisco, CA.

Willis, S.L., & Schaie, K.W. (1983b). *Fluid-crystallized ability correlates of real life tasks.* Paper presented at the annual meeting of the American Educational Research Association, Montreal, Canada.

Willis, S.L., & Schaie, K.W. (1986). Practical intelligence in later adulthood. In R.J. Sternberg & R.K. Wagner (Eds.), *Practical Intelligence: Origins of competence in the everyday world* (pp. 236–268). New York: Cambridge University Press.

Chapter Four

Age-Related Differences in Visual Information Processing: Qualitative or Quantitative?

Geoffrey R. Loftus
Pauline E. Truax
Walter W. Nelson

Numerous recent investigations have focused on age-related limitations in visual information processing. Two general types of limitations have been noted, one involving time, and the second involving space (Hoyer & Plude, 1980). With respect to time, the question is: Do older people carry out perceptual processes more slowly than younger people? With respect to space, the question is: Do older people accurately perceive information over a narrower spatial area than do younger people?

We have several goals in this chapter. Primarily, we are interested in whether age differences in visual information acquisition are quantitative or qualitative, and we present an experiment bearing on this question. Second, we demonstate how apparently temporal qualitative differences may be attributable to spatial limitations. Finally, we use our experiment to address some methodological issues; we note some shortcomings of previous methodologies, and offer a new technique to deal with these shortcomings. We begin by briefly reviewing the literature on temporal and spatial limitations in older adults.

Temporal Limitations

Temporal limitations have been investigated more extensively than spatial ones. Typical studies have used a visual backward-masking paradigm in which a brief target stimulus is followed by a mask that

---

This research was supported by National Science Foundation Grant BNS82-09617 to Geoffrey R. Loftus.

impairs the S's identification of the target. Efficiency of visual processing is usually characterized by the critical time required to escape masking effects, estimated by the interval between stimulus onset and mask onset (stimulus onset asynchrony, or SOA) that produces some criterion performance level. The general finding is that older Ss require longer SOAs. This may be taken to mean that older Ss require more time, relative to young Ss, to perform an equivalent task; that is, their processing is less efficient.

The finding of longer SOAs for older Ss has been demonstrated in many studies. A series of masking experiments reported by Walsh and his associates used single-character target stimuli. These experiments showed a slowing for older adults in both peripheral and central perceptual processes (as defined by Turvey, 1973). Walsh (1976) used a backward masking paradigm to investigate age differences in central perceptual processes. Ss viewed target and mask dichotically; that is, they viewed a target stimulus in one eye followed by a pattern mask in the other eye. The older group required a 24% longer SOA in order to achieve the same criterion level of performance. In two similar experiments, Walsh, Williams, and Hertzog (1979) found 33% and 38% increases in central processing time for older relative to younger Ss.

Peripheral processes were investigated by Walsh, Till, and Williams (1978) in a monoptic backward-masking study. Two experiments showed that older Ss needed longer SOAs to process the targets adequately. Apparently, slowing of perceptual processes occurs throughout the system.

The quantitative/qualitative issue. An age-related slowing in both peripheral and central visual processing is thus well documented. However, the reasons for this effect are unclear. One possibility is that the effect is quantitative. By this interpretation, older people acquire the same information, via the same cognitive processes, as do younger people, but at a slower pace. A second possibility is that the effect is qualitative. By this interpretation, older people acquire different kinds of information or are using less efficient information-acquisition strategies compared to younger people, or both.

How are these two possibilities to be empirically distinguished? One standard approach is to interpret the absence of a statistical interaction between age and a given independent variable as evidence that the effect of the independent variable is quantitative; that is, a quantitative effect is assumed to exist when the age difference is constant across all levels of the independent variable. Conversely, the presence of an Age × Condition interaction is cited as evidence that the effect of the condition is qualitative.

By this test, the evidence supporting either a simple quantitative or a qualitative difference between visual processing for young and old people is inconclusive. Walsh (1976) found no interaction between age and target duration on critical SOA in his dichoptic backward-masking experiment. Till (1978) found a similar lack of interaction with respect to target energy: The peripheral processing difference between age groups was constant across target energy conditions. However, in a similar paradigm, Walsh et al. (1978) did find an interaction: The younger Ss improved more quickly with increasing energy level than did the older Ss. Kline and Szafran (1975) also found stimulus duration to interact with age in a monoptic backward-masking paradigm: Young Ss improved more rapidly with increasing duration than older Ss.

Interpreting interactions. Relying on the presence or absence of a statistical interaction as evidence for quantitative or qualitative age-related differences is problematical (Anderson, 1961; Bogartz, 1976; Krantz & Tversky, 1971; Loftus, 1978, 1985a, 1985b). The major problem is that, unless the interaction is ordinal (crossover), it can be removed by applying a suitable monotonic transformation to the dependent variable. This, in turn, means that conclusions issuing from a nonordinal interaction cannot be extended to other dependent variables, or to underlying theoretical constructs, whose relationship to the dependent variable cannot be assumed stronger than monotonic. Loftus (1985b) points out a related problem, which is that conclusions based on statistical interactions are likely to be inconsistent, both within and across experiments. In the experiment we report below, we expand on this methodological issue, and suggest a somewhat different method for determining whether an obtained effect is quantitative or qualitative.

Spatial Limitations

Spatial limits impose constraints on the quantity of information that can occupy the system at any given time. The target stimuli for the Walsh et al. experiments were single characters; thus the spatial capacity was probably not a limiting factor. It is possible that any qualitative differences between the age groups involve a difference in the degree to which multiple units of information must be handled one unit at a time (serial processing) versus simultaneously (parallel processing).

Parallel processing of visual information does occur under some circumstances in young adults (Shiffrin & Schneider, 1977). However, it appears that parallel processing is more difficult for older adults. In a preliminary investigation, Walsh and Thompson (Walsh, 1975) studied age differences using a partial report procedure similar to that described by Averbach and Coriell (1961). An array of eight letters (two rows of four items) was displayed for 50 ms and followed at various delays by a visual marker designating one of the items to be reported. Before the experimental trials began, Ss practiced until they could report six out of eight items correctly when there was no delay between the array and marker. Nine young (18–31 years of age) and 10 old (60–72 years of age) Ss participated in this experiment. The difference between old and young Ss was dramatic. The practice task was simple for the young Ss; they typically reported the first eight items correctly. The older Ss, however, found the practice task much more difficult. The task was impossible for 8 of the 10 old Ss. Even after 2 hours of practice these older Ss were unable to report more than four out of eight items correctly. The 2 older subjects who reached criterion did so immediately, like the 9 younger Ss. The performance of these 2 Ss in the actual experiment was not dramatically different from that of the young. These results suggest that most older Ss cannot process large blocks of items as single perceptual events.

PRESENT EXPERIMENT: THE QUANTITATIVE SLOWING HYPOTHESIS

We now report an experiment to investigate qualitative versus quantitative differences in acquisition of visual information. The paradigm used in this experiment was very similar to that reported by Cerella, Poon, and Fozard (1982). Briefly, old and young Ss performed a relatively simple visual memory task: On each of a series of trials, an S saw a target stimulus consisting of a row of four digits for exposure durations ranging from 25 to 641 ms, followed immediately by a mask consisting of random black splotches (visual noise) on a white background. Immediately after seeing the target-mask display, the S reported as many of the digits as possible. The principle data in this paradigm take the form of a *performance curve,* which is a function relating mean proportion of reported digits to exposure duration. We assume that the rate at which a performance curve rises reflects the rate at which information is acquired from the digit array.

Based on the past data described above, we expected that young Ss would perform better than older Ss on this task. Our principle goal was to test the (null) hypothesis that the expected old/young difference is *quantitative* against the (alternative) hypothesis that the difference is *qualitative.* The logic underlying both the conceptual and empirical comparison of these hypotheses is spelled out by Loftus (1985c) and, briefly, is this. Suppose that the old/young difference is quantitative. By quantitative, we mean that older Ss in this task acquire the same information, via the same perceptual processes, as do younger Ss, but at a rate that is slower by some factor, k. This hypothesis, which we term the *quantitative slowing hypothesis,* yields a simple, but very strong prediction: It will take k times as long for older, relative to younger, Ss to reach any arbitrary performance level. Mathematically, this prediction may be expressed as

$$PY(t) = PO(kt),$$

where $PY(x)$ and $PO(x)$ refer to performance levels for young and old subjects, respectively, following an array exposed for a duration of x.

This prediction is illustrated in Figure 1(a), with k arbitrarily set to 2. To test the prediction empirically, it is convenient to plot performance as a function of duration on a log scale, rather than a linear scale, as shown in Figure 1(b). The prediction then becomes

$$PY[ln(t)] = PO[ln(k) + ln(t)].$$

That is, the performance curves for old and young subjects should be *horizontally parallel,* with the old-subject curve shifted to the right by a distance equal to $ln(k)$. Thus, if the obtained performance curves *are* horizontally parallel, the quantitative slowing hypothesis is confirmed, and k can be estimated by the horizontal difference between the curves. If the curves are not horizontally parallel, then the quantitative slowing hypothesis is disconfirmed, and a qualitative difference is inferred.[1]

Method

Subjects. Subjects were 11 old adults (5 males and 6 females, 56 to 73 years of age, mean age 64.45 years) and 11 young adults (4 males and 7 females, 18 to 28 years of age, mean age 19.75 years). Of the old Ss, 4 were parents of the experimenters, 4 were University of Washington staff members, 1 was a senior faculty member, and 3 answered an advertisement in the campus daily paper. They were paid $10 for participating. The young Ss were university undergraduates receiving course credit for their participation. All Ss (including those with corrected vision) were roughly screened for visual acuity: They saw a practice slide and had to report the top row of digits. All Ss did so with ease.

Stimuli. The stimuli were 72 12-digit arrays, prepared as black-on-white 35 mm slides. The 12 digits in each array were arranged in three rows of four digits per row. Each digit subtended 0.56° vertical $\times$ 0.28°

---

[1] We should emphasize the difference between pairs of curves that are horizontally parallel and pairs of curves that are vertically parallel. Vertical parallelism is implied by lack of interaction in a standard analysis of variance. If two curves are vertically parallel, they are generally not horizontally parallel, and vice versa.

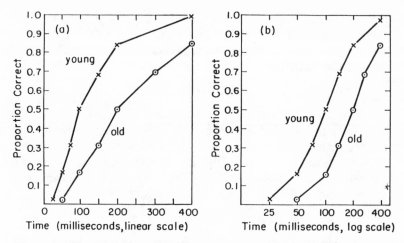

Figure 1.   Hypothetical performance curves predicted by the quantitative slowing hypothesis. In this example, old Ss take twice as long as young Ss to reach any given performance level. In the right panel, the curves are plotted on a log duration scale: The prediction is that the curves will be horizontally parallel.

horizontal. Digits were separated by 0.37° vertical and 0.74° horizontal. The digits in each array were chosen randomly with the restriction that no digit could appear more than twice in any row. On each trial, the S attempted to report the four digits from one of the three rows.

As noted, the noise mask that followed each array consisted of black visual noise on a white background. When the mask was superimposed on the digit arrays, no digits could be read from the arrays.

There was a dim adapting field continuously present during the experimental session.

Apparatus.   The apparatus is described in detail by Loftus, Gillispie, Tigre, and Nelson (1984). All slides were displayed by Kodak carousel projectors. Timing was controlled by a Gerbrands tachistoscopic shutter with rise and fall times of approximately 1 ms. Subjects responded with keys marked 0–9 on a response box. All display apparatus was enclosed in a soundproof box. All display and response-collection apparatus was under control of an Apple II computer.

Design and procedure.   Subjects were run individually. At the start of an experimental session, an S was read the instructions, and was allowed to dark-adapt for 5 min. After having the procedure explained, the S had a few trials of practice.

In the experiment proper, each S saw a total of 144 stimuli in the form of two consecutive passes through the 72 slides. We refer to each of the two 72-trial passes as a *set* of trials.

Aside from age, the only independent variable was exposure duration of the target array. Each array was shown for one of nine exposure durations, ranging from 25 ms to 641 ms, in equal log steps; each duration differed from the adjacent durations by a factor of 1.5. Exposure durations occurred randomly across the 144 trials with the restriction that, within each 72-trial set, eight arrays were displayed at each of the nine exposure durations.

Recall that each stimulus array was three rows by four columns. During each trial, the S had to report only one of the three rows. The S always knew in advance which row was to be reported. This was accomplished by blocking trials, by to-be-reported row, in 24-trial blocks. Prior to the start of each block, the S was informed which row was to be reported for that block. Additionally, a high, medium, or low tone prior to each trial reminded the S that the top, middle, or bottom row was to be reported on that trial.

On each trial, the following sequence of events occurred. First, a series of ten 30-ms-on/30-ms-off, 1,000-hz beeps signaled the start of the trial. During this warning period, a dim fixation light was displayed at the point where the middle of the upcoming array would be. This was followed by a blank (adapting field only) delay of 500 ms, followed by a 200-ms, 2,000-hz, 1,000-hz, or 250-hz tone, reminding the S to report the top, middle, or bottom row of the upcoming array. There was then another 500-ms blank delay, followed by the digit array, followed by the mask which lasted 500 ms. Immediately after the display sequence, the S attempted to type in the four digits, in correct order, guessing if necessary. Pressing a return key completed the response. If the S typed in fewer, or more, than four digits, he or she was requested to respond again. Feedback followed the S's response in the form of four 250-ms tones: Each tone was high (1,500 hz) if the corresponding digit had been correctly reported, and low (250 hz) if it had been incorrectly reported. Following feedback was a 500-ms pause prior to the start of the next trial. Ss were urged to guess as best they could, even when they were certain that they had not seen anything.

Results and Discussion

Performance curves. Average performance curves for old and young Ss will be shown below. First, however, Figure 2 provides a flavor for the individual curves. For sake of clarity, only three curves—those for the best, worst, and median Ss from both the old and young groups—are shown. These six curves are fairly typical of those from all 22 Ss.

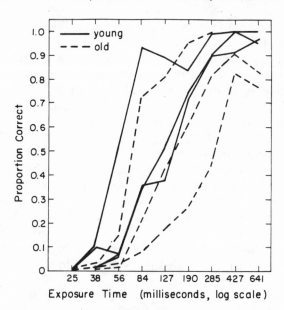

Figure 2.   Individual performance curves for three young Ss (solid lines) and three old Ss (dashed lines).

Old Ss are represented by dashed lines, and young Ss are represented by solid lines. As expected, performance was generally better for young Ss, relative to old Ss. The observed across-S variability was also greater for old relative to young Ss.

Recall the prediction of the quantitative slowdown hypothesis: On the average, old-S performance curves should be horizontally parallel to young-S performance curves. The observed individual curves for old and young Ss were not grossly nonparallel (see Figure 2). An evaluation of the prediction must therefore depend on a statistical test.

Averaging artifacts.   At this point, however, we face a problem. To make old/young horizontal comparisons, it is inappropriate to obtain, and compare, average curves across the young and across the old Ss. Figure 3 illustrates why this is so. Here, hypothetical performance curves are illustrated for two old Ss and two young Ss. The curves are as predicted by the quantitative slowing hypothesis; they are all horizontally parallel to one another. As with the observed performance curves (Figure 2) there is more variability in the old Ss, relative to the young Ss. The dashed curves in Figure 3 show the averages of the young and old Ss. Note that conclusions based on the average curves only would be incorrect: Although all the individual curves are horizontally parallel, the average curves are not. The effect of increased

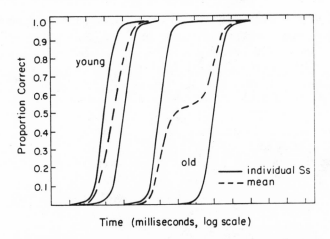

Figure 3. Hypothetical performance curves for two young Ss (left) and two old Ss (on the right). The increased old-S variability produces a systematic bias when the curves are averaged.

variability in the older Ss is to bias the average slope systematically; it is shallower. It is important to realize that the presence of this artifact does not depend on there being increased *population* variability for the older Ss; it is only necessary that there be more *sample* variability. The greater the difference in observed variability between young and old Ss, the more serious the artifact.

Cumulative normal fit to the psychometric function. We solve this problem as follows. We have found, using experienced Ss in this paradigm, that the curves shown in Figure 2 are fit reasonably well by a cumulative normal. A normal curve has only two parameters, μ, the mean, and σ, the standard deviation. Two cumulative normal curves are horizontally parallel if and only if they do not differ in σ. Our statistical strategy, therefore, was to fit each of the 22 individual performance curves by a cumulative normal, thereby estimating μ and σ for each S. A test of old/young horizontal parallelness can be accomplished by performing a *t-* test of the estimated sigmas for old and young Ss.

Accordingly, we corrected each S's nine probabilities for the guessing level of 0.1, and then transformed each corrected probability to a z-score. We then computed the best-fitting straight line through the data points relating z to log duration. From this fit, we obtained three pieces of data for each S. The first datum was the slope of the regression function, which reflects the estimate of σ (and to which we shall hereafter refer as a slope).[2] The second datum was the X-intercept of the regression function, which represents the estimate of μ. The X-intercept may be viewed as the critical time required to achieve a 50% performance level (i.e., to recall two out of the four digits), and is comparable to the critical times to escape masking (e.g., as reported by Walsh and his colleagues). We shall hereafter refer to the X-intercept as the "critical time." The third datum was the Pearson r[2]. Table 1 shows these data for the 11 old and 11 young Ss.[3] Figure 4 shows the mean performance curves for young and old Ss. These average curves were obtained by averaging the corrected-for-guessing z-score curves and transforming back to probabilities. Note that under the assumption that the z-transformed curves are linear this technique is not subject to the averaging artifact described above.

As indicated earlier, comparison of the slopes for old versus young Ss constitutes the statistical test of the quantitative slowing hypothesis. The mean slopes are 0.51 and 0.58 for old and young Ss, respectively. Although small, the difference is significant, $t(20) = 2.20$ $p < .05$, indicating that the old-S performance curves shown in Figure 2 are, on the average, slightly shallower than the young-S performance curves. The quantitative slowing hypothesis is thus disconfirmed. Apparently the difference between young and old people in this task is at least partly qualitative.

The mean critical times are 176 and 105 ms for old and young Ss, respectively. This difference is significant, $t(20) = 3.58$, $p < .05$. Recall the suggestion of Figure 2 that the older Ss appear to be more variable than the younger Ss. The observed increased variability is reflected in the across-S critical-time standard deviations of 1.49 and 1.28, respectively, for old and young Ss. However, this young/old variability difference is not significant, $F(10,10) = 2.68$.

Basis of qualitative differences.   What is the nature of the qualitative difference between old and young Ss? We will address this question in several ways. Recall first that Ss had to report a row of four digits. The pattern of responding across the four digits, i.e., the serial position curves, provide evidence for the kinds of processes that are used. For example, if information from different spatial locations were acquired

---

[2] An actual estimate of σ could be obtained by raising 1.5 to the (1/slope) power.

[3] Because the regression analyses were carried out on a log time scale, all descriptive statistics (means and standard deviations), as well as inferential statistical tests, were computed on log transforms of critical time values. For ease of discourse, mean critical times are expressed in time (ms) when they are presented in tables or in the text. Standard deviations of critical times are expressed as ratios (e.g., a mean of 100 and a standard deviation of 2.0 indicates that ±1 standard deviation ranges from 100/2.0 = 50 to 100 × 2.0 = 200).

Table 1. Summary Data for All 22 Subjects

Old Ss	Age	Slope	Critical Time	r^2
S1	64	.358	228.1	.94
S2	73	.440	278.7	.96
S3	73	.509	175.9	.91
S4	59	.419	308.0	.90
S5	65	.382	225.9	.94
S6	56	.568	232.8	.84
S7	61	.609	88.2	.89
S8	66	.547	106.7	.92
S9	72	.542	144.0	.91
S10	64	.623	124.0	.97
S11	56	.617	170.7	.92
Means	64.45	.510	175.9	.92
SDs		.096	1.49	

Young				
S1	28	.534	119.1	.90
S2	19	.588	86.5	.95
S3	19	.535	68.7	.88
S4	19	.623	135.6	.93
S5	18	.587	80.6	.92
S6	18	.533	120.3	.94
S7	18	.672	139.8	.96
S8	19	.549	139.8	.97
S9	18	.599	121.5	.97
S10	21	.597	88.2	.86
S11	22	.565	98.5	.88
Means	19.91	.580	105.6	.92
SDs		.043	1.28	

Note: Critical times are in ms, and mean critical times are geometric means.

entirely in parallel, and if there were no short-term memory limitations, then performance would not depend on serial position. Conversely, to the degree that performance *does* depend on serial position, we can conclude either that the digits are originally acquired serially or that there are short-term memory limitations, or both. Thus we ask: Do old and young Ss differ in their response pattern across the four digits?

Answering this question is not entirely straightforward because, when comparing old and young Ss with respect to serial-position effects (or any other variable), we would like to keep performance level constant. To achieve this goal, we selected, for each S, the four adjacent exposure durations that produced two performance levels below 50%, and two performance levels above 50%. We computed probability correct as a function of serial position, for old and young Ss, for these durations

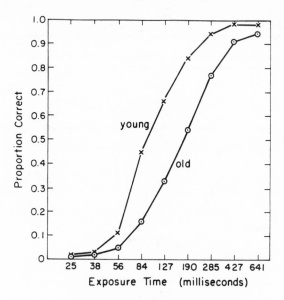

Figure 4.   Mean performance curves for old and young Ss. Averaging was done on the z- transforms of the individual curves, and the resulting mean curves were transformed back to proportions.

only. This analysis technique is somewhat unusual, in that it entails a comparison of data from systematically different exposure durations for old and young Ss—exposure durations are typically longer for older Ss. However, we assert that old/young serial-position differences can be best examined when performance, rather than exposure duration, is kept constant. Versions of this technique have been used by others for the same reason. Biederman and Tsao (1979) and Salthouse (chapter 8 of this volume) achieved equivalence across Chinese and American Ss, and across old and young Ss, respectively, by judicious subject selection. Likewise, Schoenfield and Wenger (1975) equated old/young performance in a perceptual task by differentially dark-adapting the Ss of different ages.

Table 2 shows the result of our serial-position analysis. The overall difference between old and young Ss is, of course, small; it was made to be that way. In general, performance drops over serial position. This effect was statistically significant, $F(3, 60) = 30.0$, $p < .05$, Mse = 0.007. Of primary interest is the strong crossover interaction between age and serial position, an effect that was also significant, $F(3, 60) = 6.29$, $p < .05$, Mse = 0.007. We may thus conclude that performance declines over serial position, but faster for old Ss than for young Ss. As suggested earlier, this result is consistent with a variety of possible

Table 2. Proportion Correct for Each Serial Position for Young and Old Subjects

| | Serial Position | | | | |
	1	2	3	4	Means
Young	.64	.63	.57	.53	.56
Old	.70	.65	.50	.40	.59
Means	.67	.64	.53	.47	

Table 3. Slopes and Critical Values for Old and Young Ss, for Serial Positions 1 and 2 Only, and Serial Positions 3 and 4 Only (standard deviations in parentheses)

	Serial Positions 1–2	Serial Positions 3–4
Slopes		
Old	0.559 (0.075)	0.462 (0.111)
Young	0.574 (0.051)	0.592 (0.040)
Critical Values (ms)		
Old	138 (1.41)	247 (1.80)
Young	91 (1.35)	117 (1.30)

old/young qualitative differences. We briefly sketch four: the first and second seem reasonably likely; the third and fourth seem less likely, but not entirely implausible. The present data do not allow us to distinguish among these various possibilities.

First, extraction of information from different spatial positions may be more of a parallel process for young, relative to old, Ss. Second, extracted digits may be serially placed into a short-term memory whose capacity is lower for old relative to young Ss. For example, it may be that four digits never overload short-term memory for younger Ss, but sometimes overload short-term memory for older Ss (see Sperling, 1986; Sperling & Speelman, 1970). Third, events intervening between seeing the display and reporting it may produce retroactive interference that affects the most recently stored information more severely for old than for young Ss. Fourth, Ss may make errors in striking the response keys; the causes of such motor errors may be such that later keys struck are more prone to error for older relative to younger Ss.

Is whatever causes the Age × Serial Position interaction sufficient to explain the qualitative differences between old and young Ss? To address this question, we recomputed performance curves, considering data from Serial Positions 1 and 2 only, and from Serial Positions 3 and 4 only. The results of this analysis are shown in Table 3.

For Serial Positions 3 and 4, the mean slopes for old and young Ss are 0.462 and 0.592, respectively. This difference is statistically significant, $t(20) = 3.67$, $p < .05$. Clearly, the old/young difference for Serial Positions 3 and 4 is qualitative.

For Serial Positions 1 and 2, however, the mean slopes for old and young subjects are 0.559 and 0.574, respectively. This difference is not statistically significant, $t(20) = 0.55$. Although we must exercise the usual prudence about accepting null hypotheses, we note that the observed slope difference is quite small—less than 5%. We tentatively conclude that, when only the first two serial positions are considered, the quantitative slowing hypothesis is confirmed: Old/young differences are quantitative, not qualitative.

Given this conclusion, consider the critical times for Serial Positions 1 and 2 only. Of primary importance is that the old/young difference is still quite substantial. This difference may best be characterized by noting that the mean ratio of old to young critical times is 138/91 = 1.52. Because old and young slopes are approximately equal, this ratio is approximately constant across all performance levels. The ratio can be interpreted as the degree of slowdown in information acquisition rate for old Ss relative to young Ss. That is, we may conclude that our young Ss acquire information 1.52 times faster than our older Ss.

Practice effects. We have concluded that, considering data from Serial Positions 1 and 2 only, there is no qualitative difference between old and young Ss. If all serial positions are considered, however, there *are* qualitative differences. We have already listed several possible mechanisms to explain these differences.

We now consider the possibility that whatever does underlie the qualitative differences may be attenuated with practice. Recall that each experimental session consisted of two sets of 72 trials per set. Table 4, which is organized like Table 3, shows data for Sets 1 and 2 separately. The most noteworthy result is that, whereas old and young slopes differ significantly for Set 1, $t(20) = 2.54$, $p < .05$, they do not differ significantly for Set 2, $t(20) = 1.38$. Again, we must be cautious about accepting the null hypothesis for Set 2. However, it does appear that the slope difference for old and young Ss decreases with practice.

Table 5 provides data for both serial position and practice effects. Consider young Ss first. It is evident that slopes are unaffected either by practice or by serial position. This indicates that young Ss are qualitatively invariant over both these variables. Examination of critical values, however, indicates that both variables do produce quantitative differences: Young Ss are faster by an average factor of 1.23 on Set 2 versus Set 1, and are faster by an average factor of 1.29 on Serial Positions 1–2 versus Serial Positions 3–4.

Table 4. Slopes and Critical Values for Old and Young Ss, for Set 1 Only and Set 2 Only (standard deviations in parentheses)

	Set 1	Set 2
Slopes		
Old	0.496 (0.108)	0.524 (0.108)
Young	0.588 (0.053)	0.573 (0.047)
Critical Values (ms)		
Old	189 (1.61)	166 (1.49)
Young	116 (1.28)	97 (1.31)

Table 5. Slopes and Critical Values for Old and Young Ss, for Serial Positions 1–2/Serial Positions 3–4 × Set 1/Set 2 (standard deviations in parentheses)

		Serial Position	
		1–2	3–4
Slopes			
Set 1	Old	0.555 (0.100)	0.443 (0.121)
	Young	0.589 (0.066)	0.594 (0.045)
Set 2	Old	0.563 (0.090)	0.480 (0.137)
	Young	0.560 (0.054)	0.591 (0.048)
Critical Values (ms)			
Set 1	Old	150 (1.45)	273 (2.02)
	Young	103 (1.34)	127 (1.29)
Set 2	Old	127 (1.48)	221 (1.84)
	Young	80 (1.41)	109 (1.35)

The situation is somewhat different for old Ss. For Serial Positions 1–2 only, old Ss do not differ qualitatively from young Ss, as indicated by the similar slopes. For Serial Positions 3–4, however, old Ss are qualitatively different both from young Ss *and* from themselves at Serial Positions 1–2. The slope deficit (and by assumption the qualitative differences) does attenuate with practice.

GENERAL DISCUSSION

Assessing Age Differences in Critical Processing Time

At this point, it is useful to compare explicitly the present experimental paradigm with that used in past work. In both the present paradigm and those typically used by Walsh and his colleagues (see also Turvey,

1973) the major question is: How much target processing time (critical time) is necessary to escape the effect of a noise mask? Walsh and his colleagues have defined "escaping the effect of a noise mask" to be the achievement of some arbitrary criterion performance level. In the present experiment we found, like Walsh and his colleagues, that this critical time is greater for older than for younger people.

Our paradigm may be viewed as an extension of that used by Walsh and his colleagues in that critical times are compared across *all* performance levels; this is what a horizontal comparison of performance curves (Figure 1) amounts to. We did this to test whether the expected old/young difference was qualitative or quantitative. The prediction of the quantitative slowing hypothesis was that the percent additional time required by older people (or, equivalently, the ratio of old-to-young critical times) would be independent of performance level. Note that comparison of critical times for only a single criterion performance level does not allow a test of this hypothesis.

Our experimental paradigm is very similar to that used by Cerella et al. (1982). Indeed, the major difference between our work and theirs is in the data analysis technique. Cerella et al. assumed a specific, two-stage serial scanning model, and fitted their obtained performance curves with the assumption that that model was correct. In contrast, our data analysis technique and the ensuing conclusions do not depend on any specific assumptions about the exact process of information acquisition. Thus, our conclusions may be viewed as a confirmation of Cerella et al.'s conclusions under a weaker, that is, more general, set of assumptions.

Qualitative and Quantitative Differences

Older Ss in our experiment did, indeed, require longer criterion times than did younger Ss in order to achieve any given level of performance. As indicated by the old/young difference in the psychometric function slopes, however, the ratio of old-to-young critical times was not constant across performance level, thereby disconfirming the quantitative slowing hypothesis. The difference between old and young Ss in this paradigm is at least partly qualitative.

The old/young slope difference that implied qualitative differences was small, and more detailed analyses showed that the qualitative difference is, in several respects, not very robust. First, the difference declines with practice. Second, an analysis of serial position showed that the decline in performance across serial position was substantially greater for old Ss, relative to young Ss, indicating that at least one component of the qualitative difference involved the processes by which information is acquired or integrated across spatial position. This conclusion was further confirmed by the finding that, when the first two serial positions alone are considered, the hypothesis of a strictly quantitative old/young difference cannot be rejected. In this situation the conclusion can be made (at least tentatively) that old Ss acquire the same visual information as young Ss, via the same cognitive processes, but at a rate that is about 1.5 times slower.

Application of Sperling's signal-to-noise theory. Loftus (1985c) showed that in certain circumstances reducing the luminance of visual stimuli caused the same kind of reduction in information acquisition rate as did aging in the present study. For relatively short exposure durations (under 300 ms), the reduction was quantitative, in the sense that the slopes of the psychometric functions were the same for high-luminance and low-luminance stimuli. For longer-duration stimuli, the reduction was qualitative, in the sense that the slopes were shallower for low-luminance stimuli.

Sperling (1986) proposed a signal-to-noise theory to explain these results. In Sperling's theory, decreasing luminance has the effect of adding noise to a limited-capacity serial-input channel. This causes less signal per unit time to be transmitted, which is equivalent to quantitative slowing. With increasing amounts of input information, however, the increased noise occupies space in a limited-capacity short-term memory. This effective reduction in short-term memory capacity amounts to a qualitative difference. Sperling suggested that his theory applied to any situation in which a visual stimulus is degraded by noise somewhere in the cognitive system prior to the serial input channel.

This theory suggests a tentative explanation of the present results, which would require three (testable) assumptions. First, aging must be assumed to involve addition of noise to visual stimuli at a relatively peripheral level of the visual system. Second, short-term memory capacity must be assumed to be smaller with older adults. Third, acquisition of information must be assumed to occur, at least partially, in a left-to-right order.

Given these assumptions, and Sperling's theory, consider the sequence of events in the present experimental paradigm. Acquisition of information would initially proceed with digits in the first and second serial positions. At this point, the aging deficit would occur only because of addition of noise prior to the serial input channel; such addition would cause quantitative slowing. Acquisition of additional digits, however, would tax short-term memory capacity more for older relative to younger Ss, thereby causing the qualitative difference that would result both in the shallower psychometric slopes for the older people, and in the Age × Serial Position interaction.

Levels of processing.   We make a final comment on the quantitative/ qualitative distinction that is prompted by P.B. Baltes (personal communication, 1984): A quantitative age difference at one level of cognitive processing may lead irrevocably to a qualitative difference at a higher level of processing. The major circumstance under which this will happen is that in which there is some time deadline for the completion of one process such that a subsequent process is executable only if the deadline is met. If young Ss are quantitatively faster than old Ss, then the young Ss will be more likely to meet the deadline and be able to carry out the subsequent process than the old Ss, thereby leading to a qualitative difference.

Deficits in older adults are found in many cognitive tasks that require considerably more complex strategies than the ones required in the present paradigm. It is possible, however, that in such experiments, observed qualitative differences have their roots in the sort of deficit that we have seen in initial acquisition of visual information. If this were true, then removal of the information-acquisition deficit would eliminate the qualitative differences that occur later in the cognitive system.

These considerations suggest a control in any experimental paradigm designed to investigate aging differences in which initial acquisition of visual information plays a significant role (e.g., in a Sternberg memory-scanning paradigm). The Ss in the experiment should be "handicapped" according to their rate of initial information acquisition. This could be done, for example, by differentially lowering the luminance of the stimuli (Loftus, 1985c) until the performance curves were the same for all Ss (or at least in such a way that mean old and young performance curves were the same). Such a procedure (which has occasionally been implemented; see Schoenfield & Wenger, 1975) would allow a much purer comparison of old and young Ss in more complex tasks, in the sense that eliminating initial sensory deficits would provide an isolation and examination of cognitive or strategic differences.

REFERENCES

Anderson, N.H. (1961). Scales and statistics: Parametric and nonparametric. *Psychological Bulletin, 58,* 305–316.

Averbach, E., & Coriell, H.S. (1961). Short-term memory in vision. *Bell Systems Technical Journal, 40,* 309–328.

Biederman, I., and Tsao, Y.C. (1979). On processing Chinese ideographs and English words: Some implications from Stroop-task results. *Cognitive Psychology, 11,* 125–132.

Bogartz, R.S. (1976). On the meaning of statistical interactions. *Journal of Experimental Child Psychology, 22,* 178–183.

Cerella, J., Poon, L.W., & Fozard, J.L. (1982). Age and iconic readout. *Journal of Gerontology, 37,* 197–202.
Hoyer, W.J., & Plude, D.J. (1980). Attentional and perceptual processes in the study of cognitive aging. In L.W. Poon (Ed.), *Aging in the 1980s: Psychological issues* (pp. 227–238). Washington, DC: American Psychological Association.
Kline, D.W., & Szafran, J. (1975). Age differences in backward monoptic masking. *Journal of Gerontology, 30,* 307–311.
Krantz, D.H., & Tversky, A. (1971). Conjoint-measurement analysis of composition rules in psychology. *Psychological Review, 78,* 151–169.
Loftus, G.R. (1978). On interpretation of interactions. *Memory & Cognition, 6,* 312–319.
Loftus, G.R. (1985a). Evaluating forgetting curves. *Journal of Experimental Psychology: Learning, Memory, and Cognition, 11,* 396–405.
Loftus, G.R. (1985b). Consistency and confoundings: Reply to Slamecka. *Journal of Experimental Psychology: Learning, Memory, and Cognition* (in press).
Loftus, G.R. (1985c). Picture perception: Effects of luminance level on available information and information-extraction rate. *Journal of Experimental Psychology: General, 114,* 342–356.
Loftus, G.R., Gillispie, S., Tigre, R., & Nelson, W. (1984). An Apple II-based slide projector laboratory. *Behavior Research Methods and Instrumentation, 16,* 447–453.
Schoenfield, D., & Wenger, L. (1975). Age limitations of perceptual span. *Nature, 253,* 377–378.
Shiffrin, R.M., & Schneider, W. (1977). Controlled and automatic human information processing; II. Perceptual learning, automatic attending, and a general theory. *Psychological Review, 84,* 127–190.
Sperling, G. (1960). Information available in brief visual presentations. *Psychological Monographs, 74*(Whole No. 11).
Sperling, G. (1986). A signal-to-noise theory of the effects of luminance on picture memory. *Journal of Experimental Psychology: General, 115,* 189–192.
Sperling, G., & Speelman, R.G. (1970). Acoustic similarity and auditory short-term memory: Experiments and a model. In D.A. Norman (Ed.), *Models of Human Memory* (pp. 152–202). New York: Academic Press.
Till, R.E. (1978). Age-related differences in binocular backward masking with visual noise. *Journal of Gerontology, 33,* 702–710.
Turvey, M. (1973). On peripheral and central processes in vision: Inferences from an information-processing analysis of masking with patterned stimuli. *Psychological Review, 80,* 1–52.
Walsh, D.A. (1975). Age differences in learning and memory. In D.S. Woodruff & J.E. Birren (Eds.), *Scientific perspectives and social issues.* New York: David Van Nostrand.
Walsh, D.A. (1976). Age differences in central perceptual processing: A dichoptic backward masking investigation. *Journal of Gerontology, 33,* 383–387.
Walsh, D.A., Till, R.E., & Williams, M. (1978). Age differences in peripheral visual processing: A monoptic backward masking investigation. *Journal of Experimental Psychology: Human Perception and Performance, 4,* 232–243.
Walsh, D.A., Williams, M., & Hertzog, C.K. (1979). Age-related differences in two stages of central perceptual processes: The effects of short duration targets and criterion differences. *Journal of Gerontology, 34,* 234–241.

PART II
EXPERIENCE
AND
EXPERTISE

Chapter Five

Thoughts on Expertise

Robert Glaser

In recent years, cognitive psychologists have investigated human performances that are acquired over long periods of learning and experience. These studies have contrasted the knowledge and skill of experts and novices. The data show that high levels of competence result from the interactions between knowledge structures and processing abilities. Expert performance is characterized by rapid access to an organized body of conceptual and procedural knowledge. The generalizations presented here summarize current findings on the nature of expertise.

INTRODUCTION

Information-processing studies in the 1960s and 1970s on problem solving accepted the tradition of early experimental psychology by concentrating primarily on the study of "knowledge-lean" tasks—tasks in which competence usually can be acquired over short periods of learning and experience. Studies of these tasks illuminated the basic information-processing capabilities that people employ when they behave more and less intelligently in situations where they lack any specialized knowledge and skill. The pioneering work of Newell and Simon and others richly described these general processes (such as means-end analysis, generate and test, and subgoal decomposition), but provided limited insight about the learning and thinking that require

The final version of this chapter benefited from suggestions from Matthew Lewis, postdoctoral fellow at the Learning Research and Development Center of the University of Pittsburg, currently at Carnegie-Mellon University.

This is a version of a talk given at the Social Science Research Council conference on "The Study of Expertise as a Model for Life-Span Cognitive Development." The research reported here was supported with funds from the Office of Naval Research, Personnel and Training Research Programs, Psychological Sciences Division.

a rich structure of domain-specific knowledge that is especially relevant to vocational education.

In contrast, in more recent years work has examined "knowledge-rich" tasks—tasks that require hundreds and thousands of hours of learning and experience in an area of study. Studies of expertise have attempted to sharpen this focus by describing contrasts between the performances of novices and experts. And the novices in these studies, for example, intern radiologists and electronics technicians, have engaged in learning over much longer periods than are studied in short experimental tasks.

Investigations of problem solving in knowledge-rich domains show strong interactions between structures of knowledge and cognitive processes. The results force us to think about high levels of competence in terms of this interplay between knowledge structure and processing abilities. They illuminate a critical difference between individuals who display more and less ability in particular domains of knowledge and skill. The performances of highly competent individuals indicate the possession of, rapid access to, and efficient utilization of an organized body of conceptual and procedural knowledge. Data and theory in developmental psychology, studies of expert/novice problem solving, and process analyses of high and low scorers on intelligence and aptitude test tasks show that a major component of expertise is the possession of this accessible and usable knowledge.

DEVELOPMENTAL STUDIES

To introduce a point of view, let me briefly mention some developmental studies with children. Chi, in several studies (Chi, 1978; Chi & Koeske, 1983), examined recall in children. She contrasted the performances of children with high and low knowledge in chess and those of children with high and low knowledge of dinosaur categories and features. Her results replicated, in significant ways, the early chess studies of de Groot (1965) and Chase and Simon (1973a, 1973b); high-knowledge subjects showed better memory and encoding performance than did low-knowledge individuals. And this superiority was attributed to the influence of *knowledge in content areas;* rather than to the exercise of memory capabilities as such. Changes in the organization of knowledge base appear to enable sophisticated cognitive performance.

Carey's studies of animistic thinking in young children (1985) trace the emergence of a child's concept of "alive." She documents a change from a knowledge organization centering around human characteristics (a novice point of view) to one centering around biological functions. This change resembles those typical in the development of expertise. Carey makes the point that what can be interpreted as abstract, pervasive changes in a child's reasoning and learning abilities come about as knowledge is gained in a given domain.

The acquisition of content knowledge as a factor in acquiring increasingly sophisticated problem-solving abilities is addressed in Siegler and Richards's "rule assessment" studies (1982). They conclude that "knowledge of specific content domains is a crucial dimension of development in its own right and that changes in such knowledge may underlie other changes previously attributed to the growth of capacities and strategies" (p. 930).

EXPERTISE AND ARTIFICIAL INTELLIGENCE

The evolution of artifical intelligence (AI) systems reflects the central importance of knowledge structure in expertise. Knowledge structure refers to the organization of the content of knowledge. Complete knowledge of a domain, if not organized, cannot constitute expertise. Most early work in the study of AI emphasized general problem-solving techniques to guide the search for solutions. This approach, called the "power-based strategy" by Minsky and Papert (1974), is contrasted to the "knowledge-based strategy," which emphasizes the role of well-organized knowledge representations to achieve machine intelligence. Minsky & Papert note that

> The *Power* strategy seeks a generalized increase in computational power. . . . It may look toward extensions of deductive generality, or information retrieval, or search algorithms. . . . In each case the improvement sought is . . . independent of the particular data base.
> The *Knowledge* strategy sees progress as coming from better ways to express, recognize, and use diverse and particular forms of knowledge. . . . It is by no means obvious that very smart people are that way directly because of the superior power of their general methods—as compared with average people. . . . A very intelligent person might be that way because of specific local features of his knowledge-organizing knowledge rather than because of global qualities of his "thinking." (p.59)

The necessity for a well-organized representation of knowledge is also emphasized in two reviews of expert systems for problem solving. Articles by Duda (1981) and by Stefik et al. (1982) stress that the heart of any successful reasoning system for a complex domain is the proper organization of knowledge. The lack of such an organization results in "hopelessly inefficient, naive, or unreliable" (Stefik et al., 1982) problem solvers.

Thus, in the area of AI, the problem of understanding intelligence has become increasingly focused on the large structure of domain-specific knowledge that is characteristic of experts. This was not the case in the early years of the field, when the creation of intelligent programs was identified with finding "pure" or "domain-independent" problem-solving techniques to guide the search for a solution to any problem, as with the General Problem Solver program (Newell & Simon, 1972). The techniques then elucidated, such as means-ends analysis, are clearly still part of the picture, but it was apparent early on that in realistically complex domains such techniques must engage a highly organized structure of specific knowledge. This same result is reflected in the study of human expertise.

EXPERT/NOVICE PROBLEM SOLVING

The studies of problem solving in adult experts and novices have shown fairly consistent findings in quite a variety of domains—chess play, physics, architecture, electronics, and radiological interpretation and diagnosis (Chi, Glaser, & Farr, in press). This work has shown that relations between the structure of a knowledge base and problem-solving processes are mediated through the qualilty of the representation of the problem. This problem representation is constructed by the solver on the basis of domain-related knowledge and the organization of this knowledge. The nature of this organization determines the quality, completeness, and coherence of the internal representation, which in turn determines the efficiency of further thinking.

Expert/novice research suggests that novices' representations are organized around the literal objects and events given explicitly in a problem statement. Experts' knowledge, on the other hand, is organized around inferences about principles and abstractions that subsume these factors. These principles are not apparent in the statement or the surface presentation of the problem. For example, in our studies with problems in mechanics (Chi, Feltovich, & Glaser, 1981), novices classify problems on a surface level, according to the physical properties of a situation—a spring problem or an inclined plane problem. Experts categorize problems at a higher level, in terms of applicable physics principles—a Newton's second law problem, a conservation-of-energy problem. In addition, experts know about the application of their knowledge. Their declarative information is tightly bound to conditions and procedures for its use. An intermediate novice may have sufficient knowledge about a problem situation, but lack knowledge of conditions of its applicability.

Consider the following example from a study comparing an expert's and a novice's performances in solving problems in elementary physics (Chi, Glaser, & Rees, 1982). As indicated above, previous studies had shown that the problem representations of experts were principle oriented, whereas the representations of novices were object oriented. The purpose of this follow-up study was to obtain a depiction of the difference in the representations of experts and novices. An advanced graduate student in physics (the expert) and an undergraduate just completing an elementary course with a grade of A (the novice) were given 3 mins. to tell everything they could about the concept "inclined plane," and how a problem involving an inclined plane might be solved. The networks of the novice's (H.P.) and the expert's (M.G.) elaborations of the concept "inclined plane" are shown in Figures 1 and 2, respectively. The content of their protocols are depicted by a node-link network, in which the nodes are simply the key terms mentioned and the links are unlabeled relations that join the terms mentioned contiguously. We can view each of these depictions as representing a potential schema; the terms and concepts mentioned in the protocol can be thought of as the variable (slots) of the schema.

In novice H.P.'s protocol (Figure 1), his inclined-plane schema contains numerous variables that can be instantiated, including the angle at which the plane is inclined with respect to the horizontal, whether a block is resting on the plane, and the mass and height of the block. Other variables he mentions include the surface property of the plane— whether or not it has friction, and, if it does, the coefficients of static and kinetic friction. The novice also discusses possible forces that may act on the block, for example, the drag of a pulley. At the end, he discusses the pertinence of conservation of energy, but this was not elicited as a part of a solution procedure (as will be seen in the expert's protocol). In general, one could say that the novice's inclined-plane schema is quite rich. He knows what variable ought to be specified. Hence, with a simple specification that the problem is one involving an inclined plane, he can deduce fairly accurately what the key components and entities are (e.g., friction) that such a problem would entail.

However, the casual reference to the underlying physics principle, conservation of energy, given by the novice contrasts markedly with the protocol of the expert, M.G. (Figure 2). She immediately accesses two principles that take the status of procedures, the conservation-of-energy principle and the force law. We characterize them as procedures (thus differentiating them from the novice's mention of conservation of energy) because the expert, after mentioning the force law, elaborates the condition of applicability of the procedure and then provides formulas for two of the conditions (enclosed in dashed rectangles). Following this elaboration of the principles and the conditions of applicability of one principle to inclined-plane problems (depicted in the top half of Figure 2), expert M.G. described the structural or surface

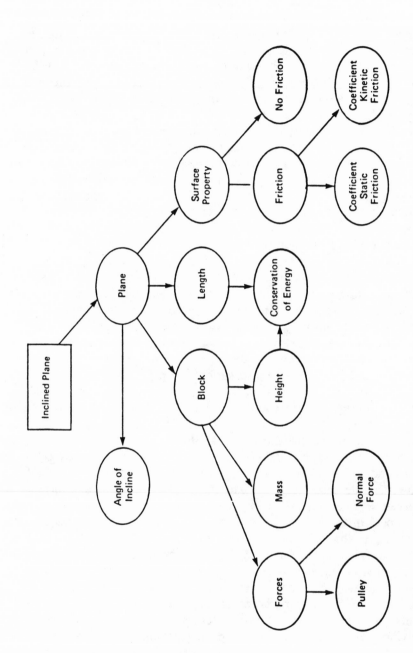

Figure 1. Network representation of a novice's schema of an inclined plane (from Chi, Glaser, & Rees, 1982).

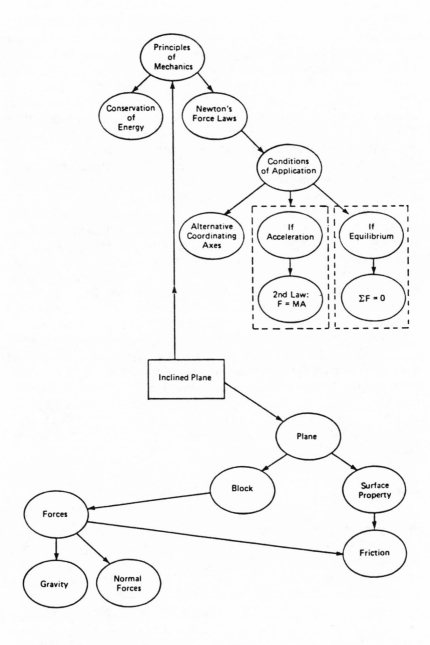

Figure 2.   Network representation of an expert's schema of an inclined plane (from Chi, Glaser, & Rees, 1982).

features of inclined-plane problems, much as novice H.P. had. Hence, it seems that the knowledge common to subjects of both skill groups pertains to the physical configuration and its properties, but that the expert has additional knowledge based on major physics laws that is relevant to the solution procedures.

Another way of viewing the difference between the novice's and expert's elaborations of the inclined plane is to note that the novice sees it as a static object; for him, it evokes not so much a description of a sequence of actions or events, but a representation of spatial relationships and a description of the configuration and its properties. The expert, on the other hand, views the inclined plane in the context of potential problem-solving procedures, that is, not so much as an inert object, but more as an entity that may serve a particular function.

As in the developmental studies, the problem-solving "difficulties" of novices can be attributed largely to the nature of their knowledge bases, and much less to the limitations of their processing capabilities, such as their inability to use general problem-solving heuristics. Novices do show effective use of heuristics; the limitations of their thinking derive from the inability to infer further knowledge from the literal cues in a problem situation. These inferences are necessarily generated in the context of a knowledge structure that experts have acquired.

In general, study of problem solving by highly competent people in rich knowledge domains provides a glimpse of the power of human thinking to use a large knowledge system in an efficient and automatic manner—particularly in ways that minimize reliance on the search heuristics identified in studies of knowledge-lean problems. Thus, a significant focus for understanding expertise is identifying the characteristics and influence of organized knowledge structures that are acquired over long periods of time.

SCHEMATA AND THEORIES

The organizations of knowledge that are developed by experts can be thought of in terms of schemata or theories of knowledge. A schema can be defined here as a modifiable information structure that represents generic structures of concepts stored in memory. Schemata represent knowledge that we experience, that is, interrelationships among objects, situations, and events. In this sense, schemata are prototypes in memory of frequently experienced situations, which individuals use to integrate and interpret instances of related knowledge. Schema theory assumes that there are schemata for recurrent situations, and that these schemata enable people to construct interpretations, representations, and perceptions of situations.

If we think of a schema as a theory or internal model that is used, matched, and tested by individuals to instantiate the situations they encounter, like a scientific theory, it is a source of representation and prediction. It enables individuals to impose meaning on a situation and to make inferences from partial information. As is the case for a scientific theory, if it fails to account for certain aspects of one's observations, it leads to learning that can modify or replace the theory. As a representation of a problem situation, it may be accompanied by rules for solution of the problem, particularly if the solver has experience with the problem type.

METACOGNITION AND GENERAL SKILLS

To temper my emphasis on structures of knowledge, I now point out that experts in various domains show self-regulatory or metacognitive capabilities that are not present in less mature or experienced learners. These abilities include knowing what one knows and doesn't know, planning ahead, efficiently apportioning one's time and attentional resources, and monitoring and editing one's efforts to solve a problem. To a large extent in experts, these self-regulatory activities are specific to a domain of knowledge. Where they appear to be generalized competencies, that is, in "generally intelligent" individuals, my hypothesis is that they become abstracted strategies after individuals use them in several fields of knowledge.

Perhaps widely competent children and adults, because of intensive exposure to different domains, employ skills that evolve as generalized cognitive processes. As general methods, however, these may be a small part of the intelligent performance shown by experts in specific fields of knowledge where they rapidly access acquired schemata and procedures. General processes may be important when an individual is confronted with problems in unfamiliar areas. However, future research may show that generalizable and transferable expertise lies in an ability to use familiar domains of knowledge for analogical and metaphorical thinking about new domains.

GENERALIZATIONS AND SPECULATIONS

I sum up my thoughts about expertise in the following paragraphs. These statements represent conclusions from research and occasional broader inferences and speculations.

1. There seems to be a *continuous development of competence;* as

experience in a field accumulates. Eventual declines in competence may be the result of conditions of experience. Competence may be limited by the environment in which it is exercised. People may attain a level of competence only insofar as it is necessary to carry out the activities or to solve problems at the given level of complexity. Conditions that extend competence may be less forthcoming as experts settle into their working situations (Chi, Glaser, & Farr, in press).

2. *Expertise seems to be very specific.* Expertise in one domain is no guarantee of expertise in others. It may be, however, that certain task domains are more generalizable than others, so that adults who are experts in applied mathematics or aesthetic design, or children who have learned measurement and number concepts, have forms of transferable expertise (Carey, 1985).

3. Experts develop *the ability to preceive large meaningful patterns.* These patterns are seen in the course of their everyday activities. Pattern recognition occurs so rapidly that it appears to take on the character of "intuitions." In contrast, the patterns novices recognize are smaller, less articulated, more literal and surface oriented, and much less related to inferences and abstracted principles. The extraordinary representational ability of experts appears to depend on the nature and organization of knowledge existing in memory. As I indicated earlier, the fact that an expert has a more coherent, complete, functional, and principled representation of knowledge than a novice necessarily implies an initial understanding of a problem that leads more easily to correct procedures and solutions (Lesgold, 1984; Chi et al., 1982).

4. *The knowledge of experts is highly procedural and goal oriented.* Concepts are bound to procedures for their application, and to conditions under which these procedures are useful. The functional knowledge of experts is related strongly to their knowledge of the goal structure of a problem. Experts and novices may be equally competent at recalling small specific items of domain-related information. But high-knowledge individuals are much better at relating these events in cause-and-effect sequences that relate to the goal and subgoals of problem solution (Voss, Greene, Post, & Penner, 1983).

5. The fast-access recognition and representational capability of experts facilitate problem perception in a way that leads to *the reduction of the role of memory search and general processing.* By contrast, novices display a good deal of search-and-processing of a general nature. Although it can be assumed that experts and novices have similar capacities available for cognitive processing, the outstanding performance of experts derives primarily from how their knowledge is structured for retrieval, pattern recognition, and inference.

6. Individuals who acquire expertise in several domains may develop *generalized thinking and problem-solving skills.* This can occur

in the course of shifting between domains so that the cognitive processes involved become decontextualized and generally applicable (Glaser, 1984). Generalizable skill may also be acquired when experts attempt to map structures and make analogies between their own domain and others (Gentner & Gentner, 1983).

7. The experience of experts enables them to develop skilled *self-regulatory processes*. These cognitive skills are manifested by proficiency in techniques of solution monitoring, by the allocation of attention, and by sensitivity to informational feedback (Brown, 1978; Gitomer & Glaser, in press). Self-regulatory processes are sometimes evidenced by the fact that experts may be slower than novices initially encoding a difficult problem, but are faster problem-solvers overall (Sternberg, 1977). The increase in self-regulatory processes is enabled as experts develop automaticity in performing the "basic operations" of a task, so that working memory is available for higher level conscious processing (Perfetti & Lesgold, 1979).

8. The precision of expert performance results from *specialized schemata* which drive their performance. These schemata incorporate goal structures that can be matched to the demands of a problem; given stated goals, experts will think only as deeply as problem goals require. Specificity of performance is evidenced by the fact that expert proficiency can be disrupted by the presentation of random (or meaningless) patterns or poorly structured problems. Under these conditions, experts lose their rapid perceptual and representational ability and resort to general problem-solving strategies (Chase & Simon, 1973a).

9. Although experts display specific domain intelligence, they do not necessarily achieve high scores on measures of general intelligence (Chase & Simon, 1973a). Both experts and novices can display good use of *general problem-solving processes*, such as generate-and-test procedures, means-end analysis, and subgoal composition. Experts use them primarily in unfamiliar situations. In solving ill-structured problems, experts employ these general methods and their thinking is less immediately driven by the principles and procedural aspects of their specific knowledge structures.

10. The development of expertise is influenced by *task demands* encountered in the course of experience and by the conditions of working situations. The cognitive models that experts acquire are constrained by environmental requirements (Scribner, 1984a, 1984b). In some domains, they develop the capability for "opportunistic planning" which is manifested by their ability to revise problem representations and to access multiple possible interpretations of a situation. In such situations, where new information is introduced, novices are less flexible. This has been particularly apparent in studies of medical diagnosis (Lesgold, Rubinson, Feltovich, Glaser, & Klopfer, in press).

This picture of expertise is probably biased by the highly structured domains in which it has been studied, and the demands of situations in which cognitive expertise has been analyzed. How do experts solve problems in "ill-structured" domains? How do different experiences lead to different forms of expertise? Hatano (Hatano & Inagaki, 1983) distinguishes between routine (or conventional) expertise and adaptive expertise. Routine experts are outstanding in terms of speed, accuracy, and automaticity of performance, and construct mental models convenient for performing their tasks, but they lack adaptability when faced with new kinds of problems. Repeated application of a procedure, with little variation, probably leads to routine expertise. Adaptive expertise requires variation and is encouraged by playful situations and in cultures where understanding is valued along with efficient performance. How might expertise develop in an understanding-oriented as compared with an efficiency-oriented environment?

FINAL REMARKS

Increased understanding of the nature of expertise challenges us to inquire how it is learned. It seems evident that expertise is acquired when people continually try to confront new situations in terms of what they know. Increasing ability to solve problems and generate new information is fostered by available knowledge that can be modified and restructured. This knowledge, when interrogated, instantiated, or falsified by novices in the course of learning and experience leads to organizations of knowledge that are the basis for the more complete schemata of experts. When teaching beginners, this might be accomplished by assessing and using relevant prior knowledge, or by providing obvious organizational schemes or temporary models as scaffolds for new information. These temporary "pedagogical theories" are regularly devised by ingenious instructors and could be incorporated more systematically into instruction. In addition, instruction should focus on the development of procedurally oriented knowledge structures that incorporate knowledge with the conditions of its use and applicability.

REFERENCES

Brown, A.L. (1978). Knowing when, where, and how to remember: A problem of metacognition. In R. Glaser (Ed.), *Advances in instructional psychology.* (Vol. 1, pp. 77–165). Hillsdale, NJ: Erlbaum.
Carey, S. (1985). Are children fundamentally different kinds of thinkers and learners

than adults? In S.F. Chipman, J.W. Segal, & R. Glaser (Eds.), *Thinking and learning skills: Current research and open questions* (Vol. 2, pp. 485–517). Hillsdale, NJ: Erlbaum.

Chase, W.G., & Simon, H.A. (1973a). Perception in chess. *Cognitive Psychology, 4,* 55–81.

Chase, W.G., & Simon. H.A. (1973b). The mind's eye in chess. In W.G. Chase (Ed.), *Visual information processing.* (pp. 215–281). New York: Academic Press.

Chi, M.T.H. (1978). Knowledge structures and memory development. In R. Siegler (Ed.), *Children's thinking: What develops?* (Vol. 1, pp. 73–96). Hillsdale, NJ: Erlbaum.

Chi, M.T.H., Feltovich, P., & Glaser, R. (1981). Categorization and representation of physics problems by experts and novices. *Cognitive Science, 5,* 121–152.

Chi, M.T.H., Glaser, R., & Farr, M. (in press). *The nature of expertise.* Hillsdale, NJ: Erlbaum.

Chi, M.T.H., Glaser, R., & Rees, E. (1982). Expertise in problem solving. In R. Sternberg (Ed.), *Advances in the psychology of human intelligence* (pp. 7–76). Hillsdale, NJ: Erlbaum.

Chi, M.T.H., & Koeske, R.D. (1983). Network representation of a child's dinosaur knowledge. *Developmental Psychology, 19,* 29–39.

de Groot, A. (1965). *Thought and choice in chess.* The Hague: Mouton.

Duda, R.O. (1981). Knowledge-based expert systems come of age. *Byte, 6* (9), 238–281.

Gentner, D., & Gentner, D.R. (1983). Flowing waters or teeming crowds: Mental models of electricity. In D. Gentner & A.L. Stevens (Eds.), *Mental Models* (pp. 99–129). Hillsdale, NJ: Erlbaum.

Gitomer, D.H. & Glaser, R. (in press). Knowledge, self-regulation and instruction. In R.E. Snow & M.J. Farr (Eds.), *Aptitude, learning, and instruction* (Vol. 3). Hillsdale, NJ: Erlbaum.

Glaser, R. (1984). Education and thinking. *American Psychologist, 39* (1), 93–104.

Hatano, G., & Inagaki, K. (1983, April). *Two courses of expertise.* Paper presented at the Conference on Child Development in Japan and the United States, Stanford, CA.

Lesgold, A.M. (1984). Acquiring expertise. In J.R. Anderson & S.M. Kosslyn (Eds.), *Tutorials in learning and memory: Essays in honor of Gordon Bower.* (pp. 31–60). San Francisco: Freeman.

Lesgold, A.M., Rubinson, H., Feltovich, P., Glaser, R. & Klopfer, D. (in press). Expertise in a complex skill: Diagnosing X-ray pictures. In M.T.H. Chi, R. Glaser, & M. Farr (Eds.), *The nature of expertise.* Hillsdale, NJ: Erlbaum

Minsky, M., & Papert, S. (1974). *Artificial intelligence.* Condon Lectures, Oregon State System of Higher Education, Eugene OR.

Newell, A., & Simon, H.A. (1972). *Human problem solving,* Englewood Cliffs, NJ: Prentice-Hall.

Perfetti, C.A., & Lesgold, A.M. (1979). Coding and comprehension in skilled reading. In L.B. Resnick & P. Weaver (Eds.), *Theory and practice of early reading,* (Vol. 1, pp. 57–84). Hillsdale, NJ: Erlbaum.

Scribner, S. (1984a). Cognitive studies of work. *Quarterly Newsletter of the Laboratory of Comparative Human Cognition, 6*(1, 2), pp. 1–50.

Scribner, S. (1984b). Studying working intelligence. In B. Rogoff & J. Lave (Eds.), *Everyday cognition: Its development in social context.* (pp. 9–41). Cambridge, MA: Harvard University Press.

Siegler, R.S. & Richards, D.D. (1982). The development of intelligence. In R.J. Sternberg (Ed.), *Handbook of human intelligence* (pp. 897–971). Cambridge, England: Cambridge University Press.

Stefik, M., Aikins, J., Balzer, R., Benoit, J., Birnbaum, L., Hayes-Roth, F., & Sacerdoti, E. (1982). The organization of expert systems, a tutorial. *Artificial Intelligence, 18,* 135–173.

Sternberg, R.J. (1977). *Intelligence, information processing, and analogical reasoning: The componential analysis of human abilities.* Hillsdale, NJ: Erlbaum.

Voss, J.F., Greene, T.R., Post, T.A. & Penner, B.C. (1983). Problem solving skill in the social sciences. In G. Bower (Ed.), *The psychology of learning and motivation: Advances in research theory* (pp. 165–215). New York: Academic Press.

Chapter Six

Theory-Guided Analysis of Mechanisms of Development and Aging Through Testing-the-Limits and Research on Expertise

Reinhold Kliegl
Paul B. Baltes

INTRODUCTION

Two central factors in theoretical explanations of cognitive change in adulthood and old age are the effects of experience and practice. These two factors also predominate in recent models of cognitive functioning in general. A good example is the expertise model in which the acquisition of expertise is described as involving long-term preoccupation with domain-specific knowledge and continuous practice of behavioral routines.

In this chapter, we propose a research framework that combines aspects of the expertise model with a life-span approach. Central to this framework are two assumptions. First, individual differences, and in particular age differences, are best studied if criterion task perfor-

This manuscript is dedicated to Helmut Coper on the occasion of his 60th birthday, in recognition of his biopsychological research on adaptivity across the life span. Research reported in this chapter has been conducted in the context of a project on expertise and aging codirected by Paul B. Baltes and Reinhold Kliegl and carried out in collaboration with Jacqui Smith and Jutta Heckhausen. Discussions with Timothy A. Salthouse, Daniel P. Keating, and Roger A. Dixon helped to clarify a number of theoretical issues. Jacqui Smith, Jutta Heckhausen, Daniel P. Keating, Timothy A. Salthouse, Ross A. Thompson, and the editors of this volume provided helpful comments on an earlier version of this chapter.

mance is assessed close to a person's limits of relevant cognitive functions. Second, it is assumed that controlled (or guided) acquisition of expertise in a laboratory setting and subsequent experimental decomposition of this expertise should yield more precise estimates of individual competence than do traditional one-time or static assessments.

We propose two research strategies that were designed to test these assumptions. Before describing this approach in more detail, we need to point out a limitation of this chapter. The empirical evidence we present is based mainly on case studies. Therefore, no strong conclusions, especially on age-comparative questions, should be drawn at present. The objective of this chapter is to advance a methodological argument rather than to report definitive data.

THEORETICAL BACKGROUND

Expertise and Reserve Capacity

Research on expert performance has emphasized the prominent role of amount and quality of permanent knowledge in cognitive processing (cf. Brown, 1982; Chi, Glaser, & Rees, 1982). However, the study of expertise has two major limitations. First, almost by definition there are few experts in specific domains. Thus the pool of possible research subjects is restricted. Second, because the acquisition of a real-life expertise usually requires many years of practice in the relevant activity, little is known about the natural developmental course of expertise. In fact, only recently has the acquisition of complex cognitive skills become a major topic of cognitive psychological research (e.g., Anderson, 1981, 1982; Chase & Ericsson, 1981).

Both the attractive and problematic sides of the expertise paradigm are illustrated when the paradigm is applied to research on aging. On the one hand, people like Arthur Rubinstein and Picasso are frequently mentioned in the study of superior older experts as exemplars of successful aging: Such people are presented as prototypes of optimized maturity (P. B. Baltes, 1984; P. B. Baltes & Kliegl, 1986). On the other hand, little is known, from a psychological perspective, about how Rubinstein and Picasso accomplished what they did and whether the cognitive processes, or the products, were truly different across their lives. Answers to such questions would add both to the study of expertise and to our understanding of successful aging (P. B. Baltes, Dittmann-Kohli, & Dixon, 1984; P. B. Baltes & Kliegl, 1986; Charness, 1981; Denney, 1984; Hoyer, 1985; Salthouse, 1985).

In principle, successful aging should be possible for the majority of healthy older adults. The achievement of a state of effective functioning involves the actualization of *reserve capacity:* The term is introduced here to communicate the notion that most people can improve, one way or another, on baseline performances. Experts are commonly defined as persons whose performance on some criterion task is far superior to that of normal persons (see, e.g., Chi et al., 1982). Experts are persons who have actualized their reserve capacity in a specific domain of functioning. Actualized reserve capacity in the form of an expertise is different from more transient or temporary types of performance improvement. Therefore, we have distinguished between baseline performance, baseline reserve capacity, and developmental reserve capacity (P. B. Baltes et al., 1984; Kliegl & Baltes, 1984).

Baseline performance denotes an individual's ability or skill inferred from his or her performance in one-time assessment under standardized conditions. Standardized conditions usually include specification of tasks, tests, instructions, and response options. Baseline reserve capacity refers to the range of baseline performance under varying conditions of demand and support. Demand and support conditions include levels of difficulty of task, variations in instruction, motivational conditions, and perhaps short-term practice. Finally, developmental reserve capacity is defined as the level and range of performance under extended periods of development (including aging) or extended periods of practice. This latter concept introduces a time and developmental dimension. We will refer to such developmental reserve capacity as latent potential (P. B. Baltes & Willis, 1982). Among the conditions qualifying under this category would be instruction and long-term acquisition of expertise.

Actualization of developmental reserve capacity should inform about latent potential and limits of functioning in old and young persons. Moreover, laboratory studies of age-related trade-offs in cognitive processes and knowledge may be used to test one important aspect of one model of successful aging called selective optimization with compensation: High levels of cognitive functioning can be preserved by restricting the area of competence and investing more and more time and effort to maintain high levels of efficiency in this narrow domain of functioning (P. B. Baltes & M. M. Baltes, 1980; P. B. Baltes et al., 1984; Dixon & Baltes, in press).

Testing-the-Limits and Research on Expertise

To illustrate the potential gained by integrating theoretical principles of the expertise paradigm and models of aging, two complementary research strategies will now be proposed. Both strategies can be seen as belonging to a methodology called testing-the-limits or learning-tests (M. M. Baltes & Kindermann, 1985; P.B. Baltes & Kliegl, 1986; Guthke,

1982; Kliegl & Baltes, 1984; Schmidt, 1971; Wiedl, 1984). The strategies proposed in this chapter differ mainly in their emphasis on theoretical specification and experimental control over criterion task performance.

The first strategy, *theory-guided synthesis* or *engineering of cognitive expertise,* is devised to identify limits in performance as subjects progress through a structured, componential training program that leads to expert performance. Concretely, we demonstrate how young and older adults with normal memory span for digits and nouns prior to training can, after training, approach the performance levels of professional mnemonists. The second strategy, *adaptivity* or *resilience testing of expert systems,* involves exposing subjects who have reached levels of expert performance to increasingly more difficult conditions until a situation is reached in which the functional reserve of the expert system is overtaxed.

One assumption underlying the combination of expertise and aging research is that iterative application of the two strategies may reveal latent potential and limits of cognitive functions more clearly than traditional aging research. A second assumption is that, if subjects perform according to the components specified by the particular theory that guided the development of the training program, it is possible to pinpoint more precisely the nature of the components involved in age-related differences.

How can actualization of developmental reserve in memory span contribute to an understanding of successful aging in general? We would like to offer three answers. First, if the question of the nature of successful aging is to be approached experimentally, we need laboratory analogs. Such analogs are easier to generate if they are based on well-defined tasks. Whether a memory expertise in digit and word span tasks is representative of more common expertises in the arts and in sports, in our opinion, is largely a matter of historical and cultural preferences.

Second, although memory span tasks may not initially appear to be very representative of the complex processes associated with successful aging, we will show that very high demands on creativity and originality lie at the roots of the memory expertise engineered in our laboratory. Actually, the displayed memory performance could be considered an epiphenomenon of creative thought. Thus, acquisition of expertise in the present paradigm changes the task from a simple to a complex and probably representative one.

Third, in principle, actualization of developmental reserve can be elicited in other cognitive processes provided that (a) there is available an explicit model of the expertise that is to be engineered so that a theory-guided training program can be devised, and (b) subjects have available adequate normal physical and motivational resources. For example, there are attempts to define wisdom as an expertise in matters of life review and life planning and to construct tasks in these domains that focus on cognitive processes such as search for relevant information and heuristics of decision (Smith, Dixon, & Baltes, in press).

Cognitive Processes and Knowledge

The interplay of cognitive processes and accumulated life experiences in the form of specialized knowledge has become the focus of attention in recent models of adult cognitive and intellectual development (P.B. Baltes et al., 1984; P.B. Baltes & Kliegl, 1986; Charness, 1981; Denney, 1984; Hoyer, 1985; Labouvie-Vief, 1982, 1985; Salthouse, 1985). A similar distinction has guided cognitive theories about differences between experts and novices (Brown, 1982; Chi et al., 1982).

In P. B. Baltes et al.'s (1984) dual-process, life-span model of intellectual functioning, the distinction between cognitive processes ("mechanics of intelligence") and various aspects of knowledge ("pragmatics of intelligence") is central because—as with Cattell's (1971) and Horn's (1982) theory of fluid and crystallized intelligence—different developmental trajectories are expected for the two components. If measured at very high levels of performance (i.e., close to maximum performance or at the level of experts), "mechanical" efficiency of cognitive processes is assumed to decline, whereas quantity and quality of select aspects of "pragmatic" knowledge might be expected to remain stable or evince even further growth with age. Growth, however, is assumed to be restricted to those select domains of knowledge that are regularly used and practiced. Primary evidence for this proposition is the differential developmental change in fluid and crystallized abilities (Cattell, 1971; Horn, 1982; Schaie & Hertzog, 1983) and Denney's (1982, 1984) work buttressing her model of intellectual aging that distinguishes between optimally exercised and unexercised abilities.

The distinction between fundamental cognitive processes and knowledge upon which these processes act has also proven to be very useful in theories about expert-novice differences. There is a consensus and some evidence (e.g., Chase & Simon, 1973; Sloboda, 1978) that experts and novices generally do not differ in fundamental cognitive processes, that is, the basic mechanics of intelligence. Rather, amount, organization, and transformation of knowledge appear to be the hallmarks of expertise (Chi et al., 1982). Consequently, there has been a shift from the emphasis on describing fundamental processes toward a focus on understanding the structure and representation of knowledge. A similar redirection in research and theoretical focus may be needed to further our understanding of developmental and individual differences in cognitive functioning in adulthood. However, to realize this objective, ways must be found to control knowledge involved in criterion tasks: Without such control, inferences about differences in cognitive processes might not be valid (Estes, 1982; Glaser, 1984; Weinert & Hasselhorn, 1986).

Age Comparisons of Peak Performance

Becoming an expert in a real-life domain is a developmental process that takes time, much practice, and preoccupation with the topic. With respect to these factors, old age may hold advantages as time lived offers a longer period of experience. In addition, however, various skills may have as a prerequisite for expert performance a certain amount or level of capacity in their component processes. Also, for some performances, components may be required and thresholds may be involved that represent necessary antecedent conditions.

It is conceivable that there may be individual (and perhaps some age-related) differences in the amount of capacity required for the development of an expertise. Thus, becoming an expert in old age may be even more difficult if certain cognitive processes such as speed of information search decline. This point can be illustrated with an example from sports: Would it be possible for an 80-year-old to jump higher than 2 m, assuming age-related decline only in basic physical resources such as muscle strength, with everything else, such as knowledge of technique and motivational level, being equal? Whereas with appropriate formal training and knowledge such a height clearly is within reach of young persons, most would agree that it should be close to impossible for an older adult.

Staying with this example for a moment, assume young and old persons are asked to jump across a bar at a height of 1 m on the basis of expert formal training and knowledge. Clearly, aging effects would be reduced because basic physical resources need not be activated to the same degree. Notice that the complexity of the task has not changed because, in principle, the same "algorithm" can be used to jump over each height. Mastering a greater height implies primarily that the task is more difficult. Thus, in the example, magnification of age differences does not arise for reasons of task structure or complexity but because of differences in task difficulty, with the more difficult one requiring more of the available reserve capacity of relevant physical processes. It follows that—holding practice and related experience constant—it may be possible to assess an individual's range of capacity in basic components by varying task difficulty independent of variation in task structure.

Advantages of Constructed Versus Naturally Acquired Expertise

There is another important point that can be communicated with reference to the high-jump example. If an expert wanted to display his or her best performance on a well-known problem, he or she would execute a highly routinized sequence of actions. Any departure from normal strategy or any switch to a different strategy would almost inevitably lead to a substantial drop in performance, perhaps only temporarily, however. For example, if a high jumper gets out of step, often the jump is not even executed. Similarly, although instruction and practice of different styles (e.g., straddle or Fosbury flop) may lead to similar achievements, a person who has trained exclusively in one of them cannot switch to another without experiencing at least a temporary drop of performance.[1]

Relatively little is known about the components or the integration of processes in real-life expert performance involving cognition. Usually experts in cognitive skills were "found in the field" and their expertise was decomposed a posteriori with the help of creative experiments (e.g., Chase & Simon, 1973). In contrast to this procedure and to the sports analogy, the present approach aims at synthesizing or constructing expertise in a laboratory setting with relevant declarative and procedural knowledge specified a priori and, consequently, under experimental control. This is a distinct and critical advantage not available in research involving real-life experts. Knowing how an expertise was acquired and how an expert-level performance is accomplished paves the way for a detailed determination of boundary conditions in criterion task performance at the level of theoretical components putatively underlying aggregated performance. Thus, rather than having to infer differences due to expertise from expert-novice performance differences in a criterion task, the constructed expertise research paradigm allows a priori prediction about expert-novice differences because the components determining performance are known. Moreover, individual differences can be assessed directly at the level of these components at various stages in the acquistion of the expertise.

Hypotheses Related to Aging and Expertise: Toward Magnification and Identification of Age Differences and Aging-Sensitive Components

In the following discussion, five sets of guiding assumptions and hypotheses that motivate our search for an alternative developmental methodology are presented (Kliegl & Baltes, 1984).

---

[1] There are expertises that are constituted by creative variations of procedures (e.g., chess, tennis). We will limit our discussion to expertises that depend on highly overlearned procedures.

First, we contend that psychometric or experimental data with one or few assessments are comparable to asking nonexperts to jump over a fairly low height such as 1 m. In addition to differences in fundamental processes and knowledge, individual and age differences in clearing such a low height may arise for an infinite number of reasons such as familiarity, motivational level, and past experience. Thus, within this normal range of functioning many alternative interpretations are plausible. The conventional approach to this problem has been to demonstrate the relevance or irrelevance of a small subset of these factors by experimental or correlational techniques. It is an open question, however, whether these strategies can ever be conclusive.

A related problem is the substantial malleability of performance under standardized one-time assessments. Results from cognitive intervention studies showed that the estimated longitudinal decline in fluid abilities can be compensated by a "life experience" of five 1-hr sessions (P. B. Baltes, Dittmann-Kohli, & Kliegl, 1986; P. B. Baltes & Willis, 1982; Willis, 1985). A comparable degree of plasticity is found in other domains of functioning of the elderly as well, such as behaviors associated with social interactions and self-care (M. M. Baltes & Kindermann, 1985; Lerner, 1984). In our view, this finding of substantial malleability is in large part due to the fact that the performances measured were not near the top but in the average range of performances. Thus, independent of how much young subjects would benefit from similar training, standard psychometric assessment does not lead to the identification of robust age differences. Data of this type are also moot with respect to reserve capacity or potential to improve. Although data from psychometric assessment were perhaps never meant to speak to notions of reserve capacity, demonstration of test-performance modifiability in short-term intervention implies that theories of aging need to incorporate notions of reserve capacity. Ignoring these results implies the rather strong assumption that amount of change due to intervention is constant across age.

Second, like Salthouse (1985; Salthouse & Somberg, 1982) we posit that measures of reserve capacity can be obtained in studies with extended practice that lead subjects to very high levels of performance. Ideally, an expertise should be constructed in a laboratory setting. The criterion of attained expertise would be a level of performance on a criterion task that may be many standard deviations better than the performance of untrained subjects. Since acquisition of a cognitive skill with extended practice seems to follow a power function, the asymptotic level could be used as an index of maximum performance (Anderson, 1982; Newell & Rosenbloom, 1981). The distinct advantage of measuring reserve capacity under conditions of extended practice and in the context of constructed expertise is that high levels of performance guarantee task execution according to theory. The experimenter knows that certain cognitive processes and specific knowledge were activated since any other strategy would fall short of such high performance levels.

Third, in analogy to the high-jump example, we postulate that larger and larger age differences in basic cognitive processes should be found with increasing task difficulty (P. B. Baltes et al., 1984; Craik, in press; Craik & Byrd, 1982; Craik & Rabinowitz, 1985; Salthouse, in press). Since construction of laboratory expertise involves the theoretical specification of a number of cognitive processes, differential sensitivity to aging-related loss should become visible. Although decline is expected on some, many cognitive processes may remain stable even under, or sometimes because of, conditions of high demand. Stability is also predicted for acquisition of new declarative knowledge.

Fourth, once an expertise is established at a stable level, we argue that it is possible to test the functional reserve, adaptivity, or resilience of the system by selectively interfering with component processes and/ or knowledge critical for correct performance on the criterion task. If these kinds of interference are possible in a quantitative, continuous manner, boundary conditions of gradual recovery versus deterioration of the expertise can be identified. Again, age effects are expected to be pronounced on such measures of resilience or adaptivity. In a review of age effects of adaptivity in thermoregulation, motility, and animal learning, Coper, Jänicke, and Schulze (1986) concluded that "a progressive reduction in adaptation to environmental conditions . . . is the most important phenomenon associated with aging" (p. 208; see also Fries & Crapo, 1981; Shock, 1977).

Fifth, we postulate that the ability to cope with challenging situations such as "loss" of a specific cognitive component process may also open the way for experimental investigations of compensatory processes. Both psychologically (Bäckman, 1984; P. B. Baltes et al., 1984; Salthouse, chapter 8 of this volume; Skinner, 1983) and physiologically (Phelps & Mazziota, 1985), the evolution of compensatory processes has been featured in accounts of effective aging. Performance recovery under more difficult or more complex conditions implies a change in kind or in efficiency of cognitive processes or in the relevant knowledge. Often these changes may involve creative transformations of the expertise leading to its reestablishment at a higher level.

Obviously, in cases of self-initiated compensatory or substitutive behaviors, subjects take their expertises beyond what they were taught in the training program and beyond the strict experimental control afforded by theory-guided synthesis. It is likely, however, that this process of restructuring is confined by the extant expertise. Especially with selective componential interference, the locus of compensatory processes is probably easily determined. Nevertheless, post hoc decompositional analysis and verbal protocols, just as in traditional research on expertise, will be required. The positive aspect, however, is that construction of expertise in a laboratory setting is expected to trigger adaptive processes of knowledge transformation and refinement which are characteristic of real-life experts.

In the next two sections, preliminary results from several case studies will be used to illustrate the interfacing of the two complementary research strategies described: theory-guided synthesis of expertise and subsequent testing of the adaptivity of this expertise. The joint application of these strategies should lead to empirical tests of the theoretical positions advanced in this section. The substantive focus is on engineered digit memory in young and old adults. More detailed information is contained in several research reports (Kliegl, Smith, & Baltes, 1986; Kliegl, Smith, Heckhausen, & Baltes, 1986a, 1986b; Smith, Kliegl, & Baltes, 1986).

THEORY-GUIDED SYNTHESIS OF MEMORY EXPERTISE

Theoretical Framework

Theory-guided synthesis of expertise involves systematic instruction and practice; one may even describe it as "shaping" the desired expertise. There are two unique aspects of this research strategy: One, a normal subject must achieve a stable level of expert performance in the course of a laboratory program. Two, the combination of cognitive processes and relevant knowledge involved in expert task performance is substantially different from those that untrained subjects bring to the task. With both conditions fulfilled, the display of expertise guarantees that the cognitive processes and domains of knowledge that constitute the theoretical components of expert performance on a criterion task were actually involved during task execution.

In digit span tasks, subjects are typically required to report in correct order a series of random digits that was presented to them once. On the average and with presentation rates of several seconds, untrained subjects can recall about seven items if they rehearse the individual digits during presentation. If, however, by chance a sequence of digits can be recoded into a meaningful element of permanent knowledge, for example one's phone number, the number of digits recalled could be substantially larger because limits associated with a rehearsal strategy apply to the number of chunks (Miller, 1956). Indeed, some form of recoding of random digits into meaningful knowledge has been the hallmark of most mnemonists (Ericsson, 1985). Similarly, two subjects who in the course of 2 years learned to recall more than 80 digits relied heavily, for example, on knowledge related to athletic running times to recode short digit sequences (Chase & Ericsson, 1981).[2] Thus, one difference between normal, untrained subjects and memory experts is that memory experts have available systematic digit-related knowledge.

Once digits are recoded into meaningful knowledge elements, more effective strategies than simple rehearsal can be employed to retain information about the order of items. A particularly useful strategy is known as the Method of Loci (cf. Bower, 1970; Yates, 1966). In the Method of Loci an overlearned sequence of geographic locations is used repeatedly (trial-invariant) as a memory peg for encoding a trial-dependent sequence of knowledge elements. Subjects are instructed to generate funny, bizarre, and dynamic images or thoughts between the to-be-remembered items and the sequentially ordered geographic locations. During recall, the geographic locations serve as retrieval cues for items and their serial position. Again, most professional mnemonists use this or similar mnemonic devices (see Bellezza, 1981, for a review). Thus, a second difference between normal, untrained subjects and memory experts is that memory experts have available special techniques that allow them to retain order information of random series of items.

Procedure

We engineered memory expertise in normal subjects using the two factors mentioned: knowledge about digits and the Method of Loci as a mnemonic strategy of encoding and retrieval. Digit-related knowledge was provided by having subjects learn a large number of historical dates. When the subjects were presented with a long series of random digits, this knowledge was used to recode consecutive digit triplets into historical dates by prefixing a 1 (e.g., 4–9–2 becomes 1492, and is associated with "Columbus discovers America"). This way, parsing a random digit sequence into digit triplets and recoding these triplets into historical events results in a random sequence of historical events. Encoding and retrieval of a random sequence of historical events should be possible with the Method of Loci.

Subjects were systematically trained in the memory expertise. First, they overlearned a specific trip around either 30 or 40 Berlin landmarks. Second, they practiced the recall of concrete nouns with this mental

---

[2] Chase and Ericsson (1981) identified three critical components of this expertise. In addition to recoding digits in elements of permanent knowledge, their subjects organized these recoded units in a trial-dependent hierarchial retrieval structure and improved on the speed with which they could carry out associated cognitive processes.

map. In a third step in our training program, subjects learned dates for 100 historical events. Finally, they attempted to integrate these components to recall strings of digits.

Subjects

So far, 1 young student (age 23 years) and 10 older adults (age range 67–78 years) have participated in 30 training sessions.[3] None of the subjects had prior experience in mnemonic strategies, and all had normal digit and word spans. Their general intelligence (Hamburg-Wechsler IQ) was 1.5 to 2 *SD* above the mean for their respective age groups. The elderly subjects were recruited from the top 20% of a positively selected sample of about 400 persons who had participated earlier in a cognitive training study on fluid-type intelligence tasks (Baltes et al., 1985). Thus, the selection strategy maximized chances of identifying mentally very fit elderly. No such special selection criteria were applied to our young subject, a personal acquaintance of members of the research team.

Results

Performance of a young adult subject.   After memorizing a map of 30 Berlin landmarks and 100 historical dates, our young subject immediately mastered the Method of Loci using concrete nouns. He also had no difficulty in employing the Method of Loci and knowledge of 100 historical events to memorize long digit lists. These were composed of random concatenation of triplets selected with replacement from the pool of 100 historical events that represented the subject's knowledge.

During the first trials our young adult correctly recalled 90 digits presented at an average self-paced rate of 12 s per digit. After 36 trials he recalled 90 digits presented at a fixed rate of 5 s per digit. Thus, after only 36 trials (and after 20 experimental sessions), with low time constraints and with suitable mnemonic techniques, the subject performed at expert level with very little instruction. Further progress of this subject will be described in a later section on adaptivity testing.

Performance of older subjects.   The 10 older subjects memorized a map with 40 Berlin landmarks. Using this map as part of the Method of Loci mnemonic, all subjects could recall more than 32 of 40 nouns,

---

[3] Another young and 2 old persons were instructed according to a different model involving recoding of digits into concrete nouns instead of historical dates (Kliegl et al., 1986). Results are in agreement with the ones presented here.

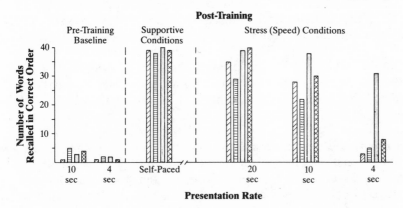

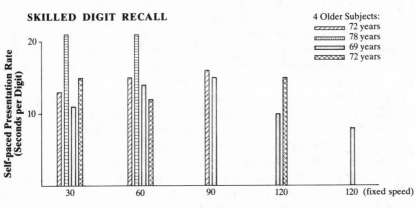

Figure 1. Magnification of individual differences in serial word recall (under speeded conditions) and digit memory (self-paced) for four subjects.

provided the study time for each word was self-determined (i.e., self-paced presentation format).

There were, however, large individual differences in the number of sessions subjects required to reach this level of performance. Only 4 of 10 elderly subjects completed all components of the training program within 30 sessions. Their post-training performances on serial recall of 40 nouns are displayed in the top part of Figure 1. These subjects showed close to perfect recall in the self-paced condition.

Like the young adult, once these older subjects had mastered the mnemonic strategy and learned the historical dates, they had little difficulty applying the model to recall long lists of digits. The performances we have observed so far are displayed in the bottom panel of

Figure 1. All 4 elderly subjects recalled correctly strings of 30 and 60 digits, respectively. Two of them succeeded also with strings of 90 and 120 digits. In all these trials, subjects determined the successive presentation of digits. The best performance we have observed was by a 69-year-old woman who correctly recalled 120 digits presented in a fixed interval of 8 s. Note that it takes 16 min to present such a long string. Preliminary as they are, these data suggest substantial developmental reserve capacity of memory processes in mentally fit old persons.

Age comparisons. Age comparisons on the basis of the present data with few subjects can, of course, illustrate only our general hypotheses. It is fair to admit that we were surprised by the ease with which our best old subject achieved her level of performance. We expected developmental reserve but not to this extent. Nevertheless, and without any intention to belittle the achievement of the best elderly person of a highly selected sample, her performance does not approach the speed of processing of our 1 young subject. Data from several other, IQ-equivalent young subjects currently in training show a similar superiority. Counter to our expectations, the best elderly subject, however, performed better than young subjects with low to average general intelligence (Kliegl et al., 1986). We predict that young subjects of equivalent intellectual and motivational level will clearly outperform the best older subjects at high levels of performance.

What about the mechanisms possibly involved in the magnification of age differences at limits of performance? None of the 10 older subjects had problems in learning 100 historical dates. Only one subject could not recall reliably the mental map of 40 locations in correct order even at the end of the training program. Our elderly subjects seemed to have difficulty in producing and encoding such images, not in principle but at the speed required for efficient performance under fast presentation rates. This was especially the case for 6 of these subjects: They required about 30 training sessions to apply the Method of Loci successfully to lists of 40 concrete nouns that were presented at subject-paced rates or at fixed rates of 20 s per word.

Individual differences among the other 4 subjects were also apparent for efficiency in the Method of Loci when nouns were presented in faster, fixed intervals (see Figure 1). In addition, these data show a strong correspondence between levels of performance in recall of nouns and recall of digits. Thus, in the present memory expertise, the formation of bizarre, funny, or dynamic images or thoughts required in the use of the Method of Loci appears to be the critical process displaying sensitivity to aging.

Thought or image formation is a rather complex cognitive process which is itself dependent on knowledge and other cognitive processes. Two complementary strategies could be advocated. First, the aging-sensitivity of thought or image formation should be cross-validated in a different criterion task. This would imply constructing an expertise, for example, in a memory-independent problem-solving task. Second, thought formation can be pushed to its limits in an extant expertise such as cognitively engineered digit memory. This might induce the need for compensatory processes and shed new light on the constituents of the cognitive process of interest. This research strategy will be illustrated in the next section.

ADAPTIVITY TESTING OF EXPERT MEMORY

Often it is difficult, if not impossible, to know whether a change in task characteristics affects difficulty or the nature of the cognitive components involved (e.g., the complexity of the system). Depending on the reserve capacity associated with relevant cognitive processes, it may affect either or both. The situation should be different if task performance is at an expert level. In this case, a person can display a high level of performance only if he or she complies with the theo-retically specified schedule of task execution (recall the example of a high jumper who will mark a personal record height only if he or she uses the practiced technique).

As long as increases in general constraints do not change the level of performance in an expertise or there are no major drops in perfor-mance, it can reasonably be assumed that task difficulty is increased without changes in the components constituting the expertise. For example, one of the elderly subjects' recall of 120 digits was not impaired by switching to a fixed presentation rate (see Figure 1). In this case, we are tapping the functional reserve of an extant system with specified components.

If we observe a significant drop in performance, limits of current functional reserve or system adaptivity are reached. In our example of increased speed of stimulus (i.e., digit) input, the drop signals either that there was not enough time to execute the required mental operations or that alternative, perhaps random or compensatory operations were invoked. Thus, a sustained drop in performance indicates that the task cannot be performed using the current level of expertise. Subsequent practice might lead to greater resilience or functional reserve due to a more efficient execution of component processes in an unchanged expert system.

The situation becomes more complicated—not unlike the typical situation in the study of real-life expertise—if environmental pressure forces a refinement of the expertise either in basic cognitive processes (e.g., combining two operations into one) or in the relevant knowledge (e.g., narrowing the spread of activated knowledge elements or elimination of irrelevant features). In this instance, separation of changes in the cognitive system from increases in efficacy of the same system may not be easily possible. Additional experiments would be needed to determine the cause of increased resilience. Nevertheless, we would anticipate that the advantage of working with well-specified laboratory expert systems continues to exist as further experimentation can be conducted against the backdrop of a well-known system of functioning.

Increasing task difficulty without changing the system is not the only way to study an expert system at its limits. Mapping functional reserve can also involve testing of single components of the system, for example, by selective interference. Two kinds of information can be gained from selectively interfering with certain components. First, any interference with a theoretically postulated component must lead to a drop in performance. If it does not, there was an error in the model specification, or automatic refinement of the expertise made this component obsolete. Selective interference serves as a validity check on the theoretical specification. The second advantage of selective interference is the possibility of experimentally inducing the need for compensatory processes and, if they materialize, their subsequent identification. Obviously, causes for improvement on a criterion task can be identified more directly if one knows where in the expertise the need for compensation existed.

The example given so far distinguished between variation in task difficulty and in the components of the system. Thus, in the following, we distinguish between testing-the-limits by variation in constraints on the criterion task and testing-the-limits by selective interference with theoretical components of the system. Note that we are primarily interested in observing and understanding two phenomena: first, why subjects cannot perform certain tasks (lack of adaptivity); and second, the adaptive processes that lead to a gradual restoration of performance after the expertise has been overtaxed by these strategies. Examples for both procedures are illustrated with data from one high-ability young subject (Kliegl et al., 1985).

Increasing Task Difficulty Within an Extant System

The first column of Table 1 specifies the parameters of a baseline expertise in digit memory at the end of a theory-guided synthesis of cognitive skill. The subject recalled correctly all 90 digits presented at a rate of 5 s per digit. Digit strings were composed by random concatenation of digit triplets based on a pool of 100 historical dates.

Table 1. Resilience Testing of an Expertise in Digit Memory

	Baseline of expertise	Intervention			
		1	2	3	4
Criterion Task					
Percentage of digits recalled in correct order[a]	100	50	50	48	80
Parameters of Expertise					
Length of digit string Compatibility with historical knowledge (%)	100				
Number of loci	30				
Order of loci	known				
Content of loci	known				
Pool size of triplets	100		25	25	100
Presentation rate (s/digit)	5	3	2	1	3
External cues at encoding	no				
External cues at recall	no				
Additional load on working memory	no				
Number of trials to restore expertise	n.a.	n.a.[b]	13	26	4

Note n.a. = not available
[a]Percentages reflect drop in first trial of intervention.
[b]Expertise was not restored after sixth trial.

There was perfect compatibility between the digit strings and the subject's historical knowledge. The expertise involved 30 loci with known order and content. Finally, the subject did not use any external cues.

The first intervention involved an increase in presentation rate to 3 s per digit. Performance dropped to 50% and was not restored during six trials in this condition. The subject reported that it took too long to decide which features of a historical event should be used for thought or image formation. Following up on this report by the subject, the next step in our training program involved identifying unique features for a subset of 25 events and having the subject memorize these. For example, instead of invoking the historical event "Crusade" to form his image, he would always use a simple "cross" when the digits corresponding to the Crusade event had to be recoded.

As a second intervention, digit strings based on random concatenation of triplets and consistent with these transformed historical events were presented at a rate of 2 s per digit. Again, performance dropped to 50%. After 13 trials, however, he could correctly recall 90 digits at this 2-s pace. The next step was to increase presentation rate to 1 s per digit. Performance was restored perfectly after 26 trials. Subsequently, we returned to the conditions of the first intervention (i.e., 100 historical dates, 3 s per digit). Performance dropped to only 80% and was restored after four trials.

This short iteration of intervention and practice illustrates how performance improved because of adaptive refinement or even transformation of knowledge. Thus, even simple manipulations of presentation rate can cause a change in expertise-relevant knowledge. It is not clear from these data to what degree there was a concomitant improvement in the efficiency of cognitive processes. Without information about the changes in relevant knowledge, an incorrect, sole attribution to increased efficiency in basic cognitive processes such as retrieval speed would have been likely.

Increasing presentation rate is but one example of increased task demands. Presenting more than 90 digits would be another. Table 1 displays a number of parameters of the expertise that could be manipulated to challenge the expertise. Since the memory expertise was constructed according to a certain model, destabilization can be induced at rather specific levels.

Selective Componential Interference

Construction of expertise implies knowledge of processes that are relevant for task execution. Following theory-guided acquisition of expertise, subjects can be prevented from using some components by experimental manipulation. In our research on digit span based on knowledge of historical dates and the Method of Loci, interference can disable, for example, the use of historical knowledge or the use of the mental walk in the Method of Loci (see also Chase & Ericsson, 1981, for similar, though a posteriori, strategies aimed at testing the cognitive processes used by their subjects).

Interference with use of historical knowledge was achieved in the present case by presenting digit strings that could not be parsed into the historical dates available in the subject's permanent knowledge. When presented with completely random sequences of digits (rather than digits compatible with the subject's knowledge of historical dates), the subject's performance fell immediately within the range of nonexperts (i.e., to about 9 digits) even with relatively slow presentation rates of 10 s per digit. Thus, historical knowledge was critical for the task. Note that the resilience or functional reserve of the expertise could be determined more precisely by manipulating the degree of compatibility between historical knowledge and digit strings.

In the present type of expertise, another example of selective componential interference can focus on the procedural component (i.e., the Method of Loci) involved in long-term memory and retrieval. Application of the Method of Loci requires knowledge of a set of landmarks and of a walk covering them in a fixed order. Our expert can easily encode 30 concrete nouns and their serial position using this technique. Interference with order of locations was achieved by prompting the subject each time a noun was presented on the screen with one of the Berlin landmarks in a new (random) order and requiring him to form an image involving noun and the prompted landmark. In addition, the subject was asked to remember the serial position of nouns. Our prediction with respect to this interference with established order of locations was the following: Forming images between nouns and land-mark prompts in unfamiliar order should lead to a complete recall of the set of nouns. Recalling them in correct order, however, should be severely impaired, unless compensatory strategies are employed.

As predicted, the subject correctly recalled 38 of 40 words and the first 18 words also in correct position. Although there was clear inter-ference with order information, performance was still remarkably high, suggesting that the subject had attempted some compensatory measures.

Toward the Study of Compensatory Processes

We have mentioned already the significance of compensatory and substitutive processes for the study of intellectual aging (Bäckman, in press; P. B. Baltes & M. M. Baltes, 1980; P. B. Baltes et al., 1984; Dixon & Baltes, in press).[4] The present pilot work illustrates how testing-the-limits of an extant expert system can be used to gain in-formation about how subjects generate compensations.

In the interference study just described, the subject was able to recall 18 words in the correct position, although our experimental effort was aimed at eliminating serial information. As noted in his verbal report, the subject had accomplished this by attempting to incorporate the serial number of the noun into the image. Thus, the image formed for the first noun and first locus prompt would involve a "1," the image for the second noun and second locus prompt a "2," and so on. This compensatory strategy worked for the first 18 nouns.

A second subject, also experienced with the Method of Loci, generated spontaneously a different compensation. She formed stories between nouns and prompted locations. To retain order information, she de-signed stories that involved a taxi driving from the prompted landmark to the location normally encoding the order information. The subject correctly recalled 34 words and 25 of them in the correct order. Again, there was a drop in performance but also successful compensation.

---

[4] This is true not only for psychological conceptions. For example, biologists (Wad-dington, 1975) and sociologists (Featherman, 1983) have argued that effective life-span development involves channeling of competence and specialization. The expertise par-adigm is a direct realization of notions about channeling and specialization.

Although these examples have only anecdotal qualities, they illustrate the interaction of specific knowledge and cognitive processes. In both cases, new elements of knowledge were incorporated in the task: numbers in the first and a taxi ride in the second example. As a consequence, image or thought formation had to synthesize three instead of two elements during each cycle.

In summary, we believe that even the few data on testing of functional reserve and adaptivity of expert systems generated important facts. Since experts strive for good performance, they are ready to demonstrate high efficacy. As long as possible, they stay within the confines of the systems and increase time-related efficacy. It appears that if within-system functioning is not sufficient, they respond with great creativity to environmental challenges of their expertise. Successful restoration may not only maintain the skill but also reestablish the expertise at a quantitatively and qualitatively higher level. This is accomplished by refinement or enlargement of specific knowledge or by increasing the efficiency of cognitive processes. Both solutions qualify as compensatory strategies which lead to an elaboration of the earlier expertise. In our view, they characterize adequately what we are likely to observe in real-life functioning.

We have not systematically collected data on old persons with respect to questions involving elaboration by compensation. Our expectation is that adaptivity testing of this kind may be especially suited to study compensatory and adaptive processes across the life span. Of particular interest is the question whether refinement of knowledge is more dependent on already available knowledge (the pragmatics of intelligence), possibly favoring older persons; or more indicative of cognitive or learning abilities (the mechanics of intelligence), which would be in line with the strengths of younger persons. At the outset, different developmental trajectories for cognitive processes and knowledge were postulated. In resilience testing of expertise, an understanding of relations and mutual dependencies between these components assumes an important role.

CONCLUSIONS

There is increasing interest in understanding the mechanisms at the basis of growth and decline in cognitive development during adulthood and old age (P. B. Baltes et al., 1984; P. B. Baltes & Kliegl, 1986; Denney, 1984; Dixon & Baltes, in press; Labouvie-Vief, 1982, 1985). It has been argued that growth and decline can be better understood if studied at limits of performance and under controlled laboratory conditions simulating real-life settings of expertise acquisition and development.

Theory-guided synthesis and subsequent systematic destabilization of complex cognitive skills were introduced as complementary testing-the-limits research strategies for assessment of developmental reserve capacity and mechanisms of functioning. Actualization of reserve capacity qualifies a person as an expert if his or her performance on a criterion task is significantly (e.g., several standard deviations) above the mean of a normal, untrained sample of comparable intellectual ability. With this criterion, theory-guided synthesis of expertise secures an advantage of experimental control over active cognitive processes on every trial of a criterion task. We presented results from case studies documenting the feasibility of this approach with young and old subjects.

Developmental reserve capacity can also be measured by indices of adaptive resilience or functional reserve. We have presented three strategies to this end: increasing task demands within the extant system, measuring the time it takes to restore the previous level of criterion task performance, and identifying the type of compensation that subjects use when the extant system is tested beyond its limits of functioning. Thus, the paradigm also offers a view at adaptive and compensatory strategies. Hypotheses about different developmental trajectories for cognitive processes and domain-specific knowledge could be assessed with such measures. Age effects may be most prominent on cognitive processes that govern the adaptive refinement of task-specific knowledge systems.

Some words of caution are in order. Once testing *beyond* the limits of an extant system has started, the further development of expertise may be to a larger degree under the subject's control than is desirable from the experimenter's point of view. Yet, aside from the argument that this departure from an extant system simulates comparable phenomena in real life, we believe that assessment of elaboration and compensation is still aided by departure from a known system. Moreover, so far our experience was that expert subjects are quite eager, interested, and possibly skilled in communicating their compensatory strategies. Of course, resources will prevent large sample studies of iterative resilience testing, but much can be learned from few subjects and efforts at obtaining verbal protocols (Ericsson & Simon, 1984). Furthermore, what was learned can subsequently be incorporated in the engineering part of newly designed research.

Presenting the general strategy of expertise construction, selective componential interference, and elaboration by triggering compensatory strategies was also placed in the context of age comparison. Available data are restricted to limit testing of an extant system by increasing task demands. Magnification of age and individual differences at limits of functioning were obtained. It was speculated that similar magnification may be obtainable if the focus is on elaboration and compensation. If the interest is in aspects of adaptivity, performing experiments at limits of performance may actually be the only way. We would like to reiterate that, in our view, the combination of theory-guided synthesis of expertise and its subsequent enhancement by systematic destabilization and fostering of compensatory strategies captures some of the dynamics of real-life situations. In this sense, we believe that our efforts aimed at simulation of expert systems in the laboratory may evince higher ecological validity than tasks of digit span initially seem to suggest. In our view, laboratory research on potential and limits in acquisition of expertise and on resilience of expertise in challenging and sometimes overtaxing situations will contribute to knowledge about changes in everyday cognitive functioning in development and aging.

REFERENCES

Anderson, J.R. (1981). *Cognitive skills and their acquisition.* Hillsdale, NJ: Erlbaum.
Anderson, J.R. (1982). Acquisition of cognitive skill. *Psychological Review, 89,* 369–406.
Bäckman, L. (in press). Varieties of memory compensation of older adults in episodic remembering. In L.W. Poon, D.C. Rubin, & B.A. Wilson (Eds.), *Everyday cognition in adult and late life.* New York: Cambridge University Press.
Baltes, M.M., & Kindermann, T. (1985). Die Bedeutung der Plastizität für die klinische Beurteilung des Leistungsverhaltens im Alter. In D. Bente, H. Coper, & S. Kanowski (Eds.), *Hirnorganische Psychosyndrome im Alter: Vol 2: Methoden zur Objektivierung pharmakotherapeutischer Wirkung* (pp. 171–184). Berlin: Springer.
Baltes, P.B. (1984). Intelligenz im Alter. *Spektrum der Wissenschaft, 5,* 46–60.
Baltes, P.B., & Baltes, M.M. (1980). Plasticity and variability in psychological aging: Methodological and theoretical issues. In G. Gurski (Ed.), *Determining the effects of aging on the central nervous system* (pp. 41–66). Berlin: Schering.
Baltes, P.B., Dittmann-Kohli, F., & Dixon, R.A. (1984). New perspectives on the development of intelligence in adulthood: Toward a dual-process conception and a model of selective optimization with compensation. In P.B. Baltes & O.G. Brim, Jr. (Eds.), *Life-span development and behavior* (Vol. 6, pp. 33–76). New York: Academic Press.
Baltes, P.B., Dittmann-Kohli, F., & Kliegl, R. (1986). *Reserve capacity of the elderly in aging-sensitive tests of fluid intelligence: Replication and extension. Psychology and Aging, 1,* 72–77.
Baltes, P.B., & Kliegl, R. (1986). On the dynamics between growth and decline in the aging of intelligence and memory. In K. Poeck (Ed.), *Neurology. Proceedings of the XIIIth World Congress of Neurology* (pp. 1–17). Heidelberg, West Germany: Springer.
Baltes, P.B., & Willis, S.L. (1982). Plasticity and enhancement of intellectual functioning in old age: Penn State's Adult Development and Enrichment Project (ADEPT). In F.I.M. Craik & S.E. Trehub (Eds.), *Aging and cognitive processes* (pp. 353–389). New York: Plenum.

Bellezza, F.S. (1981). Mnemonic devices: Classification, characteristics and criteria. *Review of Educational Research, 51,* 247–275.

Bower, G.A. (1970). Analysis of a mnemonic device. *American Scientist, 58,* 496–510.

Brown, A.L. (1982). Learning and development: The problem of compatibility, access, and induction. *Human Development, 25,* 89–115.

Cattell, R.B. (1971). *Abilities: Their structure, growth, and action.* Boston: Houghton Mifflin.

Charness, N. (1981). Aging and skilled problem solving. *Journal of Experimental Psychology: General, 110,* 21–38.

Chase, W.G., & Ericsson, K.A. (1981). Skilled memory. In J.R. Anderson (Ed.), *Cognitive skills and their acquisition* (pp. 141–189). Hillsdale, NJ: Erlbaum.

Chase, W.G., & Simon, H.A. (1973). Perception in chess. *Cognitive Psychology, 4,* 55–81.

Chi. M.T.H., Glaser, R., & Rees, E. (1982). Expertise in problem solving. In R.J. Sternberg (Ed.), *Advances in the psychology of human intelligence* (pp. 7–75). Hillsdale, NJ: Erlbaum.

Coper, H., Jänicke, B., & Schulze, G. (1986). Biopsychological research on adaptivity across the life-span of animals. In P.B. Baltes, R.M. Lerner, & D.L. Featherman (Eds.), *Life span development and behavior,* (Vol. 7, pp. 207–232). Hillsdale, NJ: Erlbaum.

Craik, F.I.M. (in press). A functional account of age differences in memory. In F. Klix & H. Hagendorf (Eds.), *Human memory and cognitive capabilities.* Amsterdam: North Holland.

Craik, F.I.M., & Byrd, M. (1982). Aging and cognitive deficits: The role of attentional resources. In F.I.M. Craik & S.E. Trehub (Eds.), *Aging and cognitive processes* (pp. 191–211). New York: Plenum.

Craik., F.I.M., & Rabinowitz, J.C. (1985). The effects of presentation rate and encoding task on age-related memory deficts. *Journal of Gerontology, 40,* 300–315.

Denney, N.W. (1982). Aging and cognitive change. In B.B. Wolman (Ed.), *Handbook of developmental psychology* (pp. 807–827). Englewood Cliffs, NJ: Prentice-Hall.

Denney, N.W. (1984). A model of cognitive development across the life span. *Developmental Review, 4,* 171–191.

Dixon, R.A., & Baltes, P.B. (in press). Toward life-span research and pragmatics of intelligence. In R.J. Sternberg & R.K. Wagner (Eds.), *Practical intelligence: Origins of competence in the everyday world.* Cambridge, England: Cambridge University Press.

Ericsson, K.A. (1985). Memory skill. *Canadian Journal of Psychology, 39,* 188–231.

Ericsson, K.A., & Simon, H.A. (1984). *Protocol analysis.* Cambridge, MA: MIT Press/ Bradford.

Estes, W.K. (1982). Learning, memory, and intelligence. In R.J. Sternberg (Ed.), *Handbook of human intelligence* (pp. 170–224). Cambridge, England: Cambridge University Press.

Featherman, D.L. (1983). Life-span perspective in social science research. In P.B. Baltes & O.G. Brim, Jr. (Eds.), *Life-span development and behavior* (Vol. 5, pp. 1–57). New York: Academic Press.

Fries, J.F., & Crapo, L.M. (1981). *Vitality and aging.* San Francisco: Freeman.

Glaser, R. (1984). Education and thinking: The role of knowledge. *American Psychologist, 39,* 93–104.

Guthke, J. (1982). The learning test concept—An alternative to the traditional static intelligence test. *The German Journal of Psychology, 6,* 306–324.

Horn, J.L. (1982). The aging of human abilities. In B.B. Wolman (Ed.), *Handbook of developmental psychology* (pp. 847–870). Englewood Cliffs, NJ: Prentice-Hall.

Hoyer, W.J. (1985). Aging and the development of expert cognition. In T.M. Schlechter

& M.P. Toglia (Eds.), *New directions in cognitive science* (pp. 69–87). Norwood, NJ: Ablex.

Kliegl, R., & Baltes, P.B. (1984). *Cognitive reserve capacity, expertise and aging.* Unpublished manuscript, Max Planck Institute for Human Development and Education, Berlin.

Kliegl, R., Smith, J., & Baltes, P.B. (1986). Testing-the-limits, expertise, and memory in adulthood and old age. In F. Klix & H. Hagendorf (Eds.), *Human Memory and cognitive capabilities* (pp. 395–407). Amsterdam: North Holland.

Kliegl, R., Smith, J., Heckhaussen, J., & Baltes, P.B. (1986a). Ausbildung zum Gedächtniskünstler: Ein experimenteller Zugang zur Überprüfung von kognitiven Theorien des Lernens and Alterns. *Unterrichtswissenschaft, 14,* 29–39.

Kliegl, R., Smith, J., Heckhausen, J., & Baltes, P.B. (1986b). *Theory-guided synthesis of an expertise: The sample case of skilled memory.* Manuscript submitted for publication.

Labouvie-Vief, G. (1982). Dynamic development and mature autonomy: A theoretical prologue. *Human Development, 25,* 161—191.

Labouvie-Vief, G. (1985). Intelligence and cognition. In J.E. Birren & K.W. Schaie (Eds.), *Handbook of the psychology of aging* (2nd ed., pp. 500–530). New York: Van Nostrand Reinhold.

Lerner, R.M. (1984). *On the nature of human plasticity.* New York: Cambridge University Press.

Miller, G.A. (1956). The magical number seven, plus or minus two. *Psychological Review, 63,* 81–97.

Newell, A., & Rosenbloom, S. (1981). Mechanisms of skill acquisition and the law of practice. In J.R. Anderson (Ed.), *Cognitive skills and their acquisition* (pp. 57–84). Hillsdale, NJ: Erlbaum.

Phelps, M.E., & Mazziotta, J.C. (1985). Positron emission tomography: Human brain function and biochemistry. *Science, 228,* 799–809.

Salthouse, T.A. (1985). *A theory of cognitive aging.* Amsterdam: North Holland.

Salthouse, T.A., & Somberg, B.L. (1982). Skilled performance: Effects of adult age and experience on elementary processes. *Journal of Experimental Psychology: General, 111,* 176–207.

Schaie, K.W., & Hertzog, C. (1983). Fourteen-year cohort-sequential analyses of adult intellectual development. *Developmental Psychology, 19,* 531–543.

Schmidt, L.R. (1971). Testing-the-Limits im Leistungsverhalten: Möglichkeiten und Grenzen. In F. Duhm (Ed.), *Praxis der klinischen Psychologie* (pp. 9–29). Göttingen, West Germany: Hogrefe.

Shock, N.W. (1977). Systems integration. In C.E. Finch & L. Hayflick (Eds.), *Handbook of the biology of aging* (pp. 639–665). New York: Van Nostrand Reinhold.

Skinner, B.F. (1983). Intellectual self-management in old age. *American Psychologist, 38,* 239–244.

Sloboda, J.A. (1978). Perception of contour in music reading. *Perception, 7,* 323–331.

Smith, J., Dixon, R.A., & Baltes, P.B. (in press). Expertise in life planning: A new approach to investigate aspects of wisdom. In M. Commons, J.D. Sinnott, F.A. Richards, & C. Amon (Eds.), *Beyond formal operations II: Adult cognitive development.* New York: Praeger.

Smith, J., Kliegl, R., & Baltes P.B. (1986). *Skilled memory: A method for studying reserve capacity in aging research.* Manuscript submitted for publication.

Waddington, C.F. (1975). *The evolution of an evolutionist.* Edinburgh, Scotland: Edinburgh University Press.

Weinert, F.E., & Hasselhorn, M. (1986). Memory development: Universal changes and individual differences. In F. Klix & H. Hagendorf (Eds.), *Human memory and cognitive capabilities.* Amsterdam: North Holland.

Wiedl, K.H. (1984). Lerntests: Nur Forschungsmittel und Forschungsgegenstand? *Zeitschrift für Entwicklungsund Pädagogische Psychologie, 16,* 245–281.

Willis, S.L. (1985). Towards an educational psychology of the adult learner. In J.E. Birren & K.W. Schaie (Eds.), *Handbook of the psychology of aging* (2nd ed., pp. 818–847). New York: Van Nostrand Reinhold.

Yates, F.A. (1966). *The art of memory.* London: Routledge & Kegan Paul.

Chapter Seven

Acquisition of Knowledge and the Decentralization of *g* In Adult Intellectual Development

William J. Hoyer

INTRODUCTION

The intent of this chapter is to propose a description of adult cognitive development that gives emphasis to the emergence of and increased differentiation of domain-ordered knowledge specializations. Research as well as theory in aging has generally overlooked the important contribution of cumulative knowledge as an antecedent of adult cognitive function. It is argued that the continuous integration of new knowledge and the increasing specialization of procedures for handling information within knowledge domains are at the core of cognitive development throughout the adult life span. Support for this position includes (a) the observation that most older adults continue to perform competently in skilled or expert domains even though standardized assessments of domain-general abilities and measures of information processing show a deficit with aging; (b) studies showing that the attentional processes of orienting, selectivity, expectancy or preparation, and automaticity serve to improve higher-level cognitive performance; and (c) studies showing the development of domain specificity or encapsulation of elementary information-processing systems (e.g., input analyzers, retrieval process) as cognitive skill level increases within knowledge domains. It is suggested that a wide variety of socio-environmental factors operating in adulthood encourage cognitive differ-

National Institute on Aging Research Grant AG 06041

entiation and the development of specializations within prescribed knowledge domains.

POINTS OF DEPARTURE

It is a generally accepted view that intelligence reflects both a person's knowledge of the world and his/her basic abilities for processing information. Although such an account of intelligence continues to be a useful one, the assumption that information processing efficiency is independent of the content of the information being processed has been questioned in recent years (e.g., Chi, 1985; Glaser, 1984; Rybash, Hoyer, & Roodin, 1986). Until recently, many developmental psychologists assumed that the development of knowledge was an outcome of age-related enlargements in intellectual capacity and improvements in general processing abilities. Chi (1978) provided one of the most striking demonstrations of the role of knowledge in cognitive development. She compared 10-year-olds and young adults on a standard memory span task and a task measuring recall memory of the positions of chess pieces. The 10-year-olds, who were skilled chess players, outperformed the young adults, who were novices at the game of chess, on the measures of memory for chess positions. These findings could not be attributed to the children being generally more intelligent or possessing better general memory skills than the younger adults.

The point that content knowledge can outweigh the effects of other age-related differences in intelligence has important implications for the study of intellectual development during the later years. Because of the amount of accumulated content knowledge and the kinds of mental abilities that are required to perform at least some adult roles (e.g., particular kinds of work), it is reasonable to question the prevailing emphasis on concepts of ability that are intended to be pure enough and general enough to cut across the particular demands of particular cognitive specializations when describing developmental changes in adult intelligence. In the information processing literature, processes which are presumed to be independent of particular knowledge domains are referred to as effortful or control processes, and in the psychometric literature, general ability or general capacity is represented by notions like Spearman's (1927) *g*, and Cattell's (1971) and Horn's (1970; Horn & Cattell, 1967) conceptions of fluid intelligence. Cattell's (1971) triadic theory of abilities posits three kinds of ability components as follows:

1. g-type capacities—general powers operating through all brain action to affect all cognitive performance. Three types of fluid or *g* abilities are the ability to grasp relations and correlations, cognitive speed, and fluency or retrieval facility.

2. provincials—powers having to do with the functioning of particular sensory and motor systems.

3. agencies—aids or acquired cognitive skills based on education and training, and proficiencies based on particular interests.

Even the multifactor theories of Thurstone (1938) and Guilford (1967), stress the domain-general nature of ability factors.

Such ability factors were not intended to represent the many kinds of specialized cognitive performances that are created through interaction with a complex and continuously changing matrix of socioenvironmental antecedents. Thus, although *g*-type abilities are fundamental to the development and acquisition of many kinds of knowledge throughout the life course, developmental theories of adult intelligence should give emphasis to the practical qualities as well as the fundamental age-ordered mechanisms that characterize adult thinking, to the factors that enable the maintenance and growth of cognitive proficiency during the adult years, and to the dynamic interaction between socio-environmental factors and the mechanisms of cognitive organization and function throughout the adult life course.

If we look at the effects of aging within particular fields (or domains) of cognitive specialization, evidence indicates that adults continue to function competently in their vocations and in their everyday avocational roles (see, e.g., Baltes, Dittmann-Kohli, & Dixon, 1984; Cole, 1979; Hoyer, 1985; Kohn & Schooler, 1978; Riley, 1983; Salthouse, Chapter 8 of this volume). The maintenance of practical intellectual functioning in old age, which is the rule rather than the exception, is at odds with the bulk of laboratory and psychometric studies reporting losses in various aspects of intellectual performance with advancing age (see, e.g., Kausler, 1982; Salthouse, 1982). A reinterpretation of the findings is offered in this chapter. This reinterpretation takes into account recent work aimed at representing human knowledge systems as computational systems, and it gives emphasis to the increased specialization of intellectual abilities and computational processes which is presumed to take place during the adult years.

There is no doubt that existing conceptualizations of adult intelligence are not representative of the competencies of adult intellectual function. Several directions have been pursued by researchers and writers attempting to emphasize the strengths of intellect during the adult years. One direction is identified with the work of writers who have critiqued the inadequacies of existing theoretical formulations and who have proposed alternative conceptualizations (e.g., Baltes, Dittmann-Kohli, & Dixon, 1984; Basseches, 1984; Denney, 1984; Hoyer, 1985; Labouvie-Vief, 1977, 1985; Sinnott, 1984). A second direction has involved the use of training procedures designed to optimize adult cognitive performance (e.g., Denney, 1979; Fozard & Popkin, 1978; Hoyer, Labouvie, & Baltes, 1973; Labouvie-Vief & Gonda, 1976; Shultz & Hoyer, 1976). Some of the best work showing the beneficial effects of training on measures of intelligence has been conducted by Baltes and Willis and their colleagues (e.g., Baltes, Dittmann-Kohli, & Kliegl, 1986; Baltes & Willis, 1982; Blieszner, Willis, & Baltes, 1981; Willis, 1985; Blieszner & Baltes, 1981). Taken together, the results of training studies suggest that non-training studies underestimate the degree of cognitive *plasticity* in the adult years. A third direction is represented by studies that give emphasis to the ecology of intelligence in later life (e.g., Cavanaugh, Kramer, Sinnott, Camp, & Markley, 1985; Denney & Palmer, 1981; Scheidt & Schaie, 1978; Scheidt & Windley, 1985; Willis & Schaie, in press). A fourth line of investigation has aimed at providing a sound methodological foundation for the analysis of intellectual aging. Work demonstrating the role of cohort factors in accounting for age-related changes in intellectual performance can be associated with this approach (e.g., Schaie, 1979, 1983). Other methodologically oriented studies aimed at explicating the differential and multidimensional nature of mental abilities have also contributed to a less pessimistic picture of adult intellectual development. The Cattell–Horn model of fluid and crystallized intelligence (see Horn, 1970) and Thurstone's model of Primary Mental Abilities (see Schaie, 1979, 1983) have been used most widely to construe intelligence as a complex system of abilities and to show that various components of the system evince distinct courses of age-related change. When tests of fluid intelligence are given to different-aged adults, age-related declines in performance are found (for reviews, see Horn, 1970, 1982). These findings are obtained on the basis of analysis of age differences in cognitive measures which are independent of substantive domains. Caution is in order in interpreting the meaning of age differences found on domain-general measures of fluid intelligence. On the one hand, such measures are presumed to provide pure assessments of ability, independent of cultural and experiential influences. On the other hand, such assessments are artificial, since they do not take into account the proposition that with age much of everyday intellectual competence may depend less on *g*-type or fluid abilities and more on context-based and routinized performance.

I am not the first to point out that the essence of intelligence in adulthood is less a matter of *g* and more a matter of knowing a lot about the world. Several writers (e.g., Baltes, Dittmann-Kohli, & Dixon, 1984; Rybash, Hoyer, & Roodin, 1986; Willis & Schaie, in press) have suggested that the fluid components of intelligence, and the fundamental information-processing abilities which appear to cut across substantive domains, may be of greater importance in accounting for aspects of intelligence in early adulthood or adolescence than in later adulthood. If cognitive processes become increasingly organized and integrated within domains of knowledge with aging (i.e., age-related experience), as proposed here, then the age-related decline in unencapusulated (i.e., fluid) measures of intelligence has importance mainly when accounting for cognitive performance in situations where past experience is largely irrelevant. Although there are only a few studies to date which take account of preexperimental knowledge differences in evaluating cognitive aging, no (or minimal) age-related declines are reported in these studies (see, e.g., Charness, in press a; Hoyer, 1985; Hultsch & Dixon, 1983; Perlmutter, 1982; Salthouse, chapter 8 of this volume). Similarly, measures of crystallized intelligence typically show little or no age-related decline (e.g., Horn, 1970).

The discrepancy between real-world observations of proficiency maintenance in late life and results showing deficits on laboratory-based measures of cognitive processing should not be superficially dismissed by reference to the crystallized/fluid distinction. Rabbitt (1977) posed the problem as follows:

> In view of the deterioration of memory and perceptual-motor performance with advancing age, the right kind of question may well be not "why are old people so bad at cognitive tasks," but rather, "how, in spite of growing disabilities, do old people preserve such relatively good performance?" (p. 623)

In other words, how is it possible to be proficient in a particular molar cognitive activity even though the components of that ability show significant deficiencies with aging? Are there new processes or abilities which serve to take the place of (or mask) age-related losses in component processes? Do the various component processes of cognition become uniquely specialized for handling particular tasks (i.e., become domain-specific) with aging? In the next section, research on attentional processes is used to address these questions.

ATTENTIONAL FACTORS WITHIN COMPUTATIONAL SYSTEMS

The study of attention is concerned with the nature of the limitations in processing information and with information selection processes. In the research on human visual information processing, the concept of attention has been used in reference to a variety of functions including alertness and arousal, automatic versus conscious or effortful processing, attention span, selectivity in the processing of particular signals (i.e., targets) relative to other stimuli (i.e., distractors), covert and overt orienting of attention, and attentional preparedness of expectancy (for a review see, e.g., Parasuraman & Davies, 1984). Although these are overlapping and relatively ill-defined functions, it is useful to view attention as a complex process involving at least these aspects. In this section, I show how various aspects of attention, particularly the functions of orienting, expectancy, and automaticity, might serve a compensatory role in intellectual performance with advancing age and experience.

Expectancy and Preparation

The development and use of expectancy and preparation can be inferred from improvements in performance as the opportunity to select stimulus information and to prepare for particular imperative events is increased. In a wide range of information-processing tasks, it has been shown that the optimal preparatory interval between a warning or precue stimulus and fast/accurate performance is age-related (e.g., Madden, 1984; Plude & Hoyer, 1985; Rabbitt & Vyas, 1980; Talland & Cairnie, 1961). In a recent series of experiments on age differences in the use of two types of expectancy information, Hoyer and Familant (in press) found no age reduction in the ability to use a priori probabilistic information to aid the spatial localization of an imperative stimulus in a visual search task. However, older adults required more time compared to younger adults (i.e., 500 ms compared to 250 ms) to process precue information preceding the onset of the imperative stimulus. Thus, when expectancy is based on a priori probabilistic information rather than on rapid processing of briefly presented information, no age differences in the use of expectancy information are obtained. In some related work (Familant, Hoyer, & Montaglione, 1984), it has been shown that expectancy information can also serve to reduce the capacity-limiting demands of stimulus uncertainty or entropy; stimulus entropy is generally more detrimental to the performance of older adults than it is to the performance of younger adults, especially in unfamiliar and complex tasks.

Salthouse (chapter 8 of this volume) has provided some clues as to how expectancy information is used by expert older typists to help them to maintain a high rate of typing. Salthouse tested younger and older typists who varied in skill level in a transcription typing task. The number of preview characters that were available while typing passages were varied, and it was found that highly skilled older typists look further ahead compared to younger typists and less skilled typists— apparently as a compensatory strategy for maintaining a high rate of typing. This result is particularly striking in contrast to the well-established finding that most psychomotor activities become slower with advancing age.

Orienting of Attention

Numerous studies have shown that advance knowledge of target location facilitates detection of a briefly presented target (e.g., Posner, Snyder, & Davidson, 1980). This orientation of attention serves to improve the processing of a stimulus occupying the attended location. Interestingly, it has been shown that shifts of mental (or covert) attention are not synonymous with oculomotor movements. Klein (1980), for example, reported that attentional shifts do not necessarily result in oculomotor readiness, and that the readiness to move one's eyes does not necessarily induce an attentional shift. Posner (1980) and Remington (1980) showed that although eye movements and shifts of attention are both affected by the location of an imperative stimulus, the orienting of covert attention actually precedes the movement of the eyes. Moreover, when eye movements are generated in the absence of a peripheral stimulus, no attention shifts are observed, suggesting that the mechanisms that control attention shifts are distinct from those that control eye movements (Remington, 1980).

Shulman, Remington, and McLean (1979) examined the nature of attentional shifts under conditions in which the eyes remained fixated at a central location. They found that stimuli located between a central cue and a peripheral target received maximal facilitation from attention at a time prior to maximal facilitation at the target. If covert attention moves in an analogue fashion as Shulman et al. have suggested, intermediate points along the path of movement should be allocated attention during the time interval between leaving a central (fixation) location and arriving at a (target location) destination. Recently, Tsal (1983) showed that cueing has the effect of attracting attention to the location of the expected target. The farther the target was from fixation, the longer it took attention to reach the target, and the longer the reaction time. If there is age-related slowing in both the covert and overt aspects of visual orienting, perhaps older adults can compensate for such limitations by using preparatory cues (see e.g. Hoyer & Familant, in press; Nissen & Corkin, 1984).

Automaticity

Some theorists take the view that abilities come about through skill acquisition or learning (e.g., Neves & Anderson, 1981). Given sufficient practice or training, there is considerable evidence to suggest that some types of information can be taken in and/or accessed from memory without placing a demand on capacity-limited abilities and processes (e.g., Schneider & Shiffrin, 1977). James (1890) expressed the view that component processes become both automatic and encapsulated as cognitive skills become highly proficient through practice as follows:

> When we are learning to walk, to ride, to swim, skate, fence, write, play, or sing, we interrupt ourselves at every step by unnecessary movements and false notes. When we are proficient, on the contrary, the results not only follow with the very minumum of muscular action requisite to bring them forth, they also follow from a single instantaneous "cue". The marksman sees the bird, and, before he knows it, he has aimed and shot. A gleam in his adversary's eye, a momentary pressure from his rapier, and the fencer finds he has instantly made the right parry and return. A glance at the musical hieroglyphics, and the pianist's fingers have rippled through a cataract of notes. (p. 119)

Recently it has been suggested that there are two general modes of attentional processing—described as *automatic* and *effortful,* or *controlled,* (e.g., Hasher & Zacks, 1979; Kahneman & Treisman, 1984; Schneider & Shiffrin, 1977). Automatic processing is fast, accurate, full-blown once initiated, and effortless in that it is not affected by capacity-limiting factors such as the demand imposed by dividing attention among simultaneous tasks or by increases in display size, memory set size, or task complexity. In contrast, effortful or controlled processing requires active, conscious control on the part of the perceiver, and it is capacity-limited in that it is affected by task complexity and information load factors. Shiffrin and Schneider (1977) used a visual/memory search paradigm to study the differences between automatic and controlled aspects of information processing. Subjects who developed an automatic target-detection strategy were unaffected by increases in the number of targets and distractors, while subjects who had to rely on controlled processing showed typical decrements as a function of these load factors. Adult age differences in automatic and controlled processing have been investigated in several studies (e.g., Madden & Nebes, 1980; Plude & Hoyer, 1981; Plude et al., 1983; Salthouse & Somberg, 1982). The main finding is that a traditional pattern of age-associated decrement is obtained under conditions requiring effortful processing, and no or minimal age differences are obtained under conditions of automatic processing. This result is consistent with our general observations that older adults show only small deficits in performing well-practiced skills, even though there may be substantial decline in performing novel tasks or in acquiring new perceptual or cognitive routines (see, e.g., Hoyer & Plude, 1980, 1982).

Compensatory Functions of Attention

The various attentional functions of automaticity, orienting, expectancy, and preparation may exert positive effects on cognitive function by restricting the search space of working memory and/or by minimizing the demands on limited capacity. The practice-related improvements in attentional function can be item-specific or general (e.g., general alertness), and either type of expectancy can benefit cognitive performance. For example, an attentional state of general preparedness can be useful in situations in which there are multiple stimulus possibilities, all or most of which are to some degree incorporated within the general expectation. Specific expectations are obviously more useful in situations in which a specific event is probable relative to other possible outcomes.

KNOWLEDGE DOMAINS AS CONCEPTUAL ENTITIES

Knowledge involves the organization of learned information in memory. Three main issues need to be considered in evaluating the role of knowledge in adult cognitive development. These are (a) knowledge representation; (b) knowledge acquisition; and (c) the actualization, availability, and use of knowledge. In examining these issues, evidence bearing on the hypothesis that a person's knowledge exerts a beneficial effect on performance by guiding the selection and processing of incoming information is presented. The richness of one's knowledge base is presumed to be a determinant of the information that is brought to bear while performing cognitive tasks.

Knowledge Representation

Contemporary cognitive theory presumes that knowledge is organized within conceptual representations. These representations can differ in many ways. One general attribute that has been used to differentiate among knowledge representations has to do with the *conceptual entities* that comprise the representation. Conceptual entities are the kinds of objects included in a particular knowledge representation that someone can think about in a relatively direct way. The term cognitive entities has been used by Flavell (1985) and others to refer to the products of cognitive development such as the use of concepts in particular domains such as mathematics. Greeno (1983) suggested that conceptual entities are important to the understanding of cognition in four ways. First, conceptual entities are important in forming and using analogies across domains. If different domains share conceptual entities, analogical reasoning is facilitated. Second, conceptual entities determine the kind of information that is available to reason about. Third, conceptual entities determine computational efficiency. Fourth, conceptual entities are used in developing expectancies and plans.

Even in domains where there are no certifiable experts, some people have vastly more experience than others through either their professions or their hobbies. It is obvious that experts know more than novices, but, in addition, expert knowledge is probably organized or structured differently. One way in which experts and novices differ is that experts have vastly more specific conceptual entities to deal with the greater number of details they know. Not only can an art historian identify more paintings, but this person also "sees more" than the novice and has refined the procedures and dimensions for appreciating as well as categorizing (identifying) objects of art. When an art historian sees a painting, he or she may see it not just as a painting, but as rendering of a particular style, a particular period, a particular technique, and so on. With experience comes a progressive refinement of meaning and the differentiation of one conceptual entity from others.

Flavell (1985) has discussed five types of developmental sequences relevant to the understanding of how conceptual entities might become differentiated as a result of experience. If X and Y represent conceptual entities and Y develops after X, Y might constitute an additional or alternative means to the same goal. Second, later-developing Y can replace earlier-developing X as an approach to a given kind of problem. Third, Y can be derived from X by differentiation, generalization, or stabilization. Fourth, X can be absorbed as a component part of a larger cognitive unit called Y. Finally, it is possible that X can develop as a facilitator of, or bridge to, Y.

In recent studies of the differences between novices and experts, it has been suggested that rapid and efficient information processing is *specific to* the kind of information represented within the knowledge domain. Experts differ from nonexperts in chess mainly in terms of component perceptual and memory abilities, and not in terms of measures of logical thinking and general problem solving (Chase & Simon, 1973; De Groot, 1965). For example, a chess master could reconstruct the positions of approximately 25 pieces from a game after having seen the display for 5 s, while a novice player could remember the locations of only about one quarter as many pieces after the same exposure. However, even though the expert was able to process large masses of domain-specific information without loss of detail, compared to the nonexpert, experts and novices did not differ from each other with regard to general (i.e., nonspecific) measures of span memory and working memory. Further, compared to less skilled players, expert players did not evidence a superiority in logical reasoning; nor did they search through more possible moves before selecting one. With regard to reasoning, the main difference between the experts and novices was that the masters spent more time considering good moves, and the novices spent more time exploring poor moves.

The pioneering work on chess skills by De Groot (1965) and Chase and Simon (1973) supports the position that component processes become specialized (or encapsulated) as a result of experience. The finding that experienced individuals can recall at a glance far more specialized information than novices can has also been reported in the domains of bridge (Charness, 1983), electronics (Egan & Schwartz, 1979) and computer programming (Jeffries, Turner, Polson, & Atwood, 1981; McKeithen, Reitman, Rueter, & Hirtle, 1981).

Another important difference between novices and experts is that experts frequently exhibit a better knowledge about which steps to use for problems belonging to particular categories; and highly skilled persons can better recognize into which category different problems should be placed. Chi, Glaser, and Rees (1982) indicated that a differential ability to categorize problems may be an important factor distinguishing novices and experts. Observed differences between experts and novices in chess, physics, and other domains have been shown to depend on the extent and organization of specific knowledge bases in long-term memory (e.g., Adelson, 1984; Bhaskar & Simon, 1977; Larkin, 1981, 1983; Simon & Simon, 1978).

Knowledge Acquisition

Knowledge acquisition is typically conceptualized as learning, and its efficiency is thought to depend on g and/or effortful information-processing skills. The processes and abilities presumed responsible for the acquisition of knowledge are generally found to decline with advancing age (see, e.g., Kausler, 1982; Salthouse, 1985a, 1985b). However, conceptualizations of knowledge acquisition need to take into account the range of learning from an effortful encoding stage to increasingly less effortful stages of proceduralization, composition, and automization (Neves & Anderson, 1981). For example, Chi and Koeske (1983) have shown that children's developing knowledge structures serve as "schemes" that enable different, perhaps more advanced, kinds of learning. Recently, Chi (1985), Glaser (1984), Keil (1981), Klahr and Siegler (1978), and others have argued that knowledge of specific content domains is a crucial dimension of development in its own right, and that knowledge development in particular areas may underlie changes previously attributed to the growth of general capacities or information-processing abilities.

Although the distinction between what is known (declarative or substantive knowledge) and the efficiency of how it is acquired or learned (procedural knowledge) is accepted by many contemporary cognitive psychologists, some recent work has challenged the usefulness of this distinction (e.g., see Fodor, 1983, 1985; Kolers & Roediger, 1984). The distinction between mental contents and mental processes is made by those advocating the view that most knowledge systems are analogous to linguistic knowing, since language is amenable to description in the form of propositional rule-based systems (see, e.g., Anderson, 1982, 1983: Collins & Loftus, 1975). Kolers and Roediger (1984) have recently reviewed the evidence bearing on the contrasting argument that the means of knowledge acquisition is specific to the means of experiencing and representing such knowledge. The position that knowledge acquisition is best described in terms of skill in manipulating specific symbol systems is consistent with the position being advanced in this chapter.

Knowledge Actualization

Knowledge actualization refers to the accumulation, access, and use of information. Knowledge actualization is presumed to depend mainly on cumulative experience. Lachman and Lachman (1980) described knowledge actualization as a type of memory of knowing that is relatively permanent, nonepisodic, and nonlinguistic, and that has been acquired through lifelong acculturation. According to Lachman and Lachman, the types of cognitive processes involved in knowledge actualization are locative processes, inferential processes, and metamemory processes. Locative processes refer to relatively automatic, unconscious, and strategy-free information-retrieval processes. Inferential processes refer to effortful, conscious, and deliberate control processes for constructing information. Metamemorial processes refer to a constellation of cognitive capacities concerned with the individual's self-assessment of and knowledge about his or her own memory processes and abilities.

Perlmutter (1980) emphasized the role of knowledge actualization in her discussion of the discrepancy between the pessimistic findings typically obtained in laboratory studies of memory aging and the numerous observations of continued high levels of competence in everyday functioning on the part of older adults. The few systematic studies which have been reported suggest that there are no age losses in knowledge-actualization processes, and that there may actually be gains in such skills and abilities with aging (see, e.g., Camp, 1985).

Availability of Knowledge

Availability or accessibility of knowledge schemata is another factor which may contribute to the domain specificity of adult intellectual function (Pollard, 1982; Tversky & Kahneman, 1973). Observed biases in selecting information for processing and in knowledge construction and retrieval may be interpreted as resulting from the application of heuristics or strategies that are optimal within the given developmental/ maturational boundaries of cognitive function (Pascual-Leone, 1984). The human cognitive system is guided by heuristics—rules of thumb or procedures for handling particular kinds of information (see, e.g., Newell & Simon, 1972). The idea that available cues provided by a problem's content and context serve to trigger a particular solution strategy may help to explain the discrepancy one finds between developmental studies of logical abstract problem-solving which show age-related decline and studies of real-life problem-solving which are less likely to show age-related decline (see Reese & Rodeheaver, 1985; Rybash et al., 1986; Sinnott, 1984).

Beliefs about what is useful renders some bodies of information available and other bodies of information unavailable. In Schoenfeld's (1983) studies of mathematical problem solving, for example, setting factors such as the desire to "look mathematical" on videotape served to establish a context within which individuals accessed and utilized some of the information at their disposal and not other information potentially at their disposal.

Knowledge schemas probably serve the function of filling-in when a perceptual task is incomplete or when there is missing information. Cognitive psychologists use this sort of evidence to argue that there is more information in the individual's perception of a physical stimulus than there is in the stimulus that prompts the perception. Research on the selectivity of information processing also suggests the importance of the individual's particular knowledge on how (and what) information is processed. In perceiving, we recognize, actively select, and subjectively interpret only part of the vast array of information to which we are exposed. Acquired knowledge determines in part the selection of items and elements for inclusion within the problem space (Newell, 1980; Newell & Simon, 1972). That is, the selectivity of input-analyzing mechanisms and processes of acquisition and encoding are in part dependent on what has already been acquired, Numerous investigators have emphasized the role of "top-down" factors in perception (e.g., Hoyer & Plude, 1982; Rock, 1983); memory (e.g., Bransford, Barclay, & Franks, 1972; Franks, Bransford, & Auble, 1982); and schematic processing (e.g., Abelson, 1981; Fiske & Kinder, 1981; Mischel, 1981; Rosch & Mervis, 1975).

The beneficial effects of having "schemas" and knowledge categories on the integration and/or storage of new information are particularly clear in the area of memory, where it has been shown that isolated pieces of information are vulnerable to forgetting unless they are integrated within schemas or domains of some type (see, e.g., Bower, Black, & Turner, 1979; Mandler & Johnson, 1977; Neisser, 1981; Nelson & Gruendel, 1981). As Neisser (1984) has pointed out, we quickly forget loosely ordered bits of information, but we seldom forget information that is part of some well-established knowledge system such as our personal history or our first language system. In studies of memory retrieval and age (e.g., Hultsch, 1971; Light & Anderson, 1983) it has been shown that isolated bits of information are more difficult to retrieve with advancing age, but that adult age differences in recall of organized information are relatively small or nonexistent (see, e.g., Hultsch & Dixon, 1984; Spilich, 1985). Thus, functionally, individuals impose an organization on incoming meaningful information. If such information is to be retained or used again, it is organized and made meaningful by combining it with information already in memory.

Are domains and schemas necessarily large bodies of knowledge or can they be relatively small or trivial? Baddeley (1982) defined a domain as an area of memory in which there are rich associative links and connections. The links which characterize particular domains of highly skilled individuals may be connected to other domains and may be divided into subdomains. The associative structure of a particular domain is not necessarily uniform across individuals who possess knowledge in this area. Domains can also be viewed as relatively discrete computational systems which include the processes and procedures for handling particular kinds of knowledge. The efficiency of processing of incoming information, and the actions and decisions that are made in response to incoming information are influenced by what is already known about the to-be-processed information. Domains become differentiated and enlarged, and new categories and domains may be formed, as a function of experience.

Gardner (1983) proposed that there are roughly seven natural domains or frames of intelligence, that information is encoded and organized into these domains, and that these domains correspond to innate brain organization. My position differs from Gardner's theory of multiple intelligences in that individuals are presumed to construct an unspecifiable number of domains of knowledge corresponding to their experience and development; thus it is suggested that people build an organization of cognition based on use of their mental capacities. From this functional perspective domains are acquired representations of areas of cognitive involvement. Although there may be some innateness to the development of some areas of knowledge (e.g., language is a likely candidate), and although properties of knowledge probably constrain the ways in which knowledge structures develop (see, e.g., Keil, 1981), I take the view that the developing individual is self-organizing with regard to the number and nature of domains. Because the antecedents of development are largely socio-environmental and person-specific in adulthood the various socio-environmental forces that affect development are uniquely processed by individuals, and should be analyzed at the level of intraindividual change across time.

By observation it seems that many older persons become increasingly proficient in specialized areas, and correspondingly less skilled at mastering and adapting to unfamiliar or domain-general cognitive tasks. That is, although the cognitive functions associated with the processing of new information show age deficits, cognitive functions involving the execution of learned knowledge in everyday situations show little or no deficit. However, it may be overly simplistic to conceptualize the kind of cognitive specialization which characterizes adult cognition in terms of an acquisition versus execution (or knowledge use) dichotomy, since the generalizability and flexibility of one's knowledge depends in part on the specific properties and characteristics of the knowledge itself. Particular domains and procedures may show a high degree of generality, whereas other domains of knowledge become increasingly specialized, and decreasingly applicable and generalizable across situations and tasks. For example, knowing mathematics can enhance one's approach to musical composition, visual design, the analysis of economic theory, or the interpretation of statistical computations of psychological data. However, one's knowledge of statistics may not benefit musical composition or the understanding of computer architecture.

Interestingly, there are individuals who have achieved extraordinary levels of performance in particular domains like mental calculation, and who (would have) scored too low to measure on general tests of ability. Scripture (1891) described the case of Tom Fuller, an illiterate slave who at age 70 years could in less than 2 minutes compute how many seconds a 70-year-old had lived, including corrections for leap years (see also Smith, 1981). Unique integrations across knowledge domains emerge through an individual's particular blendings of knowledge and ideas from different experiences. Unique integrations of disciplines and ideas are evident in all intelligent adults. Socio-environmental and historical factors determine the extent to which a particular blending warrants being dubbed as creative or exceptional.

SUMMARY

One important characteristic of adult intelligence is that it consists of an unspecifiable number of knowledge domains that correspond to what the person knows about the world. Another characteristic is that adult cognitive development is best conceptualized as the continued refinement and use of particular knowledge or cognitive specializations. The evolving sociocultural contexts of adulthood foster the continued refinement, differentiation, and use of cognitive specializations. The third point is that the requisite procedures and elementary information processes for handling information within particular domains become encapsulated. This encapsulation of computational systems enables the maintenance and/or continued development of high levels of proficiency within areas of cognitive expertise in spite of age-related declines in general processing abilities. The fourth point is that general or *g*-type measures of human ability do not give an accurate description of adult intelligence in the later years since *g*-type abilities are more predictive of one's capacity to acquire new knowledge domains and to develop relations among domains than to the continued refinement and use of knowledge within specialized domains.

The development of a knowledge-based organization of cognition in adulthood is associated with increased interindividual and intraindividual differentiation. A mature or final form of the knowledge organization is a priori unspecifiable, since it depends on the particular characteristics and constraints of knowledge domains, and on the developing individual's unique cognitive developmental history regarding particular domains. To the extent that there are interindividual uniformities and constraints in adult cognitive development, they can be attributed to (a) commonalities in the sociocultural matrix of adulthood; (b) characteristics and constraints of knowledge per se, and its organization; and (c) age-related changes in the *g*-type or effortful processes in the absence of applicable acquired knowledge.

REFERENCES

Abelson, R.P. (1981). Psychological status of the script concept. *American Psychologist, 36,*715–729.
Adelson, B. (1984). When novices surpass experts: The difficulty of a task may increase with expertise. *Journal of Experimental Psychology: Learning, Memory, and Cognition, 10,* 483–495.
Anderson, J.R. (1982). Acquisition of cognitive skill. *Psychological Review, 89,* 369–406.
Anderson, J.R. (1983). *The architecture of cognition.* Cambridge, MA: Harvard University Press.
Baddeley, A.D. (1982). Domains of recollection. *Psychological Review, 89,* 708–729.
Baltes, P.B., Dittmann-Kohli, F., & Dixon, R.A. (1984). New perspectives on the development of intelligence in adulthood: Toward a dual-process conception of selective optimization with compensation. In P.B. Baltes & O.G. Brim, Jr. (Eds.), *Life-span development and behavior* (Vol. 6, pp. 33–76). New York: Academic Press.
Baltes, P.B., Dittmann-Kohli, F., & Kliegl, R. (1986). Reserve capacity of the elderly in aging-sensitive tests of fluid intelligence: Replication and extension. *Psychology and Aging, 1,* 172–177.

Baltes, P.B., & Willis, S.L. (1982). Plasticity and enhancement of intellectual functioning in old age: Penn State's Adult Development and Enrichment Project (ADEPT). In F.I.M. Craik & S.E. Trehub (Eds.), *Aging and cognitive processes* (pp.353-389). New York: Plenum.

Basseches, M. (1984). *Dialectical thinking and adult development*. Norwood, NJ: Ablex.

Bhaskar, R., & Simon, H.A. (1977). Problem solving in semantically rich domains: An example from engineering thermodynamics. *Cognitive Science, 1,* 193-215.

Blieszner, R., Willis, S.L., & Baltes, P.B. (1981). Training research on induction ability in aging: Short-term longitudinal study. *Journal of Applied Developmental Psychology, 2,* 247-265.

Bower, G.H., Black, J.B., & Turner, T.J. (1979). Scripts in memory for text. *Cognitive Psychology, 11,* 177-220.

Bransford, J.D., Barclay, J.R., & Franks, J.J. (1972). Sentence memory: A constructive versus interpretive approach. *Cognitive Psychology, 3,* 193-209.

Camp, C.J. (1985). *Utilization of world knowledge systems*. Unpublished manuscript, University of New Orleans.

Cattell, R.B. (1971). *Abilities: Their structure, growth, and action*. Champaign, IL: Institute for Personality and Ability Testing.

Cavanaugh, J.C., Kramer, D.A., Sinnott, J.D., Camp, C.J. & Markley, R.P. (1985). Missing links and such: Interfaces between cognitive research and everyday problem solving. *Human Development, 28,* 146-168.

Charness, N. (1983). Age, skill, and bridge bidding: A chronometric analysis. *Journal of Verbal Learning and Verbal Behavior, 22,* 406-416.

Charness, N. (in press a).*Age and expertise: Responding to Talland's challenge*. In L.W. Poon, D.C. Rubin, & B.A. Wilson (Eds.),*Everyday cognition in adult and late life.* New York: Cambridge University Press.

Charness, N. (in press b). Expertise in chess, music, and physics: A cognitive perspective. In L.K. Obler & D.A. Fein (Eds.), *The neuropsychology of talent and special abilities.* New York: Guilford Press.

Chase, W.G., & Simon, H.A. (1973). Perception in chess. *Cognitive Psychology, 4,* 55-81.

Chi, M.T.H. (1978). Knowledge structures and memory development. In R.S. Siegler (Ed.), *Children's thinking: What develops?* (pp. 73-96). Hillsdale, NJ: Erlbaum.

Chi, M.T.H. (1985). Changing conception of sources of memory development. *Human Development, 28,* 50-56.

Chi, M.T.H., Glaser,R., & Rees, E. (1982). Expertise in problem solving. In R.J. Sternberg (Ed.), *Advances in the psychology of human intelligence* (pp. 7-76). Hillsdale, NJ: Erlbaum.

Chi, M.T.H., & Koeske, R.D. (1983). Network representation of a child's dinosaur knowledge. *Developmental Psychology, 19,* 29-39.

Cole, S. (1979). Age and scientific performance. *American Journal of Sociology, 84,* 958-977.

Collins, A.M., & Loftus, E.F. (1975). A spreading activation theory of semantic processing. *Psychological Review, 82,* 407-428.

De Groot, A.D. (1965). *Thought and choice in chess*. The Hague: Mouton.

Denney, N.W. (1979). Problem solving in later adulthood: Intervention research. In P.B. Baltes & O.G. Brim, Jr.(Eds.), *Life-span development and behavior* (Vol. 2, pp. 37-66). New York: Academic Press.

Denney, N.W. (1984). A model of cognitive development across the life span. *Developmental Review, 4,* 171-191.

Denney, N.W., & Palmer, A.M. (1981). Adult age differences in traditional and practical problem-solving measures. *Journal of Gerontology, 36,* 323-328.

Egan, D.E., & Schwartz, B.J. (1979). Chunking in recall of symbolic drawings. *Memory and Cognition, 7,* 149–158.

Familant, M.E., Hoyer, W.J., & Montaglione, C.J. (1984, August). *Aging, entropy, and the use of precue information.* Paper presented at the meetings of the American Psychological Association, Toronto.

Fiske, S.T., & Kinder, D.R. (1981). Involvement, expertise, and schema use: Evidence from political cognition. In N. Cantor & J.F. Kihlstrom (Eds.), *Personality, cognition, and social interaction* (pp. 171–190). Hillsdale, NJ: Erlbaum.

Flavell, J.H. (1985). *Cognitive development* (2nd ed.). Englewood Cliffs, NJ: Prentice-Hall.

Fodor, J.A. (1983). *Modularity of mind.* Cambridge, MA: MIT Press.

Fodor, J.A. (1985). Précis of *The modularity of mind. Behavioral and Brain Sciences, 8,* 1–42.

Fozard, J.L., & Popkin, S.J. (1978). Optimizing adult development: Ends and means of an applied psychology of aging. *American Psychologist, 33,* 975–989.

Franks, J.J., Bransford, J.D., & Auble, P.M. (1982). The activation and utilization of knowledge. In C. R. Puff (Ed.), *Handbook of research methods in human memory and cognition* (pp. 396–425). New York: Academic Press.

Gardner, H. (1983). *Frames of mind.* New York: Basic Books.

Glaser, R. (1984). Education and thinking: The role of knowledge. *American Pyschologist, 39,* 93–104.

Greeno, J.G. (1983). Conceptual entities. In D. Gentner & A.L. Stevens (Eds.), *Mental models* (pp. 227–252). Hillsdale, NJ: Erlbaum.

Guilford, J.P. (1967). *The nature of human intelligence.* New York: McGraw-Hill.

Hasher, L., & Zacks, R. (1979). Automatic and effortful processes in memory. *Journal of Experimental Psychology: General, 108,* 356–388.

Horn, J.L. (1970). Organization of data on life-span development of human abilities. In L.R. Goulet & P.B. Baltes (Eds.), *Life-span developmental psychology: Research and theory* (pp. 424–466). New York: Academic Press.

Horn, J.L. (1982). The aging of human abilities. In B.B. Wolman (Ed.), *Handbook of developmental psychology* (pp. 847–870). Englewood Cliffs, NJ: Prentice-Hall.

Horn, J.L., & Cattell, R.B. (1967). Age differences in fluid and crystallized intelligence. *Acta Psychologica, 26,* 107–129.

Hoyer, J.L. (1985). Aging and the development of expert cognition. In T.M. Schlechter & M.P. Toglia (Eds.), *New directions in cognitive science* (pp. 69–87). Norwood, NJ: Ablex.

Hoyer, W.J., & Familant, M.E. (in press). Adult age differences in the rate of processing expectancy information. *Cognitive Development, 2.*

Hoyer, W.J., Labouvie, G.V., & Baltes, P.B. (1973). Modification of response speed and intellectual performance in the elderly. *Human Development, 16,* 233–242.

Hoyer, W.J., & Plude, D.J. (1980). Attentional and perceptual processes in the study of cognitive aging. In L.W. Poon (Ed.), *Aging in the 1980's: Psychological issues* (pp. 227–238). Washington, DC: American Psychological Association.

Hoyer, W.J., & Plude, D.J. (1982). Aging and the allocation of attentional resources in visual information processing. In R. Sekuler, D. Kline, & K. Dismukes (Eds.), *Aging and human visual function* (pp. 245–263). New York: Liss.

Hultsch, D.F. (1971). Adult age differences in free classification and free recall. *Developmental Psychology, 4,* 338–342.

Hultsch, D.F., & Dixon, R.A. (1983). The role of pre-experimental knowledge in text processing. *Experimental Aging Research, 9,* 17–22.

Hultsch, D.F., & Dixon, R.A. (1984). Memory for text materials in adulthood. In P.B.

Baltes & O.G. Brim, Jr. (Eds.),*Life-span development and behavior* (Vol. 6, pp. 77–108). New York: Academic Press.

James, W. (1890). *Principles of psychology.* New York: Dover.

Jeffries, R., Turner, A.A., Polson, P.G., & Atwood, M.E. (1981). The processes involved in designing software. In J.R. Anderson (Ed.),*Cognitive skills and their acquisition* (pp. 255–283). Hillsdale, NJ: Erlbaum.

Kahneman, D., & Treisman, A. (1984). Changing views of attention and automaticity. In R. Parasuraman & D.R. Davies (Eds.), *Varieties of attention* (pp. 29–61). New York: Academic Press.

Kausler, D.H. (1982). *Experimental psychology of human aging.* New York: Wiley.

Keil, F.C. (1981). Constraints on knowledge and cognitive development. *Psychological Review, 88,* 197–227.

Klahr, D., & Siegler, R.S. (1978). The representation of children's knowledge. In H. Reese & L.P. Lipsitt (Eds.),*Advances in child development and behavior* (Vol. 12, pp. 61–116). New York: Academic Press.

Klein, R. (1980). Does oculomotor readiness mediate cognitive control of visual attention? In R. Nickerson (Ed.), *Attention and performance VIII* (pp. 259–276). Hillsdale, NJ: Erlbaum.

Kohn, M.L., & Schooler, C. (1978). The reciprocal effects of the substantive complexity of work and intellectual flexibility: A longitudinal assessment. *American Journal of Sociology, 84,* 24–52.

Kolers, P.A., & Roediger, H.L., III (1984). Procedures of mind. *Journal of verbal learning and verbal behavior, 23,* 425–449.

Labouvie-Vief, G. (1977). Adult cognitive development: In search of alternative interpretations. *Merrill-Palmer Quarterly, 23,* 227–263.

Labouvie-Vief, G. (1985). Intelligence and cognition. In J.E. Birren & K.W. Schaie (Eds.), *Handbook of the psychology of aging* (2nd ed., pp. 500–530). New York: Van Nostrand Reinhold.

Labouvie-Vief, G., & Gonda, J.N. (1976). Cognitive strategy training and intellectual performance in the elderly. *Journal of Gerontology, 31,* 327–332.

Lachman, J.L., & Lachman, R. (1980). Age and the actualization of world knowledge. In L.W. Poon, J.L. Fozard, L.S. Cermak, D. Arenberg, & L.W. Thompson (Eds.), *New directions in memory and aging* (pp. 313–343). Hillsdale, NJ: Erlbaum.

Larkin, J.H. (1981). Enriching formal knowledge: A model for learning to solve problems in psychics. In J.R. Anderson (Ed.), *Cognitive skills and their acquisition* (pp. 311–334). Hillsdale, NJ: Erlbaum.

Larkin, J.H. (1983). The role of problem representation in physics. In D. Gentner & A.L. Stevens (Eds.), *Mental models* (pp. 75–98). Hillsdale, NJ: Erlbaum.

Light, L.L., & Anderson, P.A. (1983). Memory for scripts in young and old adults. *Memory and Cognition, 11,* 435–444.

Madden, D.J. (1984). Data-driven and memory-driven selective attention in visual search. *Journal of Gerontology, 39,* 72–78.

Madden, D.J., & Nebes, R.D. (1980). Aging and the development of automaticity in visual search. *Developmental Psychology, 16,* 377–384.

Mandler, J.M., & Johnson, N.S. (1977). Remembrance of things parsed: Story structure and recall. *Cognitive Psychology, 9,* 111–151.

McKeithen, K.B., Reitman, J.S., Rueter, H.H., & Hirtle, S.C. (1981). Knowledge organization and skill differences in computer programmers. *Cognitive Psychology, 13,* 307–325.

Mischel, W. (1981). Personality and cognition: Something borrowed, something new? In N. Cantor & J.F. Kihlstrom (Eds.), *Personality, cognition, and social interaction* (pp. 3–19). Hillsdale, NJ: Erlbaum.

Neisser, U. (1981). John Dean's memory: A case study. *Cognition, 9,* 1–22.

Neisser, U. (1984). Interpreting Harry Bahrick's discovery: What confers immunity against forgetting? *Journal of Experimental Psychology: General, 113,* 32–35.

Nelson, K., & Gruendel, J. (1981). Generalized event representations: Basic building blocks of cognitive development. In M.E. Lamb & A.L. Brown (Eds.), *Advances in developmental psychology* (Vol.1, pp. 131–158). Hillsdale, NJ: Erlbaum.

Neves, D.M., & Anderson, J.R. (1981). Knowledge compilation: Mechanisms for the automatization of cognitive skills. In J.R. Anderson (Ed.), *Cognitive skills and their acquisitions* (pp. 57–84). Hillsdale, NJ: Erlbaum.

Newell, A. (1980). Reasoning, problem solving, and decision processes: The problem space as a fundamental category. In R. Nickerson (Ed.), *Attention and performance VIII* (pp. 693–718). Hillsdale, NJ: Erlbaum.

Newell, A., & Simon, H. (1972). *Human problem solving.* Englewood Cliffs, NJ: Prentice-Hall.

Nissen, M.J., & Corkin, S. (1984). Effectiveness of attentional cueing in older and younger adults. *Journal of Gerontology, 40,* 185–191.

Obler, L.K., & Fein, D.A. (Eds.). (in press). *The neuropsychology of talent and special abilities.* New York: Guilford Press.

Parasuraman, R., & Davies, D.R. (Eds.). (1984). *Varieties of attention.* New York: Academic Press.

Pascual-Leone, J. (1984). Growing into human maturity: Towards a metasubjective theory of adulthood stages. In P.B. Baltes & O.G. Brim, Jr. (Eds.), *Life-span development and behavior* (Vol. 3, pp. 117–156). New York: Academic Press.

Perlmutter, M. (1980). An apparent paradox about memory aging. In L.W. Poon, J.L. Fozard, L.S. Cermak, D. Arenberg, & L.W. Thompson (Eds.), *New directions in memory and aging* (pp. 345–353). Hillsdale, NJ: Erlbaum.

Perlmutter, M. (1982). The appearance and disappearance of age differences in adult memory. In F.I.M. Craik & S.E. Trehub (Eds.), *Aging and cognitive processes* (pp. 127–144). New York: Plenum.

Plude, D.J., & Hoyer, W.J. (1981). Adult age differences in visual search as a function of stimulus mapping and information load. *Journal of Gerontology, 36,* 598–604.

Plude, D.J., & Hoyer, W.J. (1985). Attention and performance: Identifying and localizing age deficits. In N. Charness (Ed.), *Aging and human performance* (pp. 47–99). London: Wiley.

Plude, D.J., Kaye, D.B., Hoyer, W.J., Post, T.A., Saynisch, M., & Hahn, M.V. (1983). Aging and visual search under consistent and varied mapping. *Developmental Psychology, 19,* 508–512.

Pollard, P. (1982). Human reasoning: Some possible effects of availability. *Cognition, 12,* 65–96.

Posner, M.I. (1980). Orienting of attention. *Quarterly Journal of Experimental Psychology, 32,* 3–25.

Posner, M.I., Snyder, C.R.R., & Davidson, B.J. (1980). Attention and the detection of signals. *Journal of Experimental Psychology: General, 109,* 160–174.

Rabbitt, P.M.A. (1977). Changes in problem solving ability in old age. In J.E. Birren & K.W. Schaie (Eds.), *Handbook of the psychology of aging* (pp. 606–625). New York: Van Nostrand Reinhold.

Rabbitt, P.M.A., & Vyas, S.M. (1980). Selective anticipation for events in old age. *Journal of Gerontology, 35,* 913–919.

Reese, H.W., & Rodeheaver, D. (1985). Problem solving and complex decision making. In J.E. Birren & K.W. Schaie (Eds.), *Handbook of the psychology of aging* (2nd ed., pp. 474–499). New York: Van Nostrand Reinhold.

Remington, R.W. (1980). Attention and saccadic eye movements. *Journal of Experimental Psychology: Human Perception and Performance, 6,* 726–744.

Riley, M.W. (1983). *Aging and society: Notes on the development of new understandings.* The Winkelman Lecture, University of Michigan, Ann Arbor.

Rock, I. (1983). *The logic of perception.* Cambridge, MA: MIT Press.

Rosch, E., & Mervis, C.B. (1975). Family resemblances: Studies in the internal structure of categories. *Cognitive Psychology, 7,* 573–605.

Rybash, J.M., Hoyer, W.J., & Roodin, P.A. (1986). *Adult cognition and aging.* New York: Pergamon.

Salthouse, T.A. (1982). *Adult cognition: An experimental psychology of human aging.* New York: Springer-Verlag.

Salthouse, T.A. (1985a). Speed of behavior and its implications for cognition. In J.E. Birren & K.W. Schaie (Eds.), *Handbook of the psychology of aging* (2nd ed., pp. 400–426). New York: Van Nostrand Reinhold.

Salthouse, T.A. (1985b). *A theory of cognitive aging.* Amsterdam: North Holland.

Salthouse, T.A., & Somberg, B.L. (1982). Skilled performance: The effects of adult age and experience on elementary processes. *Journal of Experimental Psychology: General, 111,* 176–207.

Schaie, K.W. (1979). The primary mental abilities in adulthood: An exploration in the development of psychometric intelligence. In P.B. Baltes & O.G. Brim, Jr. (Eds.), *Life-span development and behavior* (Vol. 2, pp. 67–115). New York: Academic Press.

Schaie, K.W. (1983). The Seattle Longitudinal Study: A 21-year exploration of psychometric intelligence in adulthood. In K.W. Schaie (Ed.), *Longitudinal studies of adult psychological development* (pp. 64–135). New York: Guilford Press.

Scheidt, R.J., & Schaie, K.W. (1978). A taxonomy of situations for an elderly population: Generating situational criteria. *Journal of Gerontology, 33,* 848–857.

Scheidt, R.J., & Windley, P.G. (1985). The econogy of aging. In J.E. Birren & K.W. Schaie (Eds.), *Handbook of the psychology of aging* (2 ed., pp. 245–258). New York: Van Nostrand Reinhold.

Schneider, W., & Shiffrin, R.M. (1977). Controlled and automatic human information processing. *Psychological Review, 84,* 1–66.

Schoenfeld, A.H. (1983). Beyond the purely cognitive: Belief systems, social cognitions, and metacognitions as driving forces in intellectual performance. *Cognitive Science, 7,* 329–363.

Scripture, E.W. (1891). Arithmetical prodigies. *American Journal of Psychology, 4,* 1–59.

Schultz, N.R., Jr., & Hoyer, W.J. (1976). Feedback effects on spatial egocentrism in old age. *Journal of Gerontology, 31,* 72–75.

Shriffrin, R.M., & Schneider, W. (1977). Controlled and automatic human information processing: II. Perceptual learning, automatic attending, and a general theory. *Psychological Review, 84,* 127–190.

Shulman, G.L., Remington, R.W., & McLean, J.P. (1979). Moving attention through visual space. *Journal of Experimental Psychology: Human Perception and Performance, 5,* 522–526.

Simon, D.P., & Simon, H.A. (1978). Individual differences in solving physics problems. In R.S. Siegler (Ed.), *Children's thinking: What develops?* (pp. 325–348). Hillsdale, NJ: Erlbaum.

Sinnott, J.D. (1984). Postformal reasoning: The relativistic stage. In M.L. Commons, F.A. Richards, & C. Armon (Eds.), *Beyond formal operations: Late adolescent and adult cognitive development* (pp. 298–325). New York: Praeger.

Smith, S.B. (1981). *The great mental calculators.* New York: Columbia University Press.

Spearman, C. (1927). *The abilities of man.* New York: Macmillan.

Spilich, G.J. (1985). Discourse comprehension across the span of life. In N. Charness (Ed.), *Aging and human performance* (pp. 143–190). London: Wiley.

Talland, G.A., & Cairnie, J. (1964). Aging effects on simple, disjunctive, and alerted finger reaction time. *Journal of Gerontology, 19,* 31–38.

Thurstone, L.L. (1938). *Primary mental abilities.* Chicago: University of Chicago Press.

Tsal, Y. (1983). Movements of attention across the visual field. *Journal of Experimental Psychology: Human Perception and Performance, 9,* 523–530.

Tversky, A., & Kahneman, D. (1973). Availability: A heuristic for judging frequency and probability. *Cognitive Psychology, 5,* 207–232.

Willis, S.L. (1985). Towards an educational psychology of the adult learner: Cognitive and intellectual bases. In J.E. Birren & K.W. Schaie (Eds.), *Handbook of the psychology of aging* (2nd ed., pp. 818–847). New York: Van Nostrand Reinhold.

Willis, S.L., Blieszner, R., & Baltes, P.B. (1981). Intellectual training research in aging: Modification of performance on the fluid ability of figural relations. *Journal of Educational Psychology, 73,* 41–50.

Willis, S.L., & Schaie, K.W. (in press). Practical intelligence in the elderly. In R.J. Sternberg & R.K. Wagner (Eds.), *Intelligence in the everyday world.* New York: Cambridge University Press.

Chapter Eight

Age, Experience, and Compensation

Timothy A. Salthouse

INTRODUCTION

An intriguing discrepancy exists between the competencies of older adults, assumed on the basis of everyday observations, on the one hand, and their competencies inferred from laboratory results, on the other. The laboratory results tend to portray older adults as distinctly inferior to young adults on a number of presumably basic cognitive abilities, and yet we are all aware of competent, and even remarkable, accomplishments of people well into their 60s, 70s, and beyond. One is thus faced with the question of how to account for this apparent discrepancy between the rather pessimistic results of the laboratory and the more encouraging observations of daily life.

One possible interpretation is that observations in daily life are unsystematic or biased because the activities are typically self-selected, and not representative of the entire population of potential tasks. That is, people probably tend to engage in activities in which they are reasonably competent, and try to avoid as much as possible those tasks which have proven difficult or stressful in the past. It is not clear whether the activities of daily living are inherently less difficult or complex than the tasks performed in the laboratory, but the fact that individuals are free (at least within broad limits) to choose their daily activities introduces the possibility of a self-selection bias which could drastically distort the meaning of one's observations.

A second hypothesis for the discrepancy between age trends in the laboratory and those inferred from observations of daily living is that the laboratory situation is artificial, and thus may be characterized by conditions of low motivation, high anxiety, or generally inappropriate

142

allocation of attention. Because these detrimental factors are presumably absent, or at least of considerably smaller significance, in the situations one typically encounters in the natural environment, the laboratory results may provide an unrealistic portrayal of the true capacities of older adults.

A third interpretation of the lab-life discrepancy is that laboratory tasks typically emphasize the processes of cognition while daily activities tend to reflect the prior or current products of those processes. This process-product distinction is similar to the fluid-crystallized dichotomy introduced by Horn and Cattell (1966), and the mechanics-pragmatics contrast recently proposed by Baltes, Dittmann-Kohli, and Dixon (1984). The fundamental idea in each of these conceptualizations is that there are qualitatively different types of cognition, with one exhibiting greater age sensitivity than the other. Divergent age trends in laboratory and real-life situations might be produced if the sample of abilities studied in the laboratory represents a different distribution of the two types of cognition from that involved in the activities of daily life.

A fourth hypothesis, and the one of greatest interest in the present context, is that the activities of daily living are highly practiced while tasks in the laboratory are typically quite unfamiliar. Because older adults have probably had much more experience performing activities of everyday living than young adults, if for no other reason than that they have lived 30 to 50 years longer, they can be considered to be experts in the domain of their own particular patterns of activity. It is thus conceivable that contrasts in the laboratory involve near-novice levels of performance, while those in the activities of everyday life consist of older adult experts being compared with young adult novices. This experience hypothesis is the focus of the remainder of this chapter.

A key question from the perspective of the experience hypothesis is exactly how greater experience might lead to a reduction in the magnitude of age differences in performance. Two distinct strategies have been pursued to investigate this question. One involves the direct manipulation of experience by means of the administration of training or practice in groups of young and old adults. The other strategy consists of indirectly assessing the effects of experience through an examination of detailed aspects of performance in adults of different ages who achieve the same overall level of proficiency with varying amounts of experience. Both studies involve perceptual-motor activities—an ability domain with three advantages for the purpose of this chapter. First, perceptual-motor tasks typically yield simple and objective measures of performance, often in the intrinsically meaningful scale of real time. Second, because this domain has been extensively researched, it has a number of reasonably well documented process models that can be used to facilitate the design and interpretation of research.

And third, age-related declines in perceptual-motor tasks are often among the most pronounced of any behavioral variables, thereby providing a very strong test of the potential contribution of experience in modifying the effects of aging.

EXPERIMENTAL MANIPULATION OF EXPERIENCE

The basic goal with the strategy of experimentally manipulating experience is to administer enough practice on the relevant tasks to allow the members of each age group to achieve a relatively asymptotic level of performance. Contrasts of the initial and asymptotic levels of performance could reveal that the age differences remain stable, that they increase, or that they decrease. Of course, in all cases it is important to be sensitive to artifacts of measurement such as unreliable measures early in practice or ceiling effects late in practice which might spuriously produce, or obscure, interactions of age and experience (see Salthouse, 1985).

An outcome in which age differences are reduced with practice is the most intriguing in the current context because it is consistent with the view that practice-related factors contribute to the existence of the age differences observed in the laboratory. The critical issue, however, is how such a convergent Age × Experience interaction is to be explained.

One interpretation can be termed *remediation* in that the age differences are presumed to be reduced because experience leads to the older adults "remedying" their deficit. Remediation thus implies that practice has successfully altered the critical mechanism responsible for the initial age differences in a more optimal direction in the poorer-performing older adult group. What is sometimes known as the disuse theory of cognitive aging would be supported by a remediation interpretation because this perspective postulates that a lack of recent practice on the part of older adults is responsible for many of the age differences observed in cognitive tasks.

A second interpretation can be designated *accommodation,* since in this case the critical mechanism is not directly affected by experience but instead its consequences are minimized by a shift in the manner of carrying out the relevant tasks. Accommodation is unlikely to be a major factor in simple tasks, but in more complex situations it may be manifested as a shift in one's pattern of activities or mode of performance to minimize deficit-revealing conditions.

Compensation is the term applied to a third interpretation of reduced age differences with experience because a loss in one aspect of processing could be balanced by a gain in another aspect of processing. This interpretational category differs from the previous ones in that a clear exchange is implied in which an inferiority in one processing component is accompanied by a superiority in another aspect of processing.

Notice that although remediation, accommodation, and compensation could each be responsible for interactions of age and experience, only remediation actually results in an alteration in the critical aspect of processing responsible for the initial performance differences. Because this is probably the most common interpretation of such an interaction, it is desirable to examine relevant evidence carefully to determine the plausibility of remediation as opposed to accommodation or compensation. This was an explicit goal of the study investigating the effects of practice on age differences in performance.

The study, described more fully in Salthouse and Somberg (1982), involved samples of young (age 19 to 27 years) and old (age 62 to 73 years) adults performing four distinct perceptual-motor tasks for 50 1–hr sessions over a period of several months. The tasks were embedded in a video-game context to maintain motivation across sessions, and the participants also received a bonus payment equivalent to their previous total compensation upon completion of all sessions as an incentive for continued participation. Although the subjects performed four different tasks, the one of greatest interest in the present context was a memory-scanning reaction-time task. The other tasks involved signal detection, visual discrimination, and temporal prediction of the intersection of two trajectories; but performance in the first two tasks was limited by ceiling effects in the data from the young subjects, and the measures in the third task had low reliability because they were based on a very small number of observations in each session.

A trial in the memory-scanning task consisted of the presentation of from one to four different symbols as the memory set, with the subject requested to determine as rapidly as possible whether a probe stimulus had been a member of that earlier presented memory set. Two parameters can be used to summarize performance on this task— the mean reaction time across the different set sizes, reflecting the overall level of performance, and the slope of the function relating reaction time to number of items in the memory set. This latter measure has been interpreted as an index of the time needed to perform a single comparison of an item in memory (Sternberg, 1975), and has been found to decrease considerably as a function of practice in samples of young adults (Schneider & Shiffrin, 1976).

The major results of this project are illustrated in Figure 1. This figure contains the mean reaction-time data across the 50 experimental sessions, and also the results from a 51st session administered 30 days after the 50th session. The functions are somewhat irregular because of a number of transfer conditions administered to determine the effects

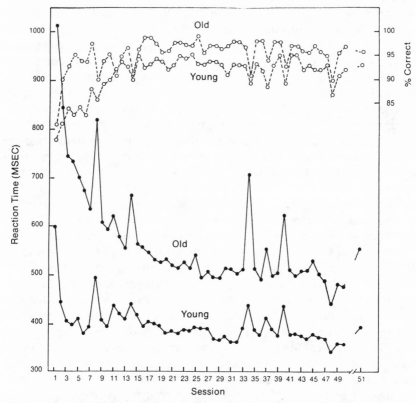

Figure 1. Mean reaction time in the memory-scanning task for young and old adults as a function of practice. Figure from "Skilled Performance: The Effects of Adult Age and Experience on Elementary Processes" by T. A. Salthouse & B. L. Somberg, 1982, *Journal of Experimental Psychology: General*, **111**, p. 188.

of switching the stimulus set, reducing the size of the probe stimuli, and so on, but it is clear that the age differences remain remarkably constant throughout 50 hrs of practice. At least with the measure of overall mean reaction time, therefore, these results suggest that the magnitude of age differences in performance are relatively stable across moderate amounts of experience. The apparent implication is that practice-related factors cannot account for much of the initial age differences in perceptual-motor performance because those differences are not substantially altered even when the individuals in each age group received practice sufficient to achieve near-asymptotic levels of performance.

The results from the slope measure were somewhat different, however, as the initial age differences were greatly attenuated, if not actually eliminated, by moderate practice. The slopes based on reaction times across set sizes 2, 3, and 4 in sessions 2 through 5 were 57.0 ms per item for the older adults and 16.5 ms per item for the young adults, but these were reduced to 15.0 and 13.5, respectively, in sessions 42 through 45.

How is the convergence of the slopes of young and old adults with practice to be interpreted? Three possibilities were outlined earlier— remediation, accommodation, and compensation. Because the slope parameter seems to reflect a unitary process, that is, the duration of a single memory comparison, the gradual reduction of the age differences could be explained as remediation of the age-related slowing deficit in this process. Accommodation and compensation are not as plausible unless an alternative means of accomplishing the memory comparison process can be identified. However, another possibility is that the age differences were attenuated because the component process indexed by the dependent variable was gradually phased out in the course of practice on the task. A commonly accepted interpretation of practice-mediated reductions in memory-scanning slope is that after extensive practice with the same assignment of stimuli to responses the memory scanning becomes automatic, possibly because of a more direct linkage between target stimulus and response category. From this perspective, therefore, the slope results imply that young and old adults are equally adept at developing automaticity of memory scannning, and consequently that the age differences are attenuated when the importance of processes responsible for those differences is greatly reduced.

This latter interpretation suggests that a category of *elimination* might be added to those of remediation, accommodation, and compensation as potential mechanisms to account for convergent interactions of age and experience. That is, if the critical processes responsible for the dependent variable cease to contribute to performance after moderate amounts of practice, then the age differences can be considered to be reduced because the relevant component has been eliminated.

To summarize, no interaction of age and experience was apparent in the measure of overall reaction time, but the age differences were reduced with practice on the slope measure. Because the slope is presumed to reflect the single process of memory scanning, accommodation and compensation interpretations seem rather implausible. However, because of the possiblity that the memory-scanning operation was eliminated after moderate practice, it is still not certain whether the interaction with the slope measure should be considered evidence of remediation of age differences in performance.

Although the results of this practice study were interesting, the study has at least two important limitations. One is that the simple nature of the experimental tasks biases the results against certain potential outcomes. For example, there is little possibility for a compensatory mechanism to emerge in very simple tasks such as choice reaction time. More complex activities in which there are a variety of different ways of performing the overall task are presumably necessary in order to provide a fair test of the compensation interpretation.

A second limitation of this, and virtually any, practice study is that it could be argued that the amount of practice provided was insufficient, and that with additional practice a different pattern of results might emerge. This is an extremely difficult criticism to overcome in studies manipulating practice in the laboratory because the amount of experimentally provided experience is necessarily limited, and yet there appear to be no limits in the amount of additional practice which continues to lead to improved performance. In other words, only a relatively small amount of practice can be administered in experimental situations, and yet performance improvements may continue indefinitely (although at progressively smaller rates) with increased practice.

In light of these reservations, it seemed desirable to consider an alternative means of investigating the effects of experience on age differences in performance. The procedure adopted capitalizes on naturally occurring experience with reasonably complex, but experimentally decomposable, real-world activities.

MOLAR EQUIVALENCE-MOLECULAR DECOMPOSITION

The molar equivalence–molecular decomposition research strategy is a variant of a procedure introduced by Charness in his studies of skilled bridge and chess players (e.g., 1979, 1981, 1983). The first step in this procedure is to obtain a moderately sized sample of adults with a wide range of ages, and across many different levels of competency on the task of interest. By careful selection of the research participants it is generally possible to obtain a sample in which the correlation between age and performance on the composite task is near 0, that is, one in which the average level of molar competency is equivalent across the age span. Unlike the case with the experimental manipulation of practice where the goal is to examine performance after ostensibly comparable amounts of practice, it is expected in this procedure that achievement of the same level of proficiency across adulthood probably requires that age and experience are positively correlated, that is, that the older adults have had more relevant experience than the young adults. However, if the activity can then be decomposed into its molecular components, age trends on the proficiency of selected components can be examined to determine the means by which a given level of molar competency is achieved at different ages. Note that the important question in this context is not what effects age has on the molar behavior, but rather whether identical mechanisms are used by all age groups to achieve the same overall level of performance.

Two outcomes from the molar equivalence–molecular decomposition strategy are particularly interesting. One pattern of results, which might be termed the *maintenance hypothesis,* is that the equivalence of molar performance is achieved because the greater experience associated with increased age leads to maintained proficiency of molecular components rather than the typical age-associated decline. In other words, the expected age-related reduction in effectiveness of molecular processes may have been prevented by the positive relationship between age and experience with the composite task. This hyothesis is consistent with both the remediation and the accommodation interpretations discussed above since experience may have "remedied" the age-related deficit found in unexperienced adults, or many older adults may have accommodated to their deficit and selected themselves out of, or into, certain occupational settings. Accommodation in this instance implies that the older adults who have continued in the relevant activity may not be very representative of their age groups, and thus the absence of an expected age difference in the molecular components may be due to differential representativeness with more highly selected individuals in the older age groups.

A second possible outcome with the molar equivalence–molecular decomposition strategy is designated the *compensation hypothesis* since a typical age-related decline might still be evident in molecular proficiency, but this decrease could be compensated for by increases in the effectiveness or efficiency of one or more metacomponential mechanisms. The nature of the metacomponential mechanisms will obviously vary across activity domains, but it will be compensatory to the extent that operation of these mechanisms allows the attainment of a high level of global proficiency despite reductions in the efficiency of component processes.

Transcription typing was the activity selected for investigation in the molar equivalence–molecular decomposition study (described in more detail in Salthouse, 1984). Three factors were influential in this decision. First, the discrete nature of the keystroke responses makes it reasonably easy to investigate. That is, typing appears integrated and continuous, and yet it culminates in distinct and separate keystrokes which can be easily timed and evaluated.

Second, the widespread use of typewriter keyboards provides access to subject populations of all ranges of skill and age. Moreover, the variations in skill can be orders of magnitude greater than that possible in laboratory tasks because of the immense amount of natural experience with real-world activities such as typing. To illustrate, although the preceding practice study involved 50 separate experimental sessions, the total number of reaction-time trials per subject was only 5,000. An average professional typist would execute this many keystrokes in about 17 min. and might be expected to produce over 2.5 million keystrokes each year.

The third reason for selecting typing as the molar activity in this study was that the activity of typing seems decomposable into components related to choice reaction time, tapping speed, and digit symbol substitution speed. For example, in both choice reaction time and transcription typing tasks the individual is required to view visually presented characters, encode them, translate them into approriate finger movements, and then execute the movements to press the appropriate key as rapidly as possible. Tapping speed is a plausible component in typing because the speed of typing is clearly limited by the rate at which one can repetitively move one's fingers. The rate of digit symbol substitution is not as obviously related to typing speed, but is similar in that both the substitution of digits into symbols and the manual typing of visually presented letters involve the rapid transcription of information presented in one form into corresponding information in another form.

The study, actually two separate studies involving very similar procedures with different samples of 34 and 40 adults, consisted of administering timed tests of transcription typing from printed copy as well as a number of specially designed tests measuring components such as reaction time, tapping speed, and digit symbol substitution rate. The typists ranged between 19 and 72 years of age and between 17 and 104 net words per min., but with no overall correlation between age and net words per min. (i.e., $r = .07$ for Study 1, and $r = -.10$ for Study 2). Age was positively correlated with cumulative experience, however, as the older typists had a greater number of months of typing-related employment than did the younger typists (i.e., $r = .51$ for Study 1, and $r = .55$ for Study 2).

Correlations between measures of component proficiency and molar competency (i.e., typing performance in net words per min), and between component proficiency and age are displayed in Table 1. The major point to be noted from these data is that the correlations with typing skill are opposite in direction to those with age. This suggests that while proficiency in the molecular processes is associated with better performance on the criterion typing task (i.e., higher typing speeds are associated with shorter reaction times or tapping intervals, and with more digit symbol substitutions), increased age is a disadvantage with each of these measures.

Another illustration of this phenomenon is presented in Figure 2, which portrays the mean interkey interval for reaction time and typing

Table 1. Component Process Correlations

	Net Words per Min		Age	
	Study 1	Study 2	Study 1	Study 2
Choice reaction times	−.18	−.36	+.46	+.62
Tapping interval	−.43	−.43	+.40	+.52
Digit symbol substitution rate	—	+.53	—	−.55

as a function of the age of the typist. (The data for this figure, and those for Figures 3, 4, and 5, are based only on the 56 typists with typing speeds above 45 net words per min to ensure that all typists were at least moderately proficient.) Notice that reaction time exhibits a sizable age trend of approximately 136 additional ms per keystroke between the 20s and 60s, whereas the age trend in typing interkey interval is virtually nonexistent. This pattern of results is clearly consistent with the compensation hypothesis described earlier since these individuals exhibited typical age-related declines in measures of component proficiency, and yet were still able to achieve the same level of molar competency.

What are the compensatory mechanisms used by older typists to achieve high levels of typing speed despite the handicap of a slower perceptual-motor speed? Several possibilities were investigated in this project, but only one measure was found to be significantly related to age. An initial hypothesis was that older typists might have developed a greater sensitivity to letter frequencies than did young typists and thus could compensate for their slower perceptual-motor speed by better matching their keystroke efficiency to the probabilities of specific letters and sequences of letters. This possibility was investigated by determining the correlation between age and measures of the effects of letter or letter-pair frequency on interkey interval during normal typing. These correlations did not differ significantly from 0, therefore suggesting that greater sensitivity to letter frequencies is unlikely as the compensatory mechanism responsible for older adults achieving the same level of typing speed as young adults in the presence of declines in the efficiency of component processes.

A second possible compensatory mechanism was the consistency of the interkey intervals during typing, on the assumption that the older experienced typists might have learned to type each keystroke at approximately equal intervals. This hypothesis was also not supported, as the correlations between age and variability of interkey interval while typing were uniformly low and not significantly different from 0.

The third compensatory mechanism investigated was the extent of

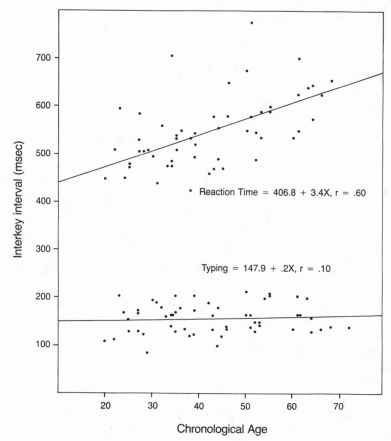

Figure 2. Median interkey intervals in choice reaction time and normal copy typing as a function of typist age.

anticipatory or preparatory processing carried out while performing normal typing. It was hypothesized that older typists might have learned to expand their "span of processing," thereby increasing the time during which a particular character can be processed. The means by which this anticipatory processing mechanism was investigated involved a special task in which typists were asked to type material from a video monitor arranged such that only a limited number of characters appeared at any given time. The number of characters, which was termed the preview window, ranged from 1 to 11 characters in increments of 2. With each successive keystroke the leftmost character was removed from the screen, the remaining characters each shifted one space to the left, and another character was added to the right of the display. The overall impression from the typist's perspective was of controlling

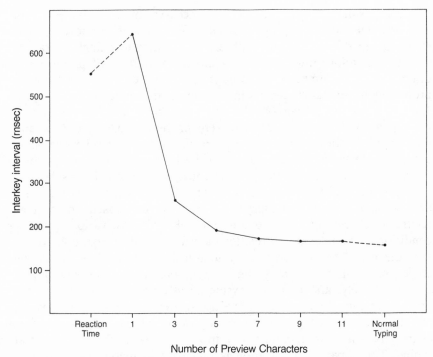

Figure 3. **Mean, across typists, of median interkey intervals in normal copy typing, typing with preview windows of 1 to 11 characters, and choice reaction time.**

a horizontally scrolling text since the material shifted at a rate determined by the interval between successive keystrokes.

Under conditions such as these, the rate of typing becomes slower with a reduction in the number of visible characters, particularly when fewer than five characters are present in the display. The value of this manipulation is that the largest preview window at which typing rate is first disrupted compared to normal typing can be used as an index of the extent of advance processing employed in normal typing. That is, if typing rate is slower with a given number of preview characters relative to normal typing, then when maintaining his or her normal rate of typing the typist must normally process more than the displayed number of characters.

The mean interkey intervals for the six preview window conditions employed, and for the typing and choice reaction time tasks, are displayed in Figure 3. Notice that the typists are performing at their normal typing rate with preview windows of 7, 9, and 11 characters, but that their performance becomes progressively more impaired with restrictions of 5, 3, and 1 visible character(s).

These results indicate that performance systematically varies from that characteristic of typing with large amounts of preview, to that characteristic of reaction time with preview limited to a single character. One can therefore infer that the relatively high rates of performance of normal typing are achieved in large part because of the simultaneous processing of several characters in advance of the character to be typed. Judging from the average results displayed in Figure 3, we find that the typists in the current sample were processing between three and four characters in advance of the character whose keystroke was being pressed since their rate did not reach the level of normal typing until at least five characters were simultaneously visible on the display.

Effects of age on this measure of anticipatory processing were examined in two complementary analyses. One was based on the correlations between age and interkey interval across the various preview conditions. The relevant correlations are illustrated in Figure 4. Notice that the correlations are virtually identical to those obtained in the choice reaction time and typing tasks at preview windows of 1 and 11, respectively, and that they systematically change from one to the other with increased preview. The age-related slowness in processing therefore becomes progressively less important as the number of preview characters is increased, culminating in no age relationship with normal typing. The apparent implication is that with increased age there is a greater reliance on anticipatory preparation which serves to minimize the limitations of slower perceptual-motor processes.

Another analysis conducted to determine the effects of age on anticipatory processing involved determining the number of characters needed to maintain a normal rate of typing for each typist, and then plotting this variable as a function of the age of the typist. As mentioned earlier, the preview-window size at which the typing rate first increases, by a criterion amount, above the rate of normal typing can be taken as a measure of the number of characters normally used in typing. I call this quantity the eye-hand span because it indicates the gap between the character whose key is currently being pressed and the character currently receiving the attention of the eyes. Figure 5 illustrates the relationship between typist age and eye-hand span in this sample of typists. Notice that there is a significant increase with age in the size of this running memory span. Typists in their 60s are relying upon an average of 4.8 characters to the right of the character being typed, while those in their 20s depend upon an average of only 2.4 characters. The difference of 2.4 characters translates into approximately 380 ms of additional preparation time available to typists in their 60s compared to typists in their 20s. This is nearly three times greater than the reaction-time differences expected across this age interval and appears

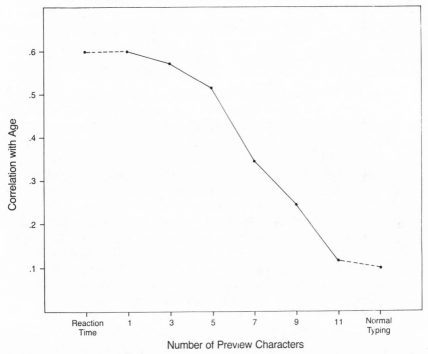

Figure 4. **Correlations between typist age and median interkey interval in normal copy typing, typing with preview windows of 1 to 11 characters, and choice reaction time.**

more than sufficient to compensate for the slower perceptual-motor processes.

The results of this typing project provide an intriguing example of the potential contribution of the molar equivalence–molecular decomposition research strategy. Young and old typists did not differ in their overall level of typing proficiency, but they were distinguishable in terms of the way in which this proficiency was achieved. Despite experience extending to decades and many millions of keystrokes, the older typists were slower at several perceptual-motor processes than were younger typists. In this respect these results are consistent with those of the practice study since the age differences are not eliminated even when the amount of experience greatly favors the older adults. However, the apparent handicap of slower perceptual-motor processes did not impair overall performance of the older typists because they seem to have adopted a strategy of anticipating more impending characters than did young typists, thereby allowing them to compensate by expanding the temporal interval over which processing could occur.

More extensive planning and preparation on the part of older adults

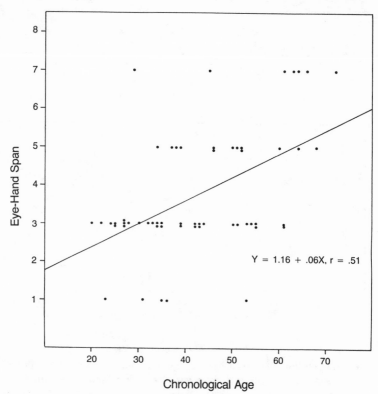

Figure 5. Eye-hand span, inferred from the largest preview window at which typing rate first deviates from that of normal typing, as a function of typist age.

is an interesting and intuitively compelling compensatory mechanism. However, quite different mechanisms might be employed in other domains and thus it is desirable to extend the molar equivalence–molecular decomposition research strategy into other ability areas.

CONCLUSION

The studies described above are concerned with only a single activity domain, and even then involved a far from exhaustive examination of important processes and mechanisms. Nevertheless, reliance on two different approaches to the issue of age and experience allows stronger and more generalized conclusions than those that would be possible if only a single research strategy had been employed.

A major conclusion is that the lab-life discrepancy in inferred age trends in cognitive competence might indeed be explainable in terms of differential experience. Adults of all ages appear to benefit from experience, and in at least one activity older adults have been found to compensate for declining abilities and thus still maintain a proficient level of overall performance. As with most studies, however, the results have led to the generation of many new and intriguing questions. For example, it is still not known whether age-related deficits in important cognitive abilities can actually be remediated, as opposed to being accommodated or compensated, through experience. The circumstances responsible for maintenance rather than compensation of extensively practiced activities are also unclear. And finally, the nature of compensation remains a puzzle, particularly the relationship between the mechanisms employed by older adults and those used by highly skilled individuals of any age.

REFERENCES

Baltes, P.B., Dittmann-Kohli, F., & Dixon, R.A. (1984). New perspectives on the development of intelligence in adulthood: Toward a dual-process conception and a model of selective optimization with compensation. In P.B. Baltes & O.G. Brim, Jr. (Eds.),*Life-span development and behavior*, (Vol. 6, pp. 33–76). New York: Academic Press.

Charness, N. (1979). Components of skill in bridge. *Canadian Journal of Psychology, 33*, 1–16.

Charness, N. (1981). Aging and skilled problem solving. *Journal of Experimental Psychology: General, 110*, 21–38.

Charness, N. (1983). Age, skill, and bridge bidding: A chronometric analysis. *Journal of Verbal Learning and Verbal Behavior, 22*, 406–416.

Horn, J.L., & Cattell, R.B. (1966). Age differences in primary mental ability factors. *Journal of Gerontology, 21*,210–220.

Salthouse, T.A. (1984). Effects of age and skill in typing. *Journal of Experimental Psychology: General, 113*, 345–371.

Salthouse, T.A. (1985). *A theory of cognitive aging.* Amsterdam: North Holland.

Salthouse, T.A., & Somberg, B.L. (1982). Skilled performance: The effects of adult age and experience on elementary processes. *Journal of Experimental Psychology: General, 111*, 176–207.

Schneider, W., & Shiffrin, R.M. (1977). Controlled and automatic human information processing: I. Detection, search, and attention. *Psychological Review, 84*, 1–66.

Sternberg, S. (1975). Memory scanning: New findings and current controversies. *Quarterly Journal of Experimental Psychology, 27, 1–32.*

Part III
Social Structure

Chapter Nine

Longevity, Social Structure, and Cognitive Aging

Ronald P. Abeles
Matilda White Riley

This chapter, written in this era of the revolution in longevity, concerns the interplay between social structures and individual aging processes, in particular those processes associated with cognitive functioning. Three questions are addressed:

1. Will increasingly long-lived people suffer inevitable declines in performance levels, or does lengthening of human lives hold potentials for continued development not yet realized?
2. To the extent that the aging process is not immutable, how are people influenced by the social structures and environments within which human aging occurs?
3. If people's lives are influenced in specific ways by social structures, to what extent can (or will) social structures be influenced, in turn, by the changes in people's lives? What consequences, in terms of individual growth and development, are likely to ensue from these reciprocal changes?

We ask these questions and, on the basis of accumulating research evidence, suggest some tentative answers.

LONGEVITY AND COGNITIVE CHANGE

The intricate relationship between social structures and aging processes can be understood against the background of unprecedented changes

The authors wish to express their gratitude for the advice and suggestions made on earlier drafts by John W. Riley, Jr., Carmi Schooler, and K. Warner Schaie.

in longevity during the 20th-century. Since the turn of the century, ever greater proportions of each successive birth cohort have survived to old age. The U.S. Bureau of the Census estimates that, among babies born in 1980, 77% could look forward to reaching age 65, as compared to about 41% in 1900 (National Center for Health Statistics, 1985; U.S. Bureau of the Census, 1984). Those surviving to age 65 could expect to live an additional 16.5 years, which is an increase of about 4.6 years over 1900 (Siegel & Taeuber, 1986). Or in other words, the proportion of 65-year-olds in 1980 who could expect to reach age 85 was more than twice the 1900 proportion (Rosenwaike, 1985). Moreover, at older ages, life expectancy has shown dramatic increases. Even those reaching age 85 could anticipate an additional 6 years of life in 1980 (Metropolitan Life Insurance Company, 1986). These are unprecedented statistics. Over two thirds of the improvement in longevity in the entire experience of Homo sapiens has taken place in the brief period since 1900 (Preston, 1976). We are in the midst of revolutionary changes in longevity with implications for individual aging and for social structures that are yet to be understood.

Longevity and Aging

From the perspective of individuals, longevity is of major importance, affecting the number of years of life that lie behind as well as ahead, both in people's own lives and in the lives of relatives and significant others (Riley & Riley, 1986).

Increased longevity prolongs a person's opportunity for accumulating social, psychological, and biological experience; maximizes a person's opportunities to complete or change the role assignments of early and middle life (e.g., change jobs, marriage partners, educational plans; take on new roles); and it prolongs a person's relationships to those significant others whose lives are likewise extended.

Also affecting the lives of individuals is the age composition of the population, which relates intimately to the social structures in which people are growing older. Over the 20th century in the United States, for example, the "aging" of the population has meant increasing the structural complexity of a person's social networks (e.g., of kinship, friendship, and community). In some families, an unheard-of four or even five generations are alive at the same time.

It should be noted that longevity and the aging population are separate and distinct phenomena. Increased longevity rates (which depend upon life-course patterns of mortality) are not necessarily coincident with an increasing proportion of old people in the population, which is influenced in the long term more by fertility than mortality. For example, toward the middle of the 21st century, when the baby-boom cohorts are replaced in the oldest age stratum by their less populous successors, the United States population will predictably become somewhat "younger." At that point, longevity may remain high for individuals, even though the proportion of old people in the population has declined.

Aging and Cognitive Decline

This revolution in longevity raises profound questions for people's lives. Will a longer life course mean that greater and greater numbers of people will be condemned to diminishing cognitive and intellectual functioning as they live longer and longer? Such a future is consonant with stereotypes of old age in which profound declines in intellectual and cognitive functioning are believed to be pervasive and inevitable. However, this stereotype is now being challenged by wide-ranging evidence (Horn & Donaldson, 1980) that will be illustrated later. Cohort studies show that many of the deficits of today's older people can be explained, not by aging, but by differences in cohort experiences (as new cohorts may be comparatively better educated, healthier, etc., than earlier ones). Longitudinal research indicates that substantial declines in many complex intellectual functions do not reliably occur until advanced old age (Schaie, 1983). Experimental investigations demonstrate that by changing the immediate social environment, old-age deficits, rather than being biologically fixed, can often be reduced or prevented (Baltes & Willis, 1982).

Aging and Cognitive Development

Alternatively, will an extended life course enable greater and greater numbers of people to develop dimensions of cognitive functioning that are unique to old age? Such dimensions may not be detected by the existing standard measures of intellectual functioning that are designed for the young and for use in schools or job entry. Yet longevity may bring its own assets in the form of components of intelligence that develop in middle or later life, such as experience-based decision-making, or interpersonal competence. One often-discussed candidate for a late developing component of intelligence is "wisdom" as a perspective for evaluating actions, setting priorities, and knowing what responses a situation requires (Clayton & Birren, 1980; Riley & Riley, 1986). Baltes and his colleagues describe wisdom as a form of intellectual development that may gradually emerge over the life course (Dittman–Kohli & Baltes, in press). They view wisdom as "an individual's ability to exercise good judgment about important but uncertain matters of life" and they compare it to professional expertise (Kliegl & Baltes, chapter 6 of this volume). As with other kinds of expertise, they argue that the development of wisdom is contingent upon (personal or vicarious) exposure to and experience with problems and their solutions. As new dimensions of intellectual functioning are conceptualized and measured, attention is being focused on how, with longer lives, and the appropriate opportunities, more people might have wisdom-developing experiences.

SOCIAL STRUCTURE AND AGING

Given that declines in cognitive functioning are not inevitable or universal for all individuals or across all domains of cognitive functioning and that the development of "wisdomlike" components is already being explored, how do social structural factors, interacting with demographic trends, affect people's cognitive and intellectual functioning as they age (Riley & Riley, 1986)? In considering this question, a distinction needs to be made between the micro and macro levels of social structure. The latter refers to the structure of large social units, such as the economy or the polity, and includes society as a whole, while the former refers to the immediate social environment in which people interact (e.g., the workplace or home). A major means by which macrosocial structures affect cognitive functioning is by allocating people to different kinds of microsocial structures in which particular social roles become open or closed as people grow older. That is, macrolevel social structure does not directly influence cognitive functioning, but is an essential component in a "two-step flow" of influence (to borrow a term from communications research). The microsocial structures are the immediate environmental forces that shape cognitive functioning.

Microstructures

Clues to the actual and potential influence on cognitive functioning of microsocial structural factors come from two different sources of evidence: longitudinal field studies and experimental laboratory investigations.

Field studies. Heavily although not exclusively on the basis of the former source, Schooler (chapter 2 of this volume) theorizes that environments characterized by complexity and rewards for cognitive effort should improve cognitive and intellectual functioning:

> The more diverse the stimuli, the greater the number of decisions required, the greater the number of considerations to be taken into account in

making these decisions; and the more ill defined and apparently contradictory the contingencies, the more complex the environment. To the degree that the pattern of reinforcement within such an environment rewards cognitive effort, individuals should be motivated to develop their intellectual capacities and to generalize the resulting cognitive processes to other situations.

This postulate is supported by diverse data, including longitudinal panel data on the effects of jobs upon cognitive functioning. Workers in jobs with microsocial structures that provide them with substantive complexity, lack of routinization, and freedom from close supervision improve in their cognitive functioning (in terms of intellectual flexibility) over a 10-year period (Kohn & Schooler, 1978, 1981, 1982). When the social environments of the home and school contain these same characteristics, they, too, promote cognitive functioning (Schooler, Kohn, Miller, & Miller, 1983; Schooler, Miller, Miller, & Richtand, 1984). Moreover, the impact of the immediate social environment on cognitive and intellectual functioning is found to be about equally great across a wide age spectrum—from children to old people (see Miller, Slomczynski, & Kohn, chapter 10 of this volume).

Another example of the effect of social structure on aging is a followup study by Schaie (1983) at four successive 7-year intervals, of adults of all ages who are members of a Seattle health maintenance organization. Among the numerous findings was the unexpected relationship to age of most types of intelligence. Contrary to conventional expectations, scarcely any individual up to age 60, and less than half of individuals even at age 80, showed reliable decrements in cognitive test performance over a 7-year period. Among individuals at the oldest ages, there was wide variability, prompting Schaie (1984) to look for explanations. Individual differences were attributable partly to cardiovascular and other diseases, but also to economic status (a macrosocial variable) and to the intellectual stimulation of the environment (a microsocial variable). Relatively lower cognitive functioning was associated with "disengaged" life-styles, namely, passive activities, few changes in professional roles, low involvement in work activities, solitary activities, few people-related activities. By contrast, the combination of high status and engagement was associated with maintaining intellectual abilities over a 14-year period (Gribbin, Schaie, & Parham, 1980; Schaie, 1983).

Experimental studies. The wide variability in performance with aging has also led to the consideration of possible experimental interventions designed to prevent or modify those declines that do occur. A growing number of experimental studies demonstrate improvements in intellectual functioning with aging when the immediate social environment is structured in particular ways: if life situations are challenging, provide incentives and opportunities for learning, and if people continue to use their skills.

Building upon Schaie's earlier field work, Baltes and Willis (1982) manipulated the immediate social environment by providing specific training opportunities in order to explore the modifiability of intellectual performance. These experiments involved people with a mean age of 70 who were living in the community, and focused on those intellectual skills (spatial orientation and inductive reasoning) in which elderly persons have been most likely to show declines in test performance. The training program consisted of five 1-hr group sessions, in which 3 to 5 subjects were given problems that increased in complexity and difficulty from one session to the next. The trainer described a problem and modeled the strategies for identifying the relational rules used in solving it, while attempting to relate the problem-solving strategies to everyday tasks (e.g., knitting, music). After a number of examples were modeled by the trainer, the subjects were asked to solve several practice problems, feedback to responses was given, and group discussion of the problems and solutions occurred. An environment was created that provided increasing intellectual challenge (cf. Schooler's "complexity"; chapter 2 of this volume), opportunities to practice skills, incentives to perform, and clear feedback on success and failure. Even though these experimental interventions were brief and short-term—very different from the massive educational exposures of younger people—the magnitude of improvement is at least large enough to recover the previous aging decline observed in longitudinal studies from age 60 to age 80. Over three quarters of the subjects showed improvement following training, and training effects endured for at least 6 months and transferred to other tests of similar types.

Other related experiments have intervened in the mechanisms that may affect intellectual performance. For example, Willis, Cornelius, Blow, and Baltes (1983) demonstrated that training can improve those attentional processes that may mediate some kinds of intellectual performance. As in the previous study, training consisted of practicing cognitive skills and of relating these abstract skills to activities in the social environments of the subjects' daily lives.

Among these related experiments, another by Schaie and Willis (Schaie & Willis, 1986; Willis, 1986; Willis & Schaie, 1986) replicates the earlier finding of the modifiability through training of older people's intellectual performance. This study adds to the earlier design by conducting the experiments on the same subjects (aged 62 to 94) whose earlier intellectual histories are known from their participation in Schaie's original Seattle longitudinal study many years earlier. Results indicate that the majority of the subjects gained significantly from training and that approximately 40% of those who had declined are returned to their predecline levels of some 14 years earlier. Moreover, while the major portion of decline can be accounted for by fewer responses (i.e., a drop in response speed), training not only increases the number of responses made, but also provides some compensation for loss in response speed by raising levels of accuracy (Schaie & Willis, 1985).

In a related vein, another illustrative study focuses upon response speed, which typically declines with aging and which is thought to reflect basic biological processes underlying cognitive functioning (see Salthouse, chapter 8 of this volume). Contrary to a purely biological perspective, Baron and his colleagues have demonstrated that, when older adults are tested under time pressure and rewards and penalties are contingent on their responses meeting specific time limits, their performance increases substantially (Baron & Menich, 1985a, 1985b; Baron, Menich, & Perone, 1983). These operant training procedures—which create a social environment in which the contingencies between behaviors and rewards are salient—bring the performance of older persons into the ranges ordinarily seen in younger persons, appreciably reducing age differences for these simple response tasks. Although these manipulations did not improve performance on more complex tasks such as discrimination learning, they do suggest that even basic processes like response speed may be affected by the microsocial structure of the environment.

Macrostructures

At the macro level, social structure influences both the kinds and the patternings of experiences to which people are exposed as a result of the roles that they occupy over their lives (see Heise, chapter 13 of this volume). This influence is most readily demonstrated in terms of the impact of socioeconomic status (SES), viewed as a position held by an individual in the larger society. SES is a strong determinant of the quality and quantity of education and of the subsequent nature of work in which people engage during their lifetime (see Walberg, chapter 11 of this volume, and Kellam, chapter 12). Thus, it affects the likelihood of being exposed to social environments that foster or inhibit particular kinds of intellectual and cognitive functioning. Besides affecting the probability of having particular experiences or being exposed to social environments, SES affects *when* significant life experiences are likely to occur (Abeles, Steel, & Wise, 1980; Hagestad & Neugarten, 1985; Hogan, 1981; see also Kellam, chapter 12 of this volume). For example, lower-SES persons are more likely to become married earlier, to have (more) children earlier, to start and leave work earlier, and to suffer from poor health and die earlier than higher-SES persons. Moreover, the sequencing of life experiences is influenced by SES. For example, lower-SES women are more likely to become teenage unmarried mothers, which is an "off-time" life event with long-lasting and mostly negative consequences for subsequent educational and occupational careers (Card, Steel, & Abeles, 1982; Presser, 1974).

Age per se is also a component of social structure, operating in a fashion similar to SES in allocating and recruiting people to roles and in evaluating their performance in those roles (Riley, Johnson, & Foner, 1972). Chronological age (or some indicant of age) is a feature not only of individuals and populations, but also of the role structures through which people move as they grow older. Like social class, age is a determinant of the kinds of social environments in which people spend their daily lives. Age affects which roles are open or closed to an individual (e.g., pupil, worker, spouse, parent, retiree), and which social networks and cultural norms will offer which opportunities or impose which demands. Age is built into the changing organization of institutions and roles through formal or informal criteria for entry and exit, through expectations of how roles are to be performed, and through sanctions for role performance. There are social rules, some with the force of norms, that govern at what age people are expected and/or allowed to engage in particular activities.

Age-graded roles, which produce "stages" in individual lives, are widely variable, but in some form they are endemic to all societies. The extraordinary range of variability is quickly suggested through comparing our own society with a premodern society in which male children from an early age help herd the cattle, young adult males are considered warriors and are not supposed to marry, and women are monopolized as wives for the polygynous elders who hold the power (Foner & Kertzer, 1978). Stages are sometimes defined by years of age; sometimes by biological or social life-course markers (e.g., puberty, the acquisition of property, attainment of adult stature, the father's retirement, or marriage of the youngest child). Thus, stages are partly—but only partly—determined by biology. For biological reasons, to be sure, very old people are generally not expected to engage in contact sports, nor preschool children to manage large organizations, nor can an arbitrary age criterion specify the appropriate age for motherhood before menarche or after menopause. Nevertheless, the "right age" to have children may be determined less by biology than by the many social and political considerations that affect the lives of the mother, the father, and the family. And all too often, old people's feelings of incompetence, their inadequate performance, even their poor health are determined, not by their potential capacity, but by restrictive regulations, practices, or erroneous beliefs that are built into the social structure and that influence the way people grow old.

Findings from many studies of the effects exerted on the aging processes by social structures—microlevel or macrolevel—as they are tested, replicated, and examined under varied conditions, can be used as clues to understanding the potential strengths and functioning of people who are growing older today. Given the proper social environment, some aspects of cognitive and intellectual functioning of *current* older people can be at least maintained and even improved. Moreover, there is evidence that *future* older people will differ from their predecessors in education, work history, diet, exercise, standard of living, medical care, and experience with chronic versus acute diseases, all of which may affect their levels of cognitive and intellectual functioning. As social structures change, people will grow old in new ways.

AGING AND CHANGING SOCIAL STRUCTURES

Because aging processes are influenced by social structures, a key issue facing society is to optimize opportunities in society for the increasing number of long-lived people. What can be done to create the kinds of places in society where older people's strengths and potentials can be sustained, enhanced, esteemed, and rewarded? The answer lies in the additional fact that social structures can also be altered. Indeed, the sheer numbers of older people are already leading to changes in both microsocial and macrosocial structure throughout the world: in work settings, educational institutions, family or tribal life, living arrangements, community facilities, health and welfare institutions.

Interplay Between Aging and Social Change

At work here is a dialectical process linking changes in the aging of individuals to changes in social structures (Riley, 1985). The evidence is clear that social structures can change individuals' lives. In turn, it is clear that as people grow old in new ways, they reshape and change the social structure.

In abstract terms, this dialectic operates along the following lines:

- In response to social change, people engage in new age-typical patterns and regularities of behavior (change in the way the aging process occurs).
- As these behavior patterns become commonplace, they are defined as age-appropriate norms and rules, reinforced by "authorities," and thereby institutionalized in the role structure of society (change in the social structure).
- In turn, these changes in age norms and social structures redirect

or otherwise alter a panoply of age-related behaviors (further change in the aging process).

Most problematic in this dialectic is how age norms are formed, not only by direct action of the state or other organizations, but also through the indirect influence of people: that is, how culturally prescribed age criteria develop as bases for role assignment and role performance in social structures, and for the definition of life stages. One means of converting behavioral regularities into normative criteria is the process of "cohort norm formation." As the members of the same cohort respond to shared experiences, they gradually and subtly develop common patterns of response, common definitions, and common beliefs, all of which crystallize into common norms about what is appropriate, proper, or true. Thus, to the extent that members of each cohort make common decisions, they exert a collective force as they move through the age-stratified society, pressing for normative adjustments in social roles and social values, and changing the shape of the age structure of society and hence of the stages of the life course. How will this dialectical process operate under today's conditions of longevity, an aging population, and a society subjected to rapid social, economic, and cultural change? Social institutions appear to be lagging behind the people who inhabit them. This raises the issue of how a new balance will be struck between the claims and the intellectual capacities of aging individuals and the shifting demands of society.

Example of Work and Retirement

Perhaps the most striking area in which social structures lag behind older people's potential for productivity over their extended lives is work. Over the 20th century, the labor-force participation of both old and young men has been eroding (the experience of women is somewhat different), and the competence of older workers for productive performance has been consistently underrated. At the turn of the century, one quarter of boys 10 to 15 years old were employed, and most men did not retire at 65 but continued to work. Since 1900, the general trend has been toward increasing concentration of economic activity in the middle adult years. In general, the average age of entry into the labor force rose, and the proportions of older people remaining in the labor force fell. In 1900, two thirds of the men 65 and over were still in the labor force. Now that proportion is only one fifth. While there is a general trend towards younger retirement ages, some variation occurs across industries and jobs. For example, manufacturing and industrial workers are more likely to be retired by age 65 than are agricultural and service workers (Parsons, 1983), whereas workers in jobs requiring cognitive skills or characterized by substantive complexity and few physical demands are less likely to retire early (Hayward & Hardy, 1985). Despite this variation, men on the average find that they are spending one quarter of their adult lifetime in retirement (Torrey, 1982).

These drastic changes in the age structure of economic roles for men offer dramatic evidence that, like the shape of the life course, retirement norms are highly mutable. The long-term societal trends in age of employment have been associated with a complex of interacting structural changes including massive secular declines in both agriculture and self-employment, extension of formal education, steadily increasing proportions of women in the labor force, establishment of age requirements for starting or discontinuing a job, and extension of public and private pension plans that afford alternative sources of income and often specify mandatory ages of retirement.

Such changes in macrolevel social structure have resulted in changes in the behaviors, attitudes, and motivations of successive cohorts of men which, in turn have altered age norms regarding work and retirement. The formation of these norms is still ongoing and evidences conflicting trends. On the one hand, age discrimination in employment constricts employment opportunities for older workers, and economic factors foster employment policies that encourage early retirement (Hutchens, 1985; Parsons, 1983, in press). On the other hand, the outlawing of mandatory retirement rules for some workers and the raising of the legal age for receiving Social Security benefits are designed to encourage the postponement of retirement (Parsons, in press). The behaviors of successive cohorts of men have yet to coalesce into definitive age norms.

Perhaps some of the ambiguity and ambivalence in the age norms for retirement reflects the failure of popular attitudes and public policy to address the question: What is retirement a transition *to?* People entering the role of retiree often have little comprehension of what the absence of work entails. They lack direction for finding new roles that could provide substitute gratifications and stimulations. Unpaid volunteer work has become an alternative activity for only a minority of old people. Expensive leisure pursuits are widely prohibited by income that is reduced with lengthening retirement. For the disabled elderly, medical care is costly and inadequate. Perhaps correctly, retirement has been called a "roleless role," lacking content and sure rewards. For some old people, this lack of content is an advantage, permitting them to escape hated jobs, to spend more time on activities they have always enjoyed, or to fashion new roles consonant with their energies, interests, and financial resources. For others, retirement is marked by lowered self-esteem, and a lack of stimulation that can lead to apathy or depression, jeopardizing vigor and continued cognitive and intellectual functioning.

Incipient Changes

As the members of successive cohorts, retiring at younger ages, are better educated and perhaps healthier than their predecessors, it seems predictable that pressures from old people and from the public will modify the existing work and retirement roles. These roles will better reflect the capabilities of older people and provide exposure to social environments that maintain and promote cognitive functioning. Scattered changes are already under way that begin to offset the lag of social structures behind the potential strengths of long-lived people. For example, older adults now drop in and out of the educational system, retraining for medicine or law, preparing for new careers, or pursuing leisure. Certain structural features of work are used to discourage early retirement; some businesses are arranging regular educational leaves, phased retirement, or pension plans that offer preretirement cultural or travel benefits; many retirees continue to work part-time; and some retirees (one-tenth of one national sample) are now becoming former retirees (Beck, 1985). Study after study suggests that the potential for involvement and participation in the larger society does not end with formal retirement—that retirement itself is not a single and irreversible event, but a process involving successive decisions. Yet the human potential still outstrips the incipient structural opportunities.

CONCLUSION

This chapter has emphasized that aging is not determined solely by biology, but rather it is seen to reflect complex interactions among social, psychological, and biological processes. This is a central premise of the life-course perspective on aging (Baltes & Willis, 1979; Featherman, 1981; Riley, 1979). It is based on a variety of scientific observations and research, including data on the considerable variation among and within individuals in age-related patterns of performance. Not everyone ages in the same way; and in any one person, behavioral or physiological systems age differently. Moreover, the variation in patterns of aging over time (e.g., aging differs from one birth cohort to the next) and across societies (e.g., aging in the urban U.S. differs from aging in rural India) demonstrates that biological forces are not operating in isolation (Riley, Abeles, & Teitelbaum, 1982). Such variations provide mounting support for our position that social structural factors play a major role in influencing the course of age-related changes and stabilities in human performance. This has been our main message. The emerging base of knowledge on aging is marked by two dramatically linked tendencies: First, we have been grossly underestimating the intellectual strengths and potentials of the added years; and second, we are only now beginning to understand that productive and rewarding roles might be provided for many longevous people in our changing society. For the future, one inference is inescapable: Increasing numbers of capable people are living in a society that offers them few meaningful roles, which foreshadow changes either in the people or in the role structures. The only real question is how roles can be structured in ways to maximize the cognitive and intellectual performance of people as they age.

REFERENCES

Abeles, R.P., Steel, L., & Wise, L.L. (1980). Patterns and implications of life-course organization. In P.B. Baltes & O.G. Brim, Jr. (Eds.), *Life-span development and behavior* (Vol. 3, pp. 307–337). New York: Academic Press.

Baltes, P.B., & Willis, S.L. (1979). Life-span developmental psychology, cognitive functioning, and social policy. In M.W. Riley (Ed.), *Aging from birth to death: Interdisciplinary perspectives* (pp. 15–46). Boulder, CO: Westview Press.

Baltes, P.B., & Willis, S.L. (1982). Plasticity and enhancement of intellectual functioning in old age: Penn State's Adult Development and Enrichment Project (ADEPT). In F.I.M. Craik & S.E. Trehub (Eds.), *Aging and cognitive processes.* (pp. 353–389). New York: Plenum.

Baron, A., & Menich, S.R. (1985a). Reaction times of younger and older men: Effects of compound samples and a prechoice signal on delayed matching-to-sample performances. *Journal of the Experimental Analysis of Behavior, 44*(1), 1–14.

Baron, A., & Menich, S.R. (1985b). Age-related effects of temporal contingencies on response speed and memory: An operant analysis. *Journal of Gerontology, 40,* 60–70.

Baron, A., Menich, S.R., & Perone, M. (1983). Reaction times of younger and older men and temporal contingencies of reinforcement. *Journal of the Experimental Analysis of Behavior, 40,* 275–287.

Beck, S.H. (1985). Determinants of labor force activity among retired men. *Research on Aging, 7*(2), 251–280.

Card, J.J., Steel, L., & Abeles, R.P. (1982). Sex differences in the patterning of adult roles as a determinant of sex differences in occupational achievement. *Sex Roles, 8*(9), 1009–1024.

Clayton, V.P., & Birren, J.E. (1980). The development of wisdom across the life-span: A reexamination of an ancient topic. In P.B. Baltes & O.G. Brim, Jr.(Eds.), *Life-span development and behavior* (Vol. 3, pp. 104–137). New York: Academic Press.

Dittmann-Kohli, F., & Baltes, P.B. (in press). Toward a neofunctionalist conception of adult intellectual development: Wisdom as a prototypical case of intellectual growth. In C. Alexander & E. Langer (Eds.), *Beyond formal operations: Alternative endpoints to human development.* New York: Oxford University Press.

Featherman, D.L. (1981). The life-span perspective in social science research. In National

Science Foundation (Ed.), *The 5-year outlook on science and technology: Source materials* (Vol. 2, pp. 621–648). Washington DC: U.S. Government Printing Office.

Foner, A., & Kertzer, D.I. (1978). Transitions over the life course: Lessons of age-set societies. *American Journal of Sociology, 83,* 1081–1104.

Gribbin, K., Schaie, K.W., & Parham, L. (1980). Complexity of the life style and maintenance of intellectual abilities. *Journal of Social Issues, 21,* 47–61.

Hagestad, G.O., & Neugarten, B.L. (1985). Age and the life course. In R.H. Binstock & E. Shanas (Eds.), *Handbook of aging and the social sciences* (2nd ed., pp. 35–93). New York: Van Nostrand Reinhold.

Hayward, M.D., & Hardy, M.A. (1985). Early retirement processes among older men. *Research on Aging, 7,* 491–515.

Hogan, D.P. (1981). *Transitions and social change: The early lives of American men.* New York: Academic Press.

Horn, J.L., & Donaldson, G. (1980). Cognitive development in adulthood. In O.G. Brim, Jr., & J. Kagan (Eds.), *Constancy and change in human development* (pp 455–529). Cambridge, MA: Harvard University Press.

Hutchens, R.M. (1985). *Hiring the older worker: An economic analysis.* Final Report to the National Institute on Aging. Unpublished manuscript, New York State School of Industrial and Labor Relations, Cornell University, Ithaca.

Kohn, M.L., & Schooler, C. (1978). The reciprocal effects of the substantive complexity of work and intellectual flexibility: A longitudinal assessment. *American Journal of Sociology, 84,* 24–52.

Kohn, M.L., & Schooler, C. (1981). Job conditions and intellectual flexibility: A longitudinal assessment of their reciprocal effects. In D.J. Jackson & E.F. Borgatta (Eds.), *Factor analysis and measurement in sociological research: A multi-dimension perspective* (pp. 281–313). Beverly Hills, CA: Sage.

Kohn, M.L., & Schooler, C. (1982). Job conditions and personality: A longitudinal assessment of their reciprocal effects. *American Journal of Sociology, 87,* 1257–1286.

Metropolitan Life Insurance Company. (1986). Recent changes in longevity. *Statistical Bulletin, 67,* 16–21.

National Center for Health Statistics. (1985). *Vital statistics of the United States, 1982* (Vol. 2, Sec. 6, Life Tables). (DHHS Publication No. PHS 85–1104.) Washington, DC: U.S. Government Printing Office.

Parsons, D.O. (1983). *The industrial demand for older workers.* Unpublished manuscript, Department of Economics, Ohio State University, Columbus.

Parsons, D.O. (in press). The employment relationship: Job attachment, work effort, and the nature of contracts. In O. Aschenfelter & R. Layard (Eds.), *Handbook of labor economics.* New York: North Holland Press.

Presser, H. (1974). Early motherhood: Ignorance or bliss? *Family Planning Perspectives, 6,* 8–14.

Preston, S.H. (1976). *Mortality patterns in national populations: With special reference to recorded causes of death.* New York: Academic Press.

Riley, M.W. (1979). Introduction: Life-course perspectives. In M.W. Riley (Ed.), *Aging from birth to death: Interdisciplinary perspectives* (pp. 3–14). Boulder, CO: Westview Press.

Riley, M.W. (1985). Overview and highlights of a sociological perspective. In A.B. Sorenson, F.E. Weinert, & L.R. Sherrod (Eds.), *Human development: Interdisciplinary Perspectives* (pp. 153–175). Hillsdale, NJ: Erlbaum.

Riley, M.W., Abeles, R.P., & Teitelbaum, M.S. (Eds.). (1982). *Aging from birth to death: Vol. 2. Sociotemporal perspectives.* Boulder, CO: Westview Press.

Riley, M.W., Johnson, M.J., & Foner, A. (1972). *Aging and society: Vol. 3: A sociology of age stratification* (pp. 3–26). New York: Russell Sage.

Riley, M.W., & Riley, J.W., Jr. (1986). Longevity and social structure: The potential of the added years. *Daedalus, 115*(1), 51–76.

Rosenwaike, I. (1985). *The extreme aged in America: A portrait of an expanding population.* Westport, CT: Greenwood Press.

Schaie, K.W. (1983). The Seattle Longitudinal Study: A 21-year exploration of psychometric intelligence in adulthood. In K.W. Schaie (Ed.), *Longitudinal studies of adult psychological development* (pp. 64–135). New York: Guilford Press.

Schaie, K.W. (1984). Midlife influences upon intellectual functioning in old age. *International Journal of Behavioral Development, 7*, 463–478.

Schaie, K.W., & Willis, S.L. (1985, March). *Cognitive training in elderly adults: Spatial orientation and reasoning.* Paper presented at the annual meeting of the Eastern Psychological Association, Boston, MA.

Schaie, K.W., & Willis, S.L. (1986). Can decline in adult intellectual functioning be reversed? *Developmental Psychology, 22*(2), 223–232.

Schooler, C., Kohn, M.L., Miller, K.A., & Miller, J. (1983). Housework as work. In M.L. Kohn & C. Schooler (Eds.), *Work and personality: An inquiry into the impact of social stratification* (pp. 242–260). Norwood, NJ: Ablex.

Schooler, C., Miller, J., Miller, K.A., & Richtand, C.N. (1984). Work for the household: Its nature and consequences for husbands and wives. *American Journal of Sociology, 90*(1), 97–124.

Siegel, J.S., & Taeuber, C.M. (1986). Demographic perspectives on the long-lived society. *Daedalus, 115*(1), 77–118.

Torrey, B.B. (1982). The lengthening of retirement. In M.W. Riley, R.P. Abeles, & M.S. Teitelbaum (Eds.), *Aging from birth to death: Vol. 2. Sociotemporal perspectives* (pp. 181–196). Boulder, CO: Westview Press.

U.S. Bureau of the Census. (1984). Demographic and socioeconomic aspects of aging in the United States. *Current Population Reports* (Series P-23, No. 138). Washington, DC: U.S. Government Printing Office.

Willis, S.L. (1986). Improvement with cognitive training: Which old dogs learn what tricks. In L.W. Poon (Ed.), *Cognition and memory in everyday life.* New York: Cambridge University Press.

Willis, S.L., Cornelius, S.W., Blow, F.C., & Baltes, P.B. (1983). Training research in aging: Attentional processes. *Journal of Educational Psychology, 75*, 257–270.

Willis, S.L., & Schaie, K.W. (1986). Training the elderly on the ability factors of spatial orientation and inductive reasoning. *Psychology and Aging, 1*(3).

Chapter Ten

Continuity of Learning-Generalization Through the Life Span: The Effect of Job on Men's Intellectual Process in the United States and Poland

Joanne Miller
Kazimierz M. Slomczynski
Melvin L. Kohn

There is an accumulating body of evidence that job conditions affect adult personality mainly through a direct process of learning and generalization—learning from the job and generalizing what has been learned to other realms of life. Although such other psychological processes as compensation and reaction formation also contribute to the effects of work on adult personality (Kohn, 1980, 1983; K. A. Miller & Kohn, 1983), the learning-generalization process is of predominant

Earlier versions of this chapter were presented to the World Congress of the International Sociological Association (Mexico City, August 1982) and the Annual Convention of the American Sociological Association (San Francisco, September 1983). The Polish survey was carried out under the auspices and with the financial support of the Polish Academy of Sciences. We are indebted to Wlodzimierz Wesolowski, who initiated the Polish study and encouraged the investigators throughout the inquiry; to Krystyna Janicka and Jadwiga Koralewicz-Sebik for collaboration in the design and administration of the Polish survey; to Bruce Roberts, Margaret Renfors, and Diane Mueller for conscientious and thoughtful research assistance; to Virginia Marbley for effectively and uncomplainingly transcribing many revisions of this paper; and to Carrie Schoenbach, Karen A. Miller, Carmi Schooler, Ronald Schoenberg, Matilda Riley, Paul Baltes, Jeylan T. Mortimer, and John A. Clausen for critical readings of earlier versions of this paper. The models in this paper were estimated by MILS, an advanced version of LISREL (Jöreskog & van Thillo, 1972) developed by Ronald Schoenberg.

importance. People who do intellectually demanding work come to exercise their intellectual prowess not only on the job but also in their nonoccupational lives (Kohn & Schooler, 1978, 1981; J. Miller, Schooler, Kohn, & K.A. Miller, 1979); they even seek out intellectually demanding activities in their leisure-time pursuits (K.A. Miller & Kohn, 1983). Moreover, people who do self-directed work come to value self-direction more highly, both for themselves and for their children, and to have self-conceptions and social orientations consonant with such value (Coburn & Edwards, 1976; Grabb, 1981; Hoff & Gruneisen, 1978; Kohn, 1969; Kohn & Schooler, 1969, 1983a; J. Miller et al., 1979; Mortimer & Lorence 1979a, 1979b; Naoi & Schooler, 1985; Slom-czynski, Miller, & Kohn, 1981). In short, the lessons of work are directly carried over to nonoccupational realms. All these findings are consistent with the sociological premise that experience in so central a domain of life as work must affect orientations to and behavior in other domains as well (Kohn & Schooler, 1973; Marx, 1964, 1971). All the findings are also consistent with the theoretical expectation that "transfer of learning" extends to a wide spectrum of psychological functioning (Gagne, 1968; see also Breer & Locke, 1965).

Learning-generalization, which we think of as equivalent to "transfer of learning," is integral to a number of psychological theories. Such concepts as the "generalized response" of reinforcement theory (e.g., Skinner, 1953), "generalized imitation" of social-learning theory (e.g., Gewirtz, 1969), and "generalized psychological pattern" of cognitive dissonance theory (e.g., Festinger, 1957) posit that knowledge and orientations acquired in one situation are generalized or transferred to other situations. According to the theory of social action, "generalization is perhaps the most important of the learning mechanisms" (Parsons, Shils, Allport, Kluckhohn, Murray, Sears, Sheldon, Stouffer, & Tolman, 1951, p. 12).

In this chapter, we ask whether learning-generalization continues throughout men's working lives. Recent work in developmental and social psychology suggests that learning, particularly as represented in "crystallized" (or synthesized) intelligence, continues throughout the life-span (for reviews and assessments of this literature, see Baltes, Dittmann-Kohli, & Dixon, 1984; Baltes & Labouvie, 1973; Horn & Donaldson, 1980, pp. 468–476). In principle, since transfer of learning is "an essential characteristic of the learning process" (Gagne, 1968, p. 68), not only initial learning but also the generalization of what has been learned should continue as workers grow older. It is nevertheless possible that learning-generalization does not occur at the same rate or to the same extent at all ages. The process may be especially pronounced in younger workers, who are at early stages of their oc-cupational careers, before they are preoccupied with family responsibilities, but may diminish as workers grow older, advance in their careers, and have changing family responsibilities. It is also possible that either learning or generalization diminishes as workers grow older, simply because of biological decrements (Horn & Donaldson, 1980, pp. 476–481; Jarvik & Cohen, 1973, pp. 227–234; but see Labouvie-Vief & Chandler, 1978; Riley & Bond, 1983). To see whether learning and the generalization of learning continue unabated throughout adult life requires an analysis of how job conditions affect the psychological functioning of workers at different ages, or stages of career, or stages of life course. This chapter attempts such an analysis. We believe that this analysis is the first systematic empirical effort to see whether learning-generalization continues to be responsive to the social-environmental conditions of natural settings as workers grow older.

We focus on what we regard as a prototypic example of learning-generalization: the relationship between occupational self-direction and intellective process. By occupational self-direction we mean the use of initiative, thought, and independent judgment in work. We focus on occupational self-direction—or, more precisely, the job conditions that facilitate or inhibit the exercise of occupational self-direction—because prior analyses have demonstrated that the experience of occupational self-direction is at the heart of what is learned from the experience of work (Kohn & Schooler, 1973, 1982). We focus on intellective process because it offers a clear-cut instance of what we mean by learning-generalization: Thinking on the job is carried over to thinking off the job. Moreover, intellective process dramatically exemplifies the learning-generalization process, for occupational self-direction has particularly strong effects on intellective process (Kohn & Schoenbach, 1983).

The analysis is cross-national: It examines the continuity of learning-generalization in two countries, Poland and the United States. For both countries we separate analyses of job conditions and intellective process for younger, middle-aged, and older men. For each country, our analysis asks: Is the relationship of job to intellective process consistent for all three age groups? As in any analysis of the relationship between social structure and personality, cross-national comparative analysis has the utility of ascertaining whether the findings in any one country are specific to the culture and to the economic and political system of that country. In an analysis of people of differing ages, there is the further advantage that even the "same" cohorts have had different experiences in different countries. When the two countries are Poland and the United States, we also have the opportunity of seeing whether the findings are consistent for a socialist and a capitalist society.

METHODS OF DATA COLLECTION AND CHARACTERISTICS OF AGE SUBSAMPLES

The original U.S. survey was based on interviews carried out in 1964 with 3,101 men, representative of all men in the United States, 16 years of age or older, who were currently employed in civilian occupations. (For detailed information, see Kohn, 1969, Appendix C.) These data provide the primary base for the U.S. analyses in this chapter. In addition, for analyses of the reciprocal effects of occupational self-direction and intellective process, we utilize a 10-year follow-up study of a representative subsample of 687 of those men originally interviewed (see Kohn & Schooler, 1983, Appendix A).

The Polish survey, conducted in 1978 with a sample of 1,557 men, was an exact replication of the main parts of the original U.S. survey (Slomczynski et al., 1981). Questions pertaining to occupational self-direction were directly adopted from the U.S. study, while those pertaining to intellective process required some modification to provide cross-cultural equivalence. When we discuss the measurement models, we shall note departures from the original American questions.

The Polish sample was a multistage probability sample, designed to represent men aged 19 to 65 years, living in urban areas and employed in civilian occupations. The sample excludes the rural peasantry because this large category—constituting more than 25% of the total Polish labor force—has no functional equivalent in the United States. However, the sample does include farmers living in proximity to urban centers, making the Polish sample more comparable to the U.S. sample than a sample fully representative of the labor force in Poland would have been. Men aged 16 to 18 were excluded because of their restricted employment status under Polish labor law; men over 65 years of age were excluded because almost all urban employees in Poland are required to retire at that age.

In our analyses for both Poland and the United States, we distinguish three age groups: 30 years of age or younger, 31 through 45, and 46 or older. Given the age distributions of our total samples, such a division is optimal for achieving subsamples of relatively equal size. If it were possible to do so, we would consider not only age, but also stage of career and stage of life course, both of which are defined by sequences of events rather than by chronology. (For pertinent discussions of life course, see Baltes, 1982; Elder, 1974; Elder & Rockwell, 1979; Riley, 1979. For pertinent discussion of stages of career, see Landinsky, 1976; Wilensky, 1961.) Since we lack the requisite data to differentiate these closely related phenomena, "age" has to stand as a proxy not only for itself, but also for stages of career and life-course (Elder, 1981).

From a historical perspective, the three Polish cohorts have had unique generational experiences. The majority of men in the oldest age group completed their elementary educations before World War II and entered the labor force before the rapid industrialization of the 1950s had begun. A critical experience for this generation was the Nazi occupation and, later, the Stalinist era, terminated by the national upheaval of the "Polish October" in 1956. Men in the intermediate age group were just entering their adult lives in the mid-1950s; at the early stages of their occupational careers, they experienced the post-October economic and political stabilization, which ended with the students' protests in 1968 and the workers' revolt in 1970. The youngest group came of age under the relative prosperity of the Gierek regime, which started showing visible cracks in 1976 during the workers' riots.

Although both the middle and the youngest age groups were educated in the common-school system introduced under the socialist regime, they differ with respect to their vocational preparation. The transition from more general to more specialized education experienced by these two age groups paralleled the economic development of the country. Forced industrialization of the 1950s—when the majority of the middle age group started to work—provided many new job opportunities for persons without specialized education. In contrast, the youngest group entered a more competitive labor market created by a declining rate of new industrial positions and a structural shift from the industrial to the service sector.

Since the U.S. men had been interviewed 14 years before the Polish men, the experiences of all three U.S. age groups are of a rather different historical era from those of their Polish counterparts. The men in the oldest age group (born in 1918 or before) had experienced the Great Depression and World War II as adults. The middle age group (men born between 1919 and 1933) includes both those for whom World War II was a childhood experience and those whose young adult lives were disrupted by wartime experience. The youngest men (born between 1934 and 1948) are essentially a post–World War II generation. As in Poland, educational requirements for many jobs increased greatly from cohort to cohort.

It is apparent that in distinguishing the same three age *groups* for Poland and the United States we are in fact comparing age *cohorts* from markedly dissimilar historical periods. This means that if we discover a different relationship between age and learning-generalization in the two countries, it will be difficult to assess precisely what explains the divergence. But if in both countries we find the effects of job conditions on intellective process to be similar for all three age groups, this will provide powerful evidence for the continuity of learninig-generalization.

MEASUREMENT OF INTELLECTIVE PROCESS

We examine two aspects of intellective process: ideational flexibility and authoritarian conservatism. These offer two distinct vantage points for looking at intellective process. Ideational flexibility is a measure of intellectual performance in the interview situation, reflecting the use of logical reasoning, ability to see both sides of an issue, and independent judgment. As such, it is a measure of how effectively a person uses his or her intellect in a relatively demanding situation; it is the thinking process, rather than the content of the task, that is at issue. Authoritarian conservatism, by contrast, is explicitly meant to measure the content of one's normative beliefs—namely, obeisance to authority and intolerance of nonconformity to the dictates of authority—rather than the process by which one came to hold those beliefs. Yet, authoritarian conservatism also reflects intellective process, for the opposite pole of intolerance is open-mindedness in one's orientation to the social world (Gabennesch, 1972; Kelman & Barclay, 1963; Kohn, 1969, pp. 189, 201–203; J. Miller, Slomczynski, & Schoenberg, 1981; Roof, 1974). By looking at both ideational flexibility and authoritarian conservatism, we assess the continuity of learning-generalization with respect to conceptually distinct, albeit closely related, aspects of intellective process.

Ideational Flexibility

In analyzing both the U.S. and the Polish data, we follow the strategy of measuring intellectual flexibility that was developed in Kohn and Schooler's (1978) longitudinal analysis of the U.S. data. We rely on a variety of indicators—including men's answers to seemingly simple but highly revealing cognitive problems, their handling of perceptual and projective tests, their propensity to "agree" when asked agree-disagree questions, and the impression they made on the interviewer during a long session that required a great deal of thought and reflection. None of these indicators is assumed to be completely valid; but we do assume that all the indicators reflect, to some substantial degree, men's flexibility in attempting to cope with the intellectual demands of complex tasks. We do not claim that an index of intellectual functioning based on such indicators measures innate intellectual ability or that intellectual flexibility evidenced in the interview situation is necessarily identical to intellectual flexibility as it might be manifested in other situations; we do not have enough information about the situational variability of intellectual functioning to be certain. We do claim that an index based on such measures reflects men's actual intellectual functioning in a nonwork situation that seemed to elicit considerable intellectual effort from nearly all respondents. We claim also that such an index transcends the criticism that "the perseverance of a youth-centric . . . measurement of intellectual aging has demonstrated, most conspicuously by its very existence, a serious gap in age- and cohort-fair assessment" (Baltes et al., 1984, p. 36); our measures are decidedly not "youth-centric."

The original U.S. measurement model of intellectual flexibility was based on seven indicators: (a) the Goodenough estimate of the respondent's intelligence (See Witkin, Dyk, Faterson, Goodenough, & Karp, 1962), based on a detailed evaluation of the Draw-a-Person Test; (b) the appraisal of Witkin et al. (1962) of sophistication of body concept in the Draw-a-Person Test; (c) a summary score for the respondent's performance on a portion of the Embedded Figures Test (see Witkin et al., 1962); (d) the interviewer's appraisal of the respondent's intelligence; (e) the frequency with which the respondent agreed when asked the many agree-disagree questions included in the interview; (f) a rating of the adequacy of his answer to the apparently simple cognitive problem: "What are all the arguments you can think of for and against allowing cigarette commercials on TV?" and (g) a rating of the adequacy of his answer to another relatively simple cognitive problem: "Suppose you wanted to open a hamburger stand and there were two locations available. What questions would you consider in deciding which of the two locations offers a better business opportunity?" In the Polish study, the last two questions have been modified. Since there are no hamburger stands in Poland, answering this question would require a different level of knowledge by Poles from that by Americans. For this reason, "kiosk" (newsstand) was substituted for "hamburger stand" in the Polish interviews, kiosks being at least as familiar to Poles as are hamburger stands to Americans. Similarly, "advertisement of goods" was substituted for "cigarette commercials," as an equivalent debatable issue. The pilot study, the fieldwork and subsequent statistical tests indicate that Polish men react to the modified questions much as their American counterparts do to the original questions.

The original U.S. model of intellectual flexibility, a longitudinal model, contained two underlying dimensions, one ideational, the other perceptual. We have produced cross-sectional analogues of that model for the total samples of both Polish and U.S. men, with paths from concepts to indicators that are very similar for the two countries. We are thus assured of the cross-national validity of the basic measurement instrument. But we cannot apply this instrument for subgroup analyses of the Polish data, for in the Polish study both indicators of the perceptual dimension—the Draw-a-Person Test and the Embedded Figures Test—were administered only to a randomly chosen subsample of 400 men. This one-fourth subsample provides too few men to divide into three age groups on which we could confidently base causal analysis. We have therefore developed measurement models for both Poland and the United States using only those indicators related to ideational flexibility (see Table 1). We have found that factor scores based on these one-dimension models of ideational flexibility correlate near unity with factor scores based on the ideational dimension of the two-dimension models (for the U.S., $r = .97$; for Poland, $r = .96$). This justifies using the simpler one-dimension model. Moreover, for both the two-dimension and one-dimension models, we have confirmed the cross-national reliability of measurement by the methods described in J. Miller et al. (1981).

A rigorous test of between-group similarities should allow the possibility that men of differing age groups vary in how their answers to the interview questions relate to the underlying concepts we wish to measure (Baltes & Labouvie, 1973, pp. 174–176; Labouvie, 1980). Thus, we construct separate measurement models of ideational flexibility for the three age groups. The resulting models are very similar to each other and to those for the total samples of both the United States and Poland (Table 1). All these models fit the data well, the chi-square per degree of freedom ranging from 0.40 to 1.00. Such differences as do exist among age groups in the relative strength of the paths from concepts to indicators are somewhat larger in Poland. To evaluate the extent to which these differences disturb the formal equivalence of measurement across age groups, we developed three models for each age group. The first is the best-fitting model for that age group (as presented in Table 1); the others impose on a particular age group the solutions for the other two age groups. We then computed factor scores for each group from its best-fitting model and from the imposed models. The correlations between these factor scores range from .88 to .94, indicating that the idiosyncratic differences in measurement among age groups are not of any great importance for causal analysis.

Authoritarian Conservatism

Authoritarian conservatism is measured by responses to questions assessing agreement or disagreement with statements advocating obeisance to authority or intolerance of nonconformity to authority. For both the U.S. and Poland, the indicators were selected from a set of 57 interview questions, including items taken from a short version (Srole, 1956) of the California F scale (Adorno, Frenkel-Brunswik, Levinson, & Sanford, 1950) and from a scale of obeisance to authority (Pearlin, 1962). Exploratory factor analyses of the U.S. and Polish data differentiated those items indicative of authoritarian conservatism from items indicative of other related dimensions of orientation (Slomczynski et

Table 1. Measurement Model of Ideational Flexibility for Three Age Groups in the United States and Poland

	U.S. Men—1964 Data				Polish Men—1978 Data			
	Age Groups			All men	Age Groups			All men
	≤30	31–45	≥46		≤30	31–45	≥46	
	Standardized Path: Concept to Indicator							
Reasons for location of a small business	.21	.29	.23	.30	.41	.49	.28	.32
Reasons for and against commercials on TV	.29	.36	.27	.32	.39	.29	.32	.31
Tendency to agree with agree-disagree questions	-.42	-.47	-.41	-.46	-.20	-.45	-.30	-.35
Interviewer's estimate of overall intelligence	.68	.66	.63	.64	.48	.43	.80	.61
Figures identified in Embedded Figures Test	.50	.56	.62	.60	.51	.62	.53	.58
Number of Cases	711	1209	1171	3101	452	575	530	1557
χ^2/df	0.83	0.50	1.00	0.42	0.84	0.40	0.77	0.57

al., 1981). A detailed cross-national analysis comparing the measurement instruments and their validity in each country is presented in J. Miller et al. (1981; see also Schoenberg, 1982). That analysis demonstrates that there are both shared and nation-specific indicators of authoritarian conservatism, but that the Polish and U.S. indices of authoritarian conservatism are conceptually equivalent and thus can be used for comparative analysis.

For the present analysis, we have constructed age-specific measurement models for Poland and the United States, using the same sets of indicators for all three age groups as for the total sample *of each country*. The patterns of responses for the separate age groups, presented in Table 2, show that although there is some variation in the relative importance of particular indicators in the several age groups, all indicators are statistically significant for all groups. In each age group in each country, endorsing absolute obedience to parents is the strongest indicator, while the weakest indicator in most age groups is extreme disapproval of women's engaging in premarital sex.

For each age group, there is a good fit of model to data, the chi-square per degree of freedom ranging from 0.65 to 1.19. Correlations between factor scores based on the best-fitting model for each age group and scores based on models imposed from other age groups are very high in both countries, ranging from .97 to .99. We therefore conclude that, for both Poland and the United States, the measurement of authoritarian conservatism is nearly invariant across age groups.

MEASUREMENT OF OCCUPATIONAL SELF-DIRECTION

Opportunities for occupational self-direction are largely determined by the substantive complexity, closeness of supervision, and routinization of the work one does (Kohn, 1969). For both the United States and Poland, information about the substantive complexity of work is based on detailed questioning of each respondent about his work with things, with data or ideas, and with people. These questions provide the basis for seven ratings of each man's job: appraisals of the complexity of his work with things, with data, and with people; an evaluation of the overall complexity of his work, regardless of whether he works primarily with data, with people, or with things; and estimates of the amount of time he spends working at each of the three types of activity. These seven ratings are treated as indicators of the underlying construct, the substantive complexity of that job.

In both studies, closeness of supervision is measured by a worker's subjective appraisals of his freedom to disagree with his supervisor, how closely he is supervised, the extent to which his supervisor tells

Table 2. Measurement Model of Authoritarian Conservatism for Three Age Groups in the United States and Poland

	U.S. Men—1964 Data				Polish Men—1978 Data			
	Age Groups			All Men	Age Groups			All men
	≤30	31–45	≥46		≤30	31–45	≥46	
	Standardized Path: Concept to Indicator							
The most important thing to teach children is absolute obedience to their parents.[a]	.55	.73	.61	.65	.66	.66	.73	.73
In this complicated world, the only way to know what to do is to rely on leaders and experts. (M)	.48	.48	.53	.52	.50	.46	.57	.53
It's wrong to do things differently from the way our forefathers did. (M)	.50	.46	.43	.44	.48	.49	.35	.40
Any good leader should be strict with people under him in order to gain their respect.	.41	.48	.50	.46	.48	.57	.60	.53
No decent man can respect a woman who has had sex relations before marriage.	.28	.35	.38	.37	.39	.44	.40	.42
Prison is too good for sex criminals; they should be publicly whipped or worse. (M)	.32	.44	.36	.39	—	—	—	—
Young people should not be allowed to read books that are likely to confuse them.	.33	.44	.36	.44	—	—	—	—
There are two kinds of people in the world: the weak and the strong.	.53	.54	.58	.62	—	—	—	—
People who question the old and accepted ways of doing things usually just end up causing trouble. (M)	.55	.60	.48	.51	—	—	—	—
One should always show respect to those in authority.	—	—	—	—	.50	.63	.65	.62
You should always obey your superiors whether or not you think they're right.	—	—	—	—	.50	.51	.55	.50
Do you believe that it's all right to do whatever the law allows, or are there some things that are wrong even if they are legal? (M)	—	—	—	—	.46	.44	.40	.42
Number of cases	711	1209	1171	3101	452	575	530	1557
X²/df	0.89	1.19	0.87	0.68	0.82	0.92	0.65	0.72

"(M)" denotes a slight modification of the American wording in the Polish interview.

[a] A high score on the indicator generally implies agreement or frequent occurrence; where alternatives are posed, the first alternative is scored high.

him what to do rather than discussing it with him, and the importance in his job of doing what one is told to do.

We use slightly different measures of routinization for the United States and Poland. For the United States, respondents' work was coded from most variable (the work involves doing different things in different ways and one cannot predict what may come up) to least variable (the work is unvaryingly repetitive). For Poland, we do not include predictability in the index, since it adds nothing to variability.

Age-specific measurement models of occupational self-direction for each country are presented in Table 3. For each age group, there is a good fit of model to data, the chi-square per degree of freedom varying between 0.72 and 2.78 for the U.S. and between 1.21 and 1.78 for Poland. The relative strengths of indicators as measures of the underlying constructs are strikingly similar for all age groups and all are statistically significant. Such differences as do exist between age-specific measurement models do not appear to disturb the conceptual equivalence of the indices. Correlations between factor scores based on the best-fitting model for a particular age group (as presented in Table 3) and those based on measurement models derived from the other age groups are in all cases near unity. We thus conclude that for workers of younger, middle, and older age the measurement models of occupational self-direction provide meaningfully patterned and conceptually equivalent indices of substantive complexity, closeness of supervision, and routinization.

LEARNING-GENERALIZATION AMONG YOUNGER, MIDDLE-AGED, AND OLDER MEN

The principal issue is whether the learning-generalization process continues at more or less the same rate throughout the life span. As evidence of learning-generalization, we look to see whether occupational self-direction affects intellective process in the predicted direction. The rationale is that using initiative, thought, and independent judgment in work is conducive to using initiative, thought, and independent judgment outside of work. More specifically, doing substantively complex work—work that in its very nature requires thought and independent judgment—should result in greater ideational flexibility and a more open-minded orientation. Close supervision, by contrast, should diminish ideational flexibility and be conducive to a rigid orientation. Finally, routinization might be expected to dull intellective functioning.

Since the Polish data are cross-sectional, we initially assume unidirectional effects of occupational self-direction on intellective process. (Later, for the U.S., we shall be able to modify this assumption and

Table 3. Measurement Model of Occupational Self-Direction for Three Age Groups in the United States and Poland

	U.S. Men—1964 Data				Polish Men—1978 Data			
	Age groups			All men	Age groups			All men
	≤30	31–45	≥46		≤30	31–45	≥46	
	Standardized Path: Concept to Indicator							
Substantive Complexity								
Complexity, work with data	.83	.85	.80	.82	.80	.89	.93	.87
Complexity, work with people	.76	.79	.75	.78	.86	.89	.87	.89
Complexity, work with things	.24	.21	.11	.25	.20	.27	.34	.25
Hours, data	.49	.47	.44	.44	.58	.62	.55	.59
Hours, people	.44	.44	.46	.43	.20	.27	.33	.29
Hours, things	-.63	-.59	-.56	-.58	-.59	-.66	-.63	-.64
Overall complexity	.85	.83	.84	.86	.79	.90	.88	.85
Closeness of Supervision								
Freedom to disagree with supervisor	.44	.46	.45	.46	.25	.32	.20	.26
R's assessment of closeness of supervision	.73	.62	.64	.65	.53	.55	.54	.55
Supervisor tells R what to do	.64	.56	.58	.59	.57	.56	.45	.58
Importance of doing what one is told	.69	.60	.66	.65	.30	.47	.35	.40
Routinization								
Variability/predictability of tasks	1.00	1.00	1.00	1.00	1.00	1.00	1.00	1.00
Number of Cases	711	1209	1171	3101	452	575	530	1557
χ^2/df	0.72	1.18	2.78	3.82	1.21	1.40	1.78	2.29

test the reciprocal relationship between occupational self-direction and intellective process.) Under the assumption of unidirectionality, we perform multiple-regression analyses, treating ideational flexibility and authoritarian conservatism as the dependent variables in parallel analyses. The conditions that facilitate or interfere with the exercise of occupational self-direction (i.e., the substantive complexity of work, routinization, and closeness of supervision) are the principal independent variables in both analyses. To statistically control social characteristics which affect both job conditions and intellective process and which thereby might result in spurious effects of job on intellective process, we include education and other pertinent social characteristics as additional independent variables[1]

The analyses (see Table 4) clearly show that occupational self-direction affects intellective process in both countries. Overall, the multiple-partial correlations of occupational self-direction and ideational flexibility (education and other pertinent social characteristics statistically controlled) are .39 for the United States and a strikingly similar .41 for Poland. The comparable multiple-partial correlations of occupational self-direction and authoritarian conservatism are .22 for the United States and a somewhat higher .29 for Poland. Of crucial importance for this analysis: The magnitudes of the multiple-partial correlations are about as great for the older as for younger and middle-aged men—in both countries and with respect to both ideational flexibility and authoritarian conservatism.

In both countries, the substantive complexity of work has the greatest effect on ideational flexibility of any of the three job conditions (see the standardized regression coefficients in Table 4), with closeness of supervision adding appreciably to its impact in Poland and modestly in the United States, and with routinization adding modestly (but significantly) in the United States. These findings are generally consistent for all age groups. For example, the standardized regression coefficients for the substantive complexity of work are consistently larger than those for closeness of supervision and routinization for all three age groups in both countries. Moreover, the unstandardized regression coefficients show that, in both countries, the magnitude of the effect

---

[1] For the United States, the pertinent social characteristics are age; urbanness and region of place raised; race; religious and national backgrounds; father's education and occupational status; maternal and paternal grandfathers' occupational status; and number of siblings. Some of the social characteristics in the U.S. analysis are omitted from the Polish analysis because they are nearly invariant in the culturally more homogeneous Polish society (namely, race, religious background, and national background), and others are omitted because the pertinent information was not collected. The social characteristics included in the Polish analysis are age, urbanness of place raised, father's educational level, and father's occupational status.

Table 4. Effects of Occupational Self-Direction on Intellective Process for Three Age Groups in the United States and Poland (controlling education and other pertinent social characteristics)

	U.S. Men—1964 Data				Polish Men—1978 Data			
	Age Groups			All Men	Age Groups			All Men
	≤30	31-45	≥46		≤30	31-45	≥46	
	Unstandardized Regression Coefficients							
Ideational Flexibility								
Substantive complexity	.022*	.021*	.027*	.028*	.090*	.040*	.055*	.040*
Closeness of supervision	-.009	-.034*	-.006	-.017*	-.118*	-.146*	.016	-.102*
Routinization	.007	-.006*	-.004*	-.013*	-.005	-.018	.004	-.006
Authoritarian Conservatism								
Substantive complexity	-.134*	-.130*	-.099*	-.121*	-.053	-.023	-.052	-.082*
Closeness of supervision	.032	.048	-.041	-.009	.614*	.661*	.991*	.644*
Routinization	.021	-.005	.039*	.058*	.045	.030	.071	.046
	Standardized Regression Coefficients								
Ideational Flexibility								
Substantive complexity	.248*	.214*	.333*	.267*	.514*	.250*	.631*	.378*
Closeness of supervision	-.041	-.105*	-.025	-.053*	-.124*	-.159*	.021	-.142*
Routinization	.076	-.046*	-.044*	-.060*	-.016*	-.043*	.018	-.022
Multiple-partial correlation	.326*	.381*	.404*	.393*	.478*	.299*	.466*	.407*
Authoritarian Conservatism								
Substantive Complexity	-.264*	-.216*	-.201*	-.225*	-.097*	-.055	-.120	-.174*
Closeness of Supervision	.025	.025	-.028	-.005	.209*	.273*	.257*	.203*
Routinization	.039	-.006	.066*	.051*	.045	.027	.067	.041
Multiple-partial correlation	.244*	.187*	.192*	.215*	.274*	.273*	.318*	.292*
Number of Cases	711	1209	1171	3101	452	575	530	1557

Note. For Poland the social characteristics are age, urbanness of place raised, and father's education and occupational status. For the U.S., social characteristics are age, urbanness and region of place raised, religious background, race, national background, father's education and occupational status, maternal and paternal grandfathers' occupational status, and number of siblings.
*Statistically significant, $p \leq .05$.

of substantive complexity on ideational flexibility is about as large for the older men as for younger and middle-aged men. The one respect in which the overall findings for ideational flexibility do not hold for all age groups is that the effect of closeness of supervision on Polish men's ideational flexibility does not seem to hold for the oldest age group, men 46 years of age and older. (The findings for authoritarian conservatism, though, belie any thought that closeness of supervision ceases to be important for intellective process in older Polish men.) This one discrepancy notwithstanding, the results for both the United States and Poland generally indicate consistent effects of job conditions on ideational flexibility for men of all ages.

As for authoritarian conservatism: In the United States, substantive complexity again has the strongest effect, with closeness of supervision of trivial importance and routinization having a statistically significant but only modest impact. In Poland, however, closeness of supervision assumes greater importance, its effect surpassing those of both substantive complexity and routinization. In principle, close supervision should increase authoritarian conservatism in both countries. In the social and political circumstances of Poland, closeness of supervision does result in authoritarian conservative beliefs; but somehow, in the social and political circumstances of the United States, closeness of supervision is overshadowed in importance by the substantive complexity of work and even by routinization.[2] We shall return, at least speculatively, to this cross-national difference. It must be emphasized, though, that *both* the U.S. and the Polish findings are entirely consistent with the learning-generalization hypothesis, the only issue being the relative importance of the substantive complexity of work and closeness of supervision for that process.

For this analysis, the focal question is whether, within each country, the pattern of relationships between job conditions and intellective process is consistent for men of different ages. The findings for both U.S. and Polish men vis-à-vis authoritarian conservatism are generally consistent for younger, middle-aged, and older men. Thus, the substantive complexity of work is of primary importance for authoritarian conservatism among U.S. men, albeit with somewhat diminished effect for the oldest men, for whom routinization has assumed increased importance. For Polish men, closeness of supervision has a statistically significant effect on authoritarian conservatism in all three age groups,

---

[2] One might think that closeness of supervision is more pertinent to authoritarian conservatism in Poland than in the United States because the indicators of authoritarian conservatism specific to Poland emphasize the centrality of authority relations (see Table 2). But if we repeat the multiple-regression analyses, using indices of authoritarian conservatism based on the same questions in both countries, the cross-national difference persists.

the magnitude of that effect being even greater among the oldest men than among younger and middle-aged men (see the unstandardized regression coefficients in Table 4). Moreover, in all three age groups the effect of close supervision surpasses the effects of substantive complexity and routinization (see the standardized coefficients in Table 4). Thus, the findings for authoritarian conservatism again show intranation, cross-age consistency.

The final finding of this analysis is decisive: The 18 statistically significant regression coefficients are all consistent in sign with the learning-generalization hypothesis. We conclude that the effects of occupational self-direction on intellective process apply consistently to younger, middle-aged, and older men. In this sense, it seems that learning-generalization occurs at all stages of career and life course. This conclusion must be hedged, though, because our analyses have thus far been cross-sectional. We have not controlled earlier levels of ideational flexibility or authoritarian conservatism. It is possible that job conditions actually affect intellective process mainly at early ages, but that, in analyses that do not control earlier levels of intellective process, these effects *appear* to continue long after they have in fact ceased. Moreover, the assumption of unidirectionality leaves open the possibility that our findings result, not from job conditions affecting intellective process, but solely from intellective process affecting selection into and modification of job conditions. For example, if younger men have less choice of job and less control over their conditions of work, they may be especially reactive to job conditions; if older men have greater job security, they may have more opportunity to affect their conditions of work. To examine such possibilities, we turn to an analysis of reciprocal effects, which requires longitudinal data. These we have for the United States, but not for Poland.

LONGITUDINAL ANALYSES OF RECIPROCAL EFFECTS

The longitudinal analyses are based on a subsample of 687 men, representative of those men in the 1964 U.S. cross-sectional survey who were aged 26 to 65 at the time of the 10-year follow-up survey in 1974. For this analysis, based on a much smaller number of men than was the cross-sectional analyses, as well as on a truncated age-range, we have divided the men into only two age groups, those 25 through 45 at the time of the follow-up survey ($N = 282$), and those 46 through 65 at that time ($N = 405$). We have deliberately used the same cutting point, age 46, to define "older" men. It should be noted, though, that these are not the same men as those in the oldest age group in the cross-sectional analyses, since the age criterion is imposed as of 10 years later.

Measurement Models

The measurement models on which the longitudinal analyses are based are similar to those previously discussed for the cross-sectional analyses, the principal differences being that the models are longitudinal, using data from both 1964 and 1974, and that we are able to use the original two-dimension measurement model of intellectual flexibility. We still focus our attention on the ideational component. In these models, the residual for each indicator in 1964 is allowed to correlate with the residual for that same indicator in 1974, a necessary practice if we are to separate the stability of the concept from overtime correlations in errors of measurement (for the rationale, see Kohn & Schooler, 1978). In developing the longitudinal measurement models for older and younger men, we followed as closely as possible the models previously developed for all men in the follow-up study (in Kohn & Schooler, 1982). We estimated the models for younger and for older men independently, retaining wherever possible the same parameters as in the corresponding longitudinal model for all men, but reestimating the magnitudes of those parameters. In general, the measurement parameters for all three models—occupational self-direction, ideational flexibility, and authoritarian conservatism—are very similar for all men, younger men, and older men; moreover, the parameters for the 1964 portions of the models are very similar to those of the cross-sectional models presented earlier in this chapter.

Causal Models

To identify the models, we treat all effects of job conditions on intellective process and of intellective process on job conditions *as if* contemporaneous, using the cross-lagged effects as instruments. This does not mean that we believe that the effects of job conditions on intellective process and of intellective process on job conditions are necessarily contemporaneous. On the contrary, past research (Kohn & Schooler, 1978, 1982) suggests that, although the effect of the substantive complexity of work on intellective process is indeed contemporaneous, the effect of intellective process on substantive complexity is actually lagged. It is nevertheless legitimate to use the cross-lagged paths as instruments to assess the *total* effects of job conditions on intellective process and the reverse. (For a discussion of the rationale and also the dangers of this procedure, see Heise, 1975, pp. 184–185.) This permits us, for example, to estimate the total effects of the substantive complexity of work on ideational flexibility and of ideational flexibility on substantive complexity, but we cannot say whether what appear to be contemporaneous effects are truly contemporaneous, lagged, or a combination of the two. Further identification is provided by allowing all of the social characteristics that were included in the cross-sectional analyses of the U.S. data (see footnote 1) to affect intellective process; only those social characteristics (namely, age, race, national and religious background) that might be seen as credentials for a mid-career job are allowed to affect current occupational self-direction.

To keep the analysis from being needlessly complex, we deliberately do not model the effects of job conditions on one another; instead we simply allow their residuals to be correlated. This means that we are not able to assess indirect effects, for instance, the indirect effect of routinization of work on ideational flexibility through routinization's effect on the substantive complexity of work. In assessing the effects of any particular job condition on intellective process, we do, however, control the effects of the other two job conditions. The models thus enable us to assess the direct reciprocal effects of job conditions and intellective process, while statistically controlling the prior states of both as well as other pertinent variables.[3]

A prototypic model of the reciprocal effects of occupational self-direction and ideational flexibility for the older men in the follow-up sample is presented in Figure 1. In this and subsequent models, the residual of each job condition is allowed to correlate with that for intellective process if that correlation proves to be statistically significant; otherwise it is fixed at 0. In this instance, the residuals of both the substantive complexity of work and of routinization prove to be significantly correlated with that for ideational flexibility.

The most important findings of this analysis are the substantial reciprocal effects of the substantive complexity of work and ideational flexibility: The substantive complexity of work decidedly affects ideational flexibility, and ideational flexibility has an even more decided impact on the substantive complexity of work. Thus, what appeared in the cross-sectional analysis to be a substantial effect of substantive complexity on ideational flexibility turns out in the longitudinal analysis to be substantial *reciprocal* effects. In the cross-sectional analysis, the modest effect of routinization on ideational flexibility turns out in the longitudinal analysis to be modest reciprocal effects—too weak to be statistically significant in either direction. Newly apparent in this anal-

---

[3] Both occupational self-direction and cognitive functioning are generated by dynamic processes. It has been shown (Schoenberg, 1977) that a static model of what, in reality, is an underlying dynamic process will underestimate the parameters but will not otherwise be misleading.

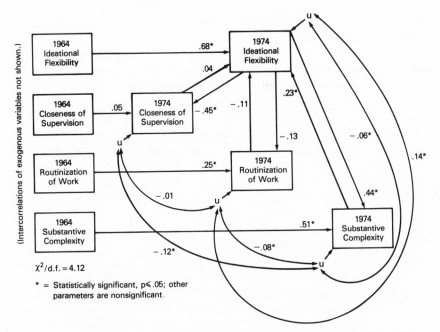

Figure 1.   Longitudinal model: Occupational self-direction and ideational flexibility, older U.S. men (paths from social characteristics and "early"
substantive complexity not shown).

ysis is that closeness of supervision—which does not significantly affect
the ideational flexibility of older men in either the cross-sectional or
the longitudinal analysis—is itself affected by older men's ideational
flexibility, with ideational flexibility leading to less closely supervised
conditions of work. The longitudinal analysis thus strikingly confi..ns
the main finding of the cross-sectional analysis, that the substantive
complexity of work continues to affect the ideational flexibility of older
men, adding that older men's ideational flexibility, in turn, affects both
the substantive complexity of their work and how closely they are
supervised.

Comparing this model to an exactly parallel model for younger men
(Table 5) shows that the reciprocal effects of the substantive complexity
of work and ideational flexibility are not only *as* strong for older as
for younger men, but may even be stronger for older men. (The
unstandardized coefficients bear out what is apparent in the standardized
coefficients shown in Table 5: The unstandardized effect of the substantive complexity of work on ideational flexibility, for example, is
.40 for older men and .06 for younger men.) Since these models are
based on relatively small numbers of cases, and are not entirely robust
under alternative specifications, we are loathe to claim an *increased*

effect for older men, but certainly there is nothing here to suggest a *diminished* effect.

Similar models for authoritarian conservatism (again see Table 5), estimated independently for older men and younger men, are entirely consistent in showing the undiminished, perhaps even stronger, effect of the substantive complexity of work for older as compared to younger men. As with ideational flexibility, the relationship between the substantive complexity of work and authoritarian conservatism, for both older and younger men, is reciprocal. In the case of authoritarian conservatism, though, the effect is predominantly *from* substantive complexity *to* authoritarian conservatism. (We find no effects of routinization of work on authoritarian conservatism, or the reverse, for either older or younger men. We cannot disaggregate the correlation between closeness of supervision and authoritarian conservatism for older men; our instruments are not strong enough.[4])

Thus, the models for both ideational flexibility and authoritarian conservatism confirm the central finding of the cross-sectional analyses—that the impact of the substantive complexity of work on intellective process continues unabated in older men. Here is convincing evidence that the cross-sectional findings are not an artifact of our not controlling "earlier" intellective process or of treating the effects of job conditions on intellective process as unidirectional. In principle, some portion of the effects of job conditions on intellective process might have occurred earlier than the time of the follow-up study, since the "contemporaneous" effects, as we have modeled them, may contain also a lagged component. However, previous analyses of the entire sample of men in the follow-up study (Kohn & Schooler, 1978, 1981) show that the effects of the substantive complexity of work on intellectual flexibility are not to any important degree a carryover from earlier times. Extrapolating, we believe that the same applies at all ages to both aspects of intellective process.

As anticipated, the longitudinal analyses do show that the effects of "earlier" intellective process are very strong; these are highly stable aspects of personality, ideational flexibility especially so. The analyses also show a substantial impact of intellective process on job conditioning. Nevertheless, the longitudinal analyses strikingly affirm the

---

[4] When working with small subsamples, one must be especially cautious about disaggregating small correlations, particularly when the instruments are weak. Fortunately, the correlations between the substantive complexity of work and intellective process are quite large and the instruments for assessing their reciprocal effects are powerful. The correlations of both closeness of supervision and routinization with intellective process, however, are smaller and the instruments are weaker (because the overtime stabilities are smaller). We can therefore be confident about our findings for substantive complexity, but must be tentative about those for routinization and closeness of supervision.

Table 5. Longitudinal Analyses: Reciprocal Effects of Occupational Self-Direction and Intellective Process

	Substantive Complexity of Work		Closeness of Supervision		Routinization of Work	
	Path to intellective process	Path from intellective process	Path to intellective process	Path from intellective process	Path to intellective process	Path from intellective process
Ideational Flexibility						
Older men (≥46)	.23*	.44*	.04	−.45*	−.11	−.13
Younger men (≤45)	.19*	.34*	−.04	−.11	−.01[a]	.12[a]
All men	.23*	.48*	.03	−.32*	−.14*	−.09
Authoritarian Conservatism						
Older men (≥46)	−.33*	−.09*	—[b]	—[b]	−.02	.05
Younger men (≤45)	−.22*	−.15*	−.04	.22*	−.02	−.02
All men	−.28*	−.09*	—[b]	—[b]	−.03	.01

Note. For older men, $N = 405$; for younger men, $N = 282$.
[a] Estimate of this parameter uncertain. (The correlation of residuals is fixed at 0; allowing a correlation of residuals—as in the models for all men and older men—creates statistical anomalies.)
[b] Not possible to disaggregate correlation between closeness of supervision and authoritarian conservatism; modeled instead as a correlation of their residuals.
* Statistically significant, $\rho \leq .05$.

causal effects of occupational self-direction, most notably that of the substantive complexity of work, on both ideational flexibility and authoritarian conservatism in older men. Job conditions contribute not only to change but also to stability (or maintenance) of personality. The longitudinal models for older men demonstrate that these processes continue to have their effects, with undiminished—perhaps even greater—magnitude, well into men's occupational careers.

SUMMARY AND DISCUSSION

The main conclusion of this research is that job conditions affect intellective process in older men just as much as in younger men. In particular, job conditions that facilitate the exercise of self-direction in work continue to enhance ideational flexibility and an open-minded, nonauthoritarian orientation, even in the oldest segment of the workforce, that is, among men aged 46 to 65. These findings are shown in both cross-sectional and longitudinal analyses for the United States. For Poland, cross-sectional analyses indicate that the findings apply as well to that country. What makes us confident, albeit not certain, that our conclusion applies as well to Poland is the consistency of the U.S. longitudinal and cross-sectional findings.

Learning and generalization from work experience occur regardless of age, and—if we may extrapolate—regardless of stages of career and life course. However, we can be confident of this conclusion only for the age segment of the male population with a very high rate of participation in the labor force. Our "oldest" group in the cross-sectional analysis is aged 46 and above, but none of the men in the Polish sample, and only a few of the men in the U.S. sample, are older than 65. In the U.S. longitudinal analysis, there is a cutoff of age 65. At that age the proportion of men who remain in the labor force drastically diminishes. To test whether the learning-generalization of work experience continues in age groups over 65 would require taking into account the selectivity of those men who remain at work. Moreover, we cannot be certain that our conclusion applies to employed women. We do have evidence that the relationships between occupational self-direction and intellective process are entirely consistent for employed U.S. men and women (J. Miller et al., 1979). But our samples of both U.S. and Polish women are too small for subgroup analysis.

Within these age and sex limitations, we have discovered notable continuity not only of the effects of job conditions on intellective process, but also of the effects of intellective process on job conditions—a continuity of reciprocal process into later stages of career and later stages of life course. Men continue to learn from their jobs and to generalize those lessons to outside-of-job reality, and men continue well into their careers to select and to mold their jobs to fit their intellective proclivities.

Since the data were collected 14 years later in Poland than in the United States, the "same" age groups actually have lived in quite different historical periods. From such data, we cannot be certain whether there are cohort or period effects on the relationships between job conditions and intellective process. For our purposes, though, the important finding is that age groups do not differ appreciably with respect to the strength of the relationship between job conditions and intellective process.

The one nonnegligible cross-national difference applies to all age groups. In the United States, uniformly for younger, middle, and older men, authoritarian conservatism is most strongly affected by the substantive complexity of work. In Poland, however, uniformly for younger, middle, and older men, authoritarian conservatism is more strongly affected by closeness of supervision. Any explanation of this cross-national difference must refer not simply to the characteristics of individuals, but also to characteristics of the countries in which these individuals live. Thus, we ask which characteristics of the political and economic systems and of the national cultures facilitate the impact of closeness of supervision on authoritarian conservatism in Poland and deter its impact in the United States. It seems to us likely that the societal authority structures and culturally grounded reactions to those structures may be crucially at issue. In Poland, because of the predominant state bureaucracy and the powerful Catholic Church, the authority structure is more salient than in the United States. It is in the self-interest of both the state bureaucracy and the Church to support all the elements of traditional Polish culture that encourage people at the bottom of the social hierarchy to obey all forms of authority; the work setting is no exception. In the United States, by contrast, it is in the self-interest of those who have institutionalized economic and political power to deemphasize, even to deny, the existence of authority structures. The impact of closeness of supervision on authoritarian conservatism may be greater in Poland than in the United States because Poles have a keener awareness of and are more receptive to hierarchical structure.

Finally, we can consider the findings of this chapter from the perspective of what they tell us about the generality of the effects of occupational self-direction on psychological functioning. These findings add substantially to the body of evidence in support of the generality of those effects (for a review of that evidence, see Kohn, 1983; Kohn & Schooler, 1983b). We have learned that occupational self-direction, particularly the substantive complexity of work, has a decided effect on ideational flexibility in Poland—a new and important piece of evidence. More generally, the findings tell us that the relationship between occupational self-direction and intellective process holds for six groups of men who have had decidedly different generational and historical experiences. The generality of the relationship is thus extended not only with respect to age, but also with respect to diversity of experience.

REFERENCES

Adorno, T.W., Frenkel-Brunswik, E., Levinson, A.J., & Sanford, R.N. (1950). *The authoritarian personality.* New York: Harper & Bros.

Baltes, P.B. (1983). Life-span development psychology: Observations on history and theory revisited. In R.M. Lerner (Ed.), *Developmental psychology: Historical and philosophical perspectives* (pp. 79–111). Hillsdale, NJ: Erlbaum.

Baltes, P.B., Dittmann-Kohli, F., & Dixon, R.A. (1984). New perspective on the development of intelligence in adulthood: Toward a dual-process conception and a model of selective optimization with compensation. In P.B. Baltes & O.G. Brim, Jr. (Eds.), *Life-span development and behavior* (Vol. 6, pp. 33–76) New York: Academic Press.

Baltes, P.B., & Labouvie, G. (1973). Adult development of intellectual performance: Description, explanation, and modification. In C. Eisdorfer & M.P. Lawton (Eds.), *The psychology of adult development and aging* (pp. 157–219). Washington, DC: American Psychological Association.

Breer, P.E., & Locke, E.A. (1965). *Task experience as a source of attitudes.* Homewood, IL: Dorsey Press.

Coburn, D., & Edwards, V.L. (1976). Job control and child-rearing values. *Canadian Review of Sociology and Anthropology, 13,* 337–344.

Elder, G.H., Jr. (1974). *Children of the Great Depression: Social change in life experience.* Chicago: University of Chicago Press.

Elder, G.H., Jr. (1981). Social history and life experience. In D.H. Eichhorn, J.A. Clausen, N. Haan, & P. Honzik (Eds.), *Present and past in middle life* (pp. 3–31). New York: Academic Press.

Elder, G.H., Jr., & Rockwell, R.C. (1979). The life course and human development: An ecological perspective. *International Journal of Behavioral Development, 2,* 1–21.

Festinger, L. (1957). *A theory of cognitive dissonance.* Evanston, IL: Row, Peterson.

Gabennesch, H. (1972). Authoritarianism as world view. *American Journal of Sociology, 77,* 857–875.

Gagne, R.M. (1968). Learning: Transfer. In D.L. Sills (Ed.), *International encyclopedia of the social sciences* (Vol. 9, pp. 168–173). New York: Macmillan/Free Press.

Gewirtz, J.L. (1969). Mechanisms of social learning: Some roles of stimulation and behavior in early human development. In D.D. Goslin (Ed.), *Handbook of socialization theory and research* (pp. 57–212). Chicago: Rand McNally.

Grabb, E.G. (1981). The ranking of self-actualization values: The effects of class, stratification, and occupational experiences. *The Sociological Quarterly, 22,* 373–383.

Heise, D.R. (1975). *Causal analysis.* New York: Wiley.

Hoff, E.H., & Gruneisen, V. (1978). Arbeitserfahrungen, Erziehungseinstellungen, und Erziehungsverhalten von Eltern. In H. Lukesch & K. Schneewind (Eds.), *Familiare Sozialisation: Probleme, Ergebnisse, Perspektiven* (pp. 239–252). Stuttgart, West Germany: Klett-Cotta.

Horn, J.L., & Donaldson, G. (1980). Cognitive development in adulthood. In O.G. Brim, Jr., & J. Kagan (Eds.), *Constancy and change in human development* (pp. 455–529). Cambridge, MA: Harvard University Press.

Jarvik, L.F., & Cohen, D. (1973). A behavioral approach to intellectual changes with aging. In C. Eisdorfer & M.P. Lawton (Eds.), *The psychology of adult development and aging* (pp. 220–280). Washington, DC: American Psychological Association.

Jöreskog, K.G., & van Thillo, M. (1972). LISREL: A general computer program for estimating a linear structural equation system involving multiple indicators of unmeasured variables. *Research Bulletin* No. 72–56. Princeton, NJ: Educational Testing Service.

Kelman, H.C., & Barclay, J. (1963). The F scale as a measure of breadth of perspective. *Journal of Abnormal and Social Psychology, 67,* 608–615.

Kohn, M.L. (1969). *Class and conformity: A study in values.* Homewood, IL: Dorsey Press (2d ed. 1977, University of Chicago Press).

Kohn, M.L. (1980). Job complexity and adult personality. In N.J. Smelser & E.H. Erikson (Eds.), *Themes of work and love in adulthood* (pp. 193–210). Cambridge, MA: Harvard University Press.

Kohn, M.L. (1983). Unresolved interpretive issues. In M.L. Kohn & C. Schooler (Eds.), *Work and personality: An inquiry into the impact of social stratification* (pp. 291–312). Norwood, NJ: Ablex.

Kohn, M.L., & Schoenbach, C. (1983). Class, stratification, and psychological functioning. In M.L. Kohn & C. Schooler (Eds.), *Work and personality: An inquiry into the impact of social stratification* (pp. 154–189). Norwood, NJ: Ablex.

Kohn, M.L., & Schooler, C. (1969). Class, occupation, and orientation. *American Sociological Review, 34,* 659–678.

Kohn, M.L., & Schooler, C. (1973). Occupational experience and psychological functioning: An assessment of reciprocal effects. *American Sociological Review, 38,* 97–118.

Kohn, M.L., & Schooler, C. (1978). The reciprocal effects of the substantive complexity of work and intellectual flexibility: A longitudinal assessment. *American Journal of Sociology, 84,* 24–52.

Kohn, M.L., & Schooler, C. (1981). Job conditions and intellectual flexibility: A longitudinal assessment of their reciprocal effects. In D.J. Jackson & E.C. Borgatta (Eds.), *Factor analysis and measurement in sociological research: A multi-dimensional perspective* (pp. 281–313). London: Sage.

Kohn, M.L., & Schooler, C. (1982). Job conditions and personality: A longitudinal assessment of their reciprocal effects. *American Journal of Sociology, 87,* 1257–1286.

Kohn, M.L., & Schooler, C. (Eds.). (1983a). *Work and personality: An inquiry into the impact of social stratification.* Norwood, NJ: Ablex.

Kohn, M.L., & Schooler, C. (1983b). The cross-national universality of the interpretive model. In M.L. Kohn & C. Schooler (Eds.), *Work and personality: An inquiry into the impact of social stratification* (pp. 281–295). Norwood, NJ: Ablex.

Labouvie, E.W. (1980). Identity versus equivalence of psychological measures and constructs. In L.W. Poon (Ed.), *Aging in the 1980s: Psychological issues* (pp. 493–502). Washington, DC: American Psychological Association.

Labouvie-Vief, G., & Chandler, M.J. (1978). Cognitive development and life-span developmental theory: Idealistic versus contextual perspectives. In P.B. Baltes (Ed.), *Life-span development and behavior* (Vol. 1, pp. 181–210). New York: Academic Press.

Ladinsky, J. (1976, March). *Notes on the sociological study of careers.* Paper presented at the Social Science Research Council Conference on Occupational Careers Analysis, Greensboro, NC.

Marx, K. (1964). *Early writings* (T.B. Bottomore, Ed. & Trans.). New York: McGraw-Hill.

Marx, K. (1971). *The Grundrisse* (D. McLennan, Ed. & Trans.). New York: Harper & Row.

Miller, J., Schooler, C., Kohn, M.L., & Miller, K.A. (1979). Women and work: The psychological effects of occupational conditions. *American Journal of Sociology, 85,* 66–94.

Miller, J., Slomczynski, K.M., & Schoenberg, R.J. (1981). Assessing comparability of measurement in cross-national research: Authoritarian conservatism in different sociocultural settings. *Social Psychology Quarterly, 44,* 178–191.

Miller, K.A., & Kohn, M.L. (1983). The reciprocal effects of job conditions and the intellectuality of leisure-time activities. In M.L. Kohn & C. Schooler (Eds.), *Work and personality: An inquiry into the impact of social stratification* (pp. 217–241). Norwood, NJ: Ablex.

Mortimer, J. T., & Lorence, J. (1979a). Work experience and occupational value socialization: A longitudinal study. *American Journal of Sociology, 84,* 1361–1385.

Mortimer, J.T., & Lorence, J. (1979b). Occupational experience and the self-concept: A longitudinal study. *Social Psychology Quarterly, 42,* 307–323.

Naoi, A., & Schooler, C. (1981, August). *Occupational conditions and psychological functioning in Japan.* Paper presented at the annual meeting of the American Sociological Association, Toronto, Canada.

Naoi, A., & Schooler, C. (1985). Occupational conditions and psychological functioning in Japan. *American Journal of Sociology, 90,* 729–752.

Parsons, T., Shils, E.A., Allport, G.W., Kluckhohn, C., Murray, H.A., Sears, R.B., Sheldon, R.C., Stouffer, S.A., & Tolman, E.C. (1951). Some fundamental categories of the theory of action: A general statement. In T. Parsons & E.A. Shils (Eds.), *Toward a general theory of action* (pp. 3–29). Cambridge, MA: Harvard University Press.

Pearlin, L.I. (1962). Alienation from work: A study of nursing personnel. *American Sociological Review, 27,* 314–326.

Riley, M.W. (Ed.). (1979). *Aging from birth to death: Interdisciplinary perspectives.* Washington, DC: American Association for the Advancement of Science.

Riley, M.W., & Bond, K. (1983). Beyond ageism: Postponing the onset of disabililty. In M.W. Riley, B.B. Hess, & K. Bond (Eds.), *Aging in society: Selected reviews of recent research* (pp. 243–252). Hillsdale, NJ: Erlbaum.

Roof, W.C. (1974). Religious orthodoxy and minority prejudice: Causal relationship or reflection of localistic work view? *American Journal of Sociology, 80,* 643–664.

Schoenberg, R.J. (1977). Dynamic models and cross-sectional data: The consequences of dynamic misspecification. *Social Science Research, 6,* 133–144.

Schoenberg, R.J. (1982). Multiple indicator models: Estimation of unconstrained construct means and their standard errors. *Sociological Methods & Research, 10,*421–433.

Skinner, B.F. (1953). *Science and human behavior.* New York: Macmillan.

Slomczynski, K.M., Miller, J. & Kohn, M.L. (1981). Stratification, work, and values: A Polish–United States comparison. *American Sociological Review, 46,* 720–744.

Srole, L. (1956). Social integration and certain corollaries: An exploratory study. *American Sociological Review, 21,* 709–716.

Wilensky, H.L. (1961). Orderly careers and social participation: The impact of work history on social integration in the middle mass. *American Sociological Review, 26,* 521–539.

Witkin, H.A., Dyk, R.B., Faterson, H.F., Goodenough, D.R., & Karp, S.A. (1962). *Psychological differentiation: Studies of development.* New York: Wiley.

Chapter Eleven

Learning and Life-Course Accomplishments

Herbert J. Walberg

To gain a broad perspective of learning and accomplishments, this chapter draws together the quantitatively synthesized results and major findings from several disciplines that bear upon learning, namely, economics, psychology, and sociology. My intention is to provide factual background for a synoptic view of the production of learning and its contribution to human development and accomplishments over the life span. My purpose is to compare the quantitative magnitudes of effects of educative factors not only on immediate academic learning but on real-world outcomes in adult life. The financial and human costs and benefits of education and their policy implications are also considered. Accordingly, this chapter is divided into seven sections:

1. The Value of Academic Learning
2. Education Effects on Learning
3. Education and Adult Accomplishments
4. Economic Returns to Education
5. Socioeconomic Status and Other Attainments
6. National Economic Vitality
7. Conclusions and Policy Implications

For several reasons this chapter concentrates on learning in the first several decades of life. Most learning takes place at this period in the life course; language, habits, tastes, job skills, and much else are largely formed by age 30; and such early investments in learning pay dividends over a long period. Considerable research on learning in this period has been conducted and quantitatively synthesized (Walberg, 1984a). Learning processes in later adult life, moreover, can be hypothesized to be similar in principle to those of the formative years.

THE VALUE OF ACADEMIC LEARNING

First, it is important to recognize that much of what we know about the causes and effects of learning is restricted to a great extent to what can be measured on academic and nonacademic tests. These tests may be comprised of oral, essay, or multiple-choice questions; but their common feature is the measurement of knowledge, skills, and the like through words. Thus, investigations of causes and effects of education and other stimulating experience are often confined to verbal achievement. Perhaps this preoccupation is short-sighted, but a reasonable case can be made that the primary medium of education, work, and life is language. Those who do well at it can be expected to be successful at the many tasks that require language competence over the life span.

Bormuth (1978) concluded that verbal activities consume much time and are of immense importance in adult work and leisure. In a 1971 survey of about 5,000 people aged 16 and over, 87% of those gainfully employed reported that they had to read as part of their jobs; and typical working people read for 141 min per day as part of their jobs, or about 29% of the work day. Since the national wage bill in 1971 was $859 billion, Bormuth estimated that U.S. workers earned $253 billion for on-the-job reading. In addition, considerable leisure activity is spent on reading. Of the total sample, for example, 73% reported having read a newspaper the previous day; the mean reading time for this activity was 33 min. Thus, the estimated time devoted to reading and its imputed value are huge.

How demanding is the typical reading task? Diehl and Mikulecky's (1980) case studies assessed the literacy requirements of a broad range of 100 occupations and high schools. They interviewed and tested 107 adults ranging from a lawyer and other professionals to assembly-line operatives and stonecutters in a sample of 26 workplaces within a 70-mile radius of Bloomington, Indiana, including Indianapolis.

They found that general on-the-job reading is sometimes repetitive; many reading materials can be seen as continuous reminders rather than demanding verbal tasks. On-the-job technical reading, however, is often demanding, even more demanding than reading in high schools, as indicated by other surveys reviewed by the authors. Technical workers encountered a wider variety of reading materials, read them more competently and comprehended them in greater depth than did the students. Professional workers read an even greater range of materials and read them more competently than technical workers and students. All groups of workers, moreover, saw reading as more important to their success than did the students.

Aside from verbal demands alone, Kohn and Schooler (1983) showed that intellectually stimulating work contributes to cognitive development in adult life. Follow-up surveys conducted as recently as 1973 of a 687-respondent subsample first tested in 1964 showed that intellectually and socially demanding jobs fostered continuing growth in intellectual functioning. Other surveys show that adult motivation and language activity foster test achievement (Frederick & Walberg, 1980), although all three are predicted by stimulating family and educational experience in childhood (Walberg & Tsai, 1983).

What can be measured on verbal tests is neither unimportant nor a complete indication of educational accomplishment and preparation for adult life. Such tests indicate little about the perseverance, creativity, integrity, social sensitivity, team skills, and other learning goals that educators, parents, and students in English and U.S. surveys consistently rank above verbal achievement as such (Raven, 1981).

Extracting information from verbal media, however, may constitute a quarter or third of adult work and may currently amount to about $500 billion per year in compensated adult time. If verbal skills fostered in school, such as writing, listening, and speaking, as well as literacy activities in childhood and adult leisure, are added, then their value is immense, and the time they take may be the biggest slice of waking life. Improvements in verbal-educational skills by increasing educational productivity in schools and in leisure and work settings may be very much in the individual and national interest.

In addition, there is little evidence to show that improving verbal test achievement sacrifices other valuable traits. Evidence cited later in the chapter suggests that, to the extent verbal and other symbol-manipulative skills are more deeply and widely learned in educational and occupational experience, national welfare and economic productivity may, in fact, be increased. On the other hand, verbal skills hardly guaranteee integrity, social sensitivity, character, parental expertise, and on-the-job competence, although they may contribute to such desirable adult characteristics.

It seems ironic that schooling and other educative experiences, which constitute such a large fraction of human time and which may have immense consumption and investment value, are so narrowly and poorly measured. Much more information is available on automobiles— for example, base price, accessory and maintenance costs; information on speed, safety, size, and reliability; and ratings on styling and handling. Comparatively little information of this kind is available on the costs and benefits of education. For this reason the estimates of educational costs, effects, and benefits in the following sections of this chapter are limited.

EDUCATION EFFECTS ON LEARNING

It would seem that administrative, economic, organizational, and sociological differences among schools would make for large differences in how much students learn. Large bodies of quantitatively synthesized literature in these fields, however, contradict this plausible hypothesis. Learning is more a function of proximal social-psychological environments in which children and adults spend most of their time.

School Input-Output Analyses

For the past several decades, economists and sociologists have analyzed easily available administrative and organizational variables on schools and school districts. Perhaps, surprisingly, this corpus of research is inconsistent in attempting to show that such school variables are associated with higher productivity of learning.

Averch, Carroll, Donaldson, Kiesling, and Pincus (1972) were the first to conduct a systematic effort to synthesize research on school input-output indexes. These Rand economists tabulated the results of 19 studies of such costly inputs as teacher qualifications and experience, pupil-teacher and teacher-administrator ratios, and the age and facilities of school buildings. Their conclusion: "Research has not identified a variant of the existing system that is consistently related to students' educational outcomes" (p. 10).

They emphasized that their findings did not mean that "nothing works" but that "Nothing consistently and unambiguously makes a difference in student outcomes" (p. 10). They further concluded that increasing expenditures on traditional educational practices is unlikely to improve educational outcomes and that educational expenditures, in fact, might be reduced without deterioration in outcomes.

Bridge, Judd, and Moock (1979) later compiled the evidence on the (regression-estimated) effects of 35 administrative, financial, and sociological inputs as revealed in 28 large-scale surveys. Only socioeconomic status of students' parents showed consistently positive correlations with learning (p. 200).

The latest and most comprehensive synthesis on the effect of capital inputs and expenditures on achievement also shows inconsistent effects. From a quantitative synthesis of 130 studies, Hanushek (1981) concluded: "The available evidence suggests that there is no relationship between expenditures and achievement of students and that such traditional remedies as reducing class sizes or hiring better trained teachers are unlikely to improve matters" (p. 19).

The basis of Hanushek's conclusion is a tabulation of the number of positive and negative, significant and nonsignificant regression coefficients of expenditures per student and other costly inputs in predicting student test scores and other educational outcomes. The inputs included expenditures per student; teacher-student ratios; teacher salaries, education, and experience; and quality indexes of facilities and administrators. Of the 554 significance tests of the coefficients for the seven indicators (which are, of course, the main determinants of educational costs), an average of 82.4% was insignificant. Ignoring significance and examining the sign of the coefficients alone reveals that several costly indicators are more often negatively than positively associated with test scores; larger classes and less well educated teachers, for example, were more often associated with higher test scores than smaller classes and better educated teachers.

Why should input-output studies show such inconsistent effects and fail to reach policy-relevant conclusions? One answer is weak methodology. The studies are ill informed of one another and of past research; they omit relevant variables and include those which are easily collectible; they often omit, for example, ability and the characteristics of students' home environment. They are correlational rather than experimental, and cross-sectional rather than longitudinal.

Inputs and outputs, furthermore, are often measured at the school or even district level rather than the class and individual student levels. Such aggregation, in view of within-school variations of resource allocation, hides educational effects on individual students that are well demonstrated at the classroom level (and discussed here in a subsequent section).

Diminishing Returns

Even given the various methodological weaknesses of input-output studies, it still remains puzzling why school inputs that many parents and educators believe indicate educational quality are insignificantly associated with learning outcomes. Cross-national research suggests that modern developed countries may have gone beyond the range in which gross school inputs make much difference. Increasing "school quality" beyond this range may lead to diminishing returns.

Nearly all quantitatively synthesized input-output research on learning comes from North America; but Heyneman and Loxley (1983) recently put research on school and teacher effects into an illuminating international perspective. They explored diverse institutional influences on student achievement in Africa, Asia, Latin America, and the Middle East as well as in modern developed countries.

Primary school children in advanced countries learned substantially more per given time unit in school than did children in poor countries. Nonetheless, the lower the national income in the 29 countries in the analysis, the weaker the relative influence of socioeconomic status on achievement and the larger the influence of gross school and teacher inputs. From data collected by the International Association for the Evaluation of Educational Achievement, school quality indexes such as teacher qualifications and experience accounted for only about 30% of the accountable achievement variance in advanced countries; but these indexes acounted for 80–90% in such countries as Thailand, Colombia, and India. Thus, an extra, added increment of gross school quality—a dollar, year of study, or a textbook—may increase learning more in developing countries such as Thailand than in affluent countries such as in Sweden.

Educational Productivity

A vast literature of some 4,000 psychological studies of the past half century contains estimates of the quantitative correlations and effects of the proximate factors that bear directly on student learning within and outside school. During the past 5 years these studies have been quantitatively synthesized (see Walberg, 1984a, for detailed description). The estimates show that nine psychological factors produce much larger and more consistent effects than class size, staff salaries, expenditures per student, and other crude indicators of quality.

The nine factors appear to require optimization to increase affective, behavioral, and cognitive learning. Potent, consistent, and widely generalizable, these factors fall into three groups:

Student aptitude includes

1. ability or prior achievement as measured by the usual standardized tests;
2. development as indexed by chronological age or stage;
3. motivation or self-concept as indicated by personality tests or the student's willingness to persevere intensively on learning tasks.

Instruction includes

4. the amount of time students spend in learning, and
5. the quality of the instructional experience, including psychological and curricular aspects.

Four environmental factors also consistently affect learning: the educationally-stimulating, psychological climates of

6. the home;
7. classroom social group;
8. the peer group outside school;
9. minimum leisure-time television viewing.

The first five aspects of student aptitude and instruction are prominent in the educational models of Benjamin S. Bloom, Jerome Bruner, John B. Carroll, Robert Glaser, and others (see Walberg, 1984, for a comparative analysis); each appears necessary for learning in school; without at least a small amount of each, the student may learn little. Large amounts of instruction and high degrees of ability, for example, may count for little if students are unmotivated or instruction is unsuitable.

These five essential factors, however, are only partly alterable by educators since, for example, the curriculum in terms of lengths of time devoted to various subjects and activities is somewhat determined by diverse economic, political, and social forces. Ability and motivation, moreover, are influenced by parents, by prior learning, and by students' contributions. Thus, educators are unlikely to raise achievement substantially by just their own efforts.

The psychological climate of the classroom group; enduring affection and academic stimulation in the home; an out-of-school peer group with learning interests, goals, and activities—these influence learning in two ways. Students learn from them directly. These factors, moreover, indirectly benefit learning by raising student ability, motivation, and responsiveness to instruction. In addition, about 10 hr (not the more typical 30) weekly of television viewing seem optimal for learning, perhaps because more television time displaces homework and other educationally and developmentally constructive activities outside school.

The major causal influences flow from aptitude, instruction, and psychological environment to learning. These factors also influence each other. Early achievement appears to raise not only the stock but the rate of learning. Called the "Matthew effect" after the "rich getting richer" passage of the Bible, the phenomenon appears fairly pervasive; children who start well at academic work and other endeavors gain at a faster rate and thereby gain increasingly larger advantages as they grow older. It seems that early success may increase motivation and also attract parental and teaching attention to the possibility of developing high talent and accomplishment. Complex reciprocal causation or mutual enhancement of ability, motivation, instruction, and stimulating environments over the early life course probably account for the Matthew effect (Walberg & Tsai, 1983).

The first five essential factors appear to substitue, compensate for, or trade-off for one another at diminishing rates of return. Immense quantities of time, for example, may be needed to bring about a moderate amount of learning if motivation, ability, or instructional quality is minimal. Thus, no single essential factor overwhelms the others; all appear important.

Although the other four factors are consistent statistically or experimentally controlled correlates of academic learning, they may directly supplement as well as indirectly influence the essential classroom factors. In either case, the powerful influences of out-of-school factors, especially the home environment, must be considered.

The 12 years of 180 6-hr days in elementary and secondary school add up to only 13% of the waking, potentially educative time of the first 18 years of life. If more of the 87% of the student's waking time nominally under the control of parents that is spent outside school were to be spent in academically stimulating conditions in the home and peer group, then the total amount of student's total learning time might be dramatically raised beyond the 13% of time spent in conventional American schools.

For instance, the average of 28 hr a week spent viewing television by high school students might usefully be added to the mere 4 or 5 hr a week of homework (Walberg & Shanahan, 1983). Europeans and Japanese believe homework helps learning; empirical results of American research support this belief.

Quantitative syntheses of about 4,000 experimental and quasi-experimental studies suggest that these generalizable factors are the chief influences on cognitive, affective, and behavioral learning (Walberg, 1984a). The productive factors were also probed for their significance in promoting learning in three large sets of survey data on elementary and high school students—the National Assessment of Educational Progress, The High School and Beyond Study, and the International Studies of Educational Achievement (Walberg, 1984b; Walberg & Shanahan, 1983). Collectively, the various studies suggest that the three groups of previously defined nine factors are powerful and consistent in influencing learning, and they can be altered or influenced by educators.

Curriculum or Content Effects

Students learn the content or subject matter they are taught or to which they are naturally exposed in environments other than classrooms; if they remain unexposed to content, they do not learn it. French children, for example, learn to speak French as a consequence of exposure to spoken French and practice with their families and other social groups. American children, however, rarely master French (except when they live with French-speaking families) because their exposure or language environment, even with a few years of French content in formal courses, is limited in time and the demanding standards of the real world.

For this reason, most American children would score as mentally retarded on standard French intelligence tests, not only because the tests are largely composed of vocabulary and language-skill items but also because the instructions themselves are in a foreign language; they would also do poorly on French achievement tests. These examples illustrate the large differences in performance attributable to widely varying exposures to subject-matter content in educative environments that are far greater than ordinarily observed within countries. Whether the content is more deliberately contrived as in schools or less contrived as in homes and other social settings, it powerfully determines what is learned.

Even environmentalists have overlooked the obvious dependence of small estimates of variance of intelligence that are arbitrarily attributable to limited content variation; in the previous examples, of course, the intelligence or achievement variance attributable to environment would be nearly 100%. For the present discussion, however, the important point is that exposure to content, in formal courses or in natural social settings, determines the substance of what is learned. It is a point that social scientists and even educators have given short shrift.

The evidence for it is massive and compelling. For example, the International Association for the Evaluation of Educational Achievement (known as the IEA) first showed the powerful effects of content exposure on learning. Although such exposure may not vary much within countries, especially those with strong central ministries of education such as France and Japan, it varies widely among countries. The IEA group measured such exposure in various ways, such as number of courses, hours of lessons during the year, standards, and test items covered in classes.

These exposure indexes were among the strongest and most consistent correlates of learning within and among countries. Even controlled for psychological productivity factors (although they may be counted as manifestations of amount and quality of instruction as discussed previously), such indexes typically produced large weights in multiple regressions; and such results were demonstrated in achievement tests in civics, English and French as foreign languages, literature, mathematics, reading comprehension, and science (Postlethwaite, 1975, pp. 28–29).

The National Assessment of Educational Progress (NAEP), given every few years to elementary and secondary school students in the United States, offers further evidence of the powerful effects of content exposure. Although the effects emerge in regression analyses of data at all age levels in reading, social studies, and science (Walberg, 1984a), they can be most clearly seen in high school mathematics (Horn & Walberg, 1984), since there is reasonable consensus about what constitutes the subject matter, as in, say, trigonometry as opposed to civics or literature.

On the NAEP mathematics test for 17-year-olds, for example, the scores correlated .63 with the rated rigor of the highest course taken (ranging from consumer mathematics to calculus), and .62 with the number of mathematics courses completed in high school. These correlations probably come close to the upper limit that might be indicated by content or exposure measures within the ordinary range of variation.

The regression weights for such curriculum exposure indexes were highly significant when controlled for socioeconomic status and most of the psychological productivity factors. But it cannot be inferred, of course, that educators and society can massively raise achievement by simply mandating higher standards and required courses; students may lack the ability and motivation to master Greek, physics, higher mathematics, and other demanding courses.

Japan's world-class test scores in relatively culture-free subjects such as mathematics and science appear to derive not from high standards alone. Concerted, persevering effort by students and families, as well as rigorous meritocratic tests for admission to elite Japanese universities (which insure life-long careers in top corporations and government bureaucracies), seem to be other causes of their high performance (Walberg, 1983).

EDUCATION AND ADULT ACCOMPLISHMENTS

It may be assumed that the first 4–6 years of schooling are necessary to acquire literacy, numeracy, and some basic knowledge and skills needed to function in modern society. Beyond this, of what use is further education? The usual view is that additional education promotes acquisition of knowledge and skills useful in the pursuit of subsequent education, work, and leisure. In accord with this view, it is clear that people with more education do better in these respects, although it is less clear that education is the cause of their success.

Real-World Accomplishments

Another view is that the usual academic courses of classroom lectures, discussions, homework, and the like merely promote the acquisition of academic facts and concepts, which are measured and graded on the usual verbal-educational tests, but which have little to do with other present and future accomplishments in "the real world." This view is consistent with the statistical facts that measured intelligence predicts grades and standardized achievement scores; but none of these has much to do with the student's other accomplishments or adult success.

In a large, varied group of working scientists, for example, no association of indexes of professional accomplishments such as patents, publications, and prizes was found with their verbal and mathematical aptitude tests, achievement tests in their field of concentration, and grades in science courses. Neither Bloom (1963) nor Helson and Crutchfield (1970) found associations of IQ and other mental abilities with distinguished accomplishments, as rated by knowledgeable peers in samples of chemists and mathematicians. Hoyt (1966) reviewed studies relating grades and later occupational success in business, engineering, medicine, and scientific research, and found no association. In Great Britain, Hudson (1960) similarly found no association of academic and scientific distinction; and the same lack of association has been found in samples of architects, artists, writers, and other occupations (see, for example, Taylor & Baron, 1963).

Research on high school students shows the same absence of association. Their grades and test scores predict college grades, but neither predict nonclassroom accomplishments in the humanities and sciences at either level. Nonclassroom accomplishments during the high school years, however, predicted with a modest degree of accuracy similar accomplishments in college and in adult life after the college years (Munday & Davis, 1974; Richards, Holland, & Lutz, 1967).

In an Educational Testing Service report, the College Entrance Examination Board questioned reviews of such research and defended the use of standardized tests for college admission. It summarized 275 studies from colleges; business, graduate, law, and medical schools; and business, industrial, governmental, and medical settings, all of which related prior characteristics to learning outcomes such as grade-point averages, degree attainment, and performance ratings in leadership, science, and musical, dramatic, literary and graphic arts.

Prior indicators including recommendations, interviews, and measures of interest and personality were nearly useless in predicting either academic or nonacademic accomplishments (among eight median correlations the highest was .28, which accounted for less than 8% of the variance). "Biodata," or responses to questions about life experiences, predicted academic and nonacademic outcomes (.43 and .35, respectively), but they are impractical for competitive academic selection since they are easily faked. The only substantial prediction was the familiar academic outcomes from prior grades and test scores (.60, which on average accounted for 36% of the variance).

Granting that asking a testing agency about the value of tests is like asking a barber if you need a haircut, it seems incontrovertible that tests and prior grades predict subsequent grades with moderate accuracy. Grades, however, have little or no value in predicting subsequent success.

Grades in Higher Education

Grades are one indication of educational accomplishment. Surveys of grades and adult outcomes, though restricted to higher education, provide little evidence that good students by this index turn out much better than their peers. In 35 studies of business, military, and civil-service people, as well as teachers, professors, scientists, physicians, and nurses, grades accounted for 2.4% of the variance in income, self-rated happiness, and job satisfaction, numbers of patents and publications, and effectiveness rating by peers and supervisors (Samson, Graue, Weinstein, & Walberg, 1984).

All these groups, of course, are more homogeneous than the general population in abilities indexed by grades that presumably make for personal and career success; such small variance limits covariance and therefore predictive validity. Having a degree, moreover, even though one's grades were poor, probably ensures greater special competence and leads to somewhat higher income on average than that of a comparable person without such a degree. Still, the low correlations inspire little confidence that added effort to achieve higher grades results in greater competence than that gained by specific training, on-the-job experience, and character traits.

Perhaps employers may be quite rational in assigning only moderate importance to grades in making decisions. Surveys of employers indicate that, beyond some fairly minimal academic competencies, responsibility, social skills, and the like are weighed heavily (Walberg & Sigler, 1975).

Crain's (1984) recent national survey of 1,283 recruitment and employment personnel showed that 94% rated dependability as "extremely important" in hiring high school graduates; 82% rated proper attitudes about work and supervisors similarly, and 74% rated teamwork also as "extremely important." Smaller percentages gave ratings of extreme importance to cognitive skills such as rapid learning, 57% reading materials as difficult as a daily newspaper, 56%; reading complex material, 22%; and handling complex calculations, 11%.

In Plato's triumvirate of affect, cognition, and behavior, hearts—for some purposes—may deserve even more attention than minds and hands, at least more than the academy seems willing to credit. Yet, at the other end of the cognitive-skill spectrum, limited verbal skill can be a substantial handicap to an individual, corporation, or nation. The Conference Board's (1984) survey of about 500 human-resource and public-affairs executives showed that most agree that many newly hired high school graduates have difficulty in reading and understanding instructions and in expressing themselves clearly to coworkers and supervisors.

Table 1. Validity of Several Assessments in Predicting Supervisor Ratings.
Occupational Level and Predictors

Entry Level	
Ability composite	.53
Job tryout	.44
Biographical inventory	.37
Reference check	.26
Experience	.18
Interview	.14
Training and experience ratings	.13
Academic achievement	.11
Education	.10
Interest	.10
Age	-.01
On-the-job Level	
Work sample test	.54
Ability composite	.53
Peer ratings	.49
Experience ratings	.49
Job knowledge test	.48
Assessment center	.43

Note. Compiled from Hunter & Hunter (1984, pp. 90–91).

Occupational Tests

Hunter and Hunter (1984) found, moreover, that cognitive knowledge and skills are the best predictors of job success. They reviewed studies of efficiency induced by using cognitive ability tests to select employees. Such tests increase efficiency by allocating the most able applicants to occupational positions. High selection validity, that is, predictability of job performance from test scores, makes for financial savings in public and private organizations. Hunter and Hunter estimated, for example, that if the Philadelphia Police Department were to drop the use of its cognitive selection test for entry-level officers and choose them at random, it would cost the city government $170 million over a decade.

For jobs in the federal government, they estimated that the substitution of criteria other than cognitive tests for entry-level hiring would cost from $3.1 billion (job tryout) to $15.9 billion (age) in lost productivity per year. They further estimated that the productivity differences between avoidance and complete use of cognitive tests for the U.S. workforce as a whole for 1980 would amount to at least $80 billion, equal to total corporate profits for the year.

Such estimates are based on performance criteria such as supervisor ratings, work samples, and production records. Hunter and Hunter's (1984) compilation of validity coefficients documents the impressive record of cognitive paper-and-pencil tests. Table 1 shows the predictability of (attenuation-corrected) supervisor ratings for (a) entry-level-jobs and (b) promotion or certification of the currently employed.

Ability composite tests, which can be given in as little as a half hour by untrained clerks, are by far the most valid for entry-level prediction. Interviews, on which much reliance is placed, are far lower in validity, and combining them with ability tests would raise the validity at most only from current employees; moreover, ability tests predict supervisor ratings nearly as well as the best on-the-job assessments of present performance.

Microeconomics of Learning and Life

How is it that students might actually be rational in avoiding academic work at full capacity? How can cognitive skills predict job performance when grades do not? Some answers are offered next, and the questions will be raised again in conclusion. Human behavior may appear irrational if our views are too narrow to realize the full costs, benefits,and risks of means and goals (Becker, 1981). Economists frequently examine the simultaneous maximization of utility of several values by several means, which are often viewed as working jointly or substituting for one another. Economists who have studied several educational factors and outcomes simultaneously have shown trade-offs among them. In an unpublished report Staaf, for example, found evidence that, at the college level, more efficient educational technologies such as the supplementary distribution of lecture notes reduced the time costs of students in a course. It should not be assumed, however, that students necessarily allocated the saved time to learn more; they actually pursued otherwise foregone leisure and work on other courses.

Staaf also found that some students trade a D in a required general course for a B in their majors because of personal interest or because of its employment value. Such rationally calculating students may be valued more than straight A students, even in academia. Staaf quotes Riesman's (unpublished) comments on the kind of student most likely to be recommended for jobs, advanced training, or fellowships: "Not too obedient . . . a bit rebellious, a bit offbeat . . . were the students likely to appeal to a faculty member who had not entirely repressed a rebelliousness of his own that had led him to be a teacher in the first place, a faculty member who was looking for signs of life, even if they gave him a bit of trouble at times. To be sure, such a student had to do well in something to earn this response, but he was often better off to have written a brilliant paper or two than to have divided his time, as an investment banker his money, among a variety of subjects."

In a sense, students, like other humans, are utility maximizers. They rationally modify their productive activities to raise their total utility at minimum total costs depending on their consumption preferences, prices of outputs (say, their value to subsequent employers), monetary and nonmonetary costs of inputs, and their comparative advantages. College students rationally chose to buy prepared lecture-notes, while skipping lectures for one course at the cost of a lower grade to gain time for more interesting courses and leisure. Widening the latitude of student choice in the educational production process increases both production and consumption efficiency.

It may be similarly rational for students to pursue leisure, hobbies, dating, and friendships in youth since complete devotion to academic education is an uncertain or risky investment. Socialization activities, moreover, may have greater consumption value in youth, as well as investment value returned in maturity, since knowing how to get along with others may be as economically important as specific knowledge that can be acquired efficiently while working, rather than in courses.

Perhaps even the study of the great miscellany of Western civilization and the uncommon personalities and thoughts that characterize the liberal arts in secondary and higher education may be similarly justifiable, like youth socialization, as an investment. The value of such study above vocational and professional training may lie in the confidence fostered in mastering the old, the new, and the odd; and in gaining a critical, yet empathic understanding of diverse viewpoints of others while retaining selfhood and self-direction. All of this, of course, would be better to take on evidence than on faith.

ECONOMIC RETURNS TO EDUCATION

Economists have assembled evidence on the investment value of the amount or degree of education. They distinguish between "social returns" to the nation's income and "private returns" to the individual, since decisions about education may be considered from the point of view of public policy or private choice.

An example of returns calculation may be helpful in understanding what economists have in mind. The private returns to a 4-year high school education are estimated by dividing the difference between existing post-tax earnings of high school and elementary school graduates by the sum of foregone earnings and the private, unsubsidized costs of education. Social returns are calculated using pretax earnings (since, from a public point of view, taxes are transfer payments counted in the national income) and the full costs, including public subsidies of the individual's education.

Monetary Returns

In his widely noted book *The Over-Educated American,* Freeman (1976) estimated that the social rates of short-term returns for a college education declined from 11–14% from 1950 through 1970 to about 7.5%–9.5% in the 1970s. Because of a possible surplus of degreed young people, he speculated that the decline in the relative rate of return to college graduates since the mid-1970s may persist.

McMahon and Wagner (1982), however, argued that longer-term rates of return provide more valid estimates because the labor market needs time to adjust to changes in educational standards, and because the superior returns of more education may not show up for a decade or so beyond graduation. Using long-term rates of return, they showed no decline in the relative market value of a high school or college education since 1958. In fact, from 1958 through 1976, the social returns to a college education, about 12–16% have been superior and more stable than returns of stocks listed on the New York Stock Exchange (which centered around 0–3% and were often negative during the period).

McMahon and Wagner further showed that, despite the higher opportunity costs of foregone earnings of those admitted to select professions, private rates of return are highest in medicine, law, and engineering-technical fields. They are lowest in the clergy and in natural science, social science, and education fields.

Analysis of social returns to education in other countries provides a basis of comparison with U.S. results. Psacharopoulos's (1983) analyzed social returns to education in 44 developing, intermediate, and advanced countries. The average returns were all positive and range from about 10% (required for World Bank investment loans for physical-capital investments) to considerably higher rates.

These educational investments in human capital, however, like many other increases in factors of production, show diminishing returns. Primary education in developing countries pays the highest returns, and higher education in advanced countries pays the least. As Psacharopoulos (1983) points out, education in primary schools and in elementary textbook subjects is cheaper to provide and consumes less valuable human capital than advanced, technical education.

All such monetary-returns comparisons may underestimate the full benefit of education because they omit its consumption value; for example, joy in learning, as well as the later psychological satisfaction with work it may confer (Lucas, 1977). They may also overestimate the complete benefit by failing to calculate time and pleasure given up in youth to pursue a select profession and also given up in later family life and friendships to pursue demanding careers. As the next section indicates, however, such subjective factors and nonmonetary returns are exceedingly difficult to estimate.

Nonmonetary Returns

Michaels (1982) points out that education may raise "productivity in non-labor-market activities and thereby provides non-monetary benefits" (p. 141). "Yet here, as elsewhere in this research area, one has the impression that a rather low burden of proof regarding a nonmarket productivity effect is imposed" (p. 131). In other words, as in much nonexperimental research, the burden of proof lies with opinion or "theory" rather than varied, stringent tests of hypotheses. Some results and uncertainties, however, are worth considering.

Education appears to increase knowledge of personal asset management and propensity to save. The more highly educated adopt new products more quickly; more highly educated women are more likely to use contraception and have fewer unplanned children. A high school education apparently raised a scaled index of married men's health by 3.5%, holding age constant, and 1.2%, holding constant prior health status, socioeconomic status, measured ability, income, obesity, and wife's schooling. Each additional year of higher education raises the probability of excellent health by an estimated 1%.

Yet, as Michaels (1982) indicates, these small associations may be accounted for not by the direct effects of schooling but by the rational use of the more valuable (income-imputed) time of the more highly educated. Because their time is more costly, "the more educated have an incentive to be relatively well informed. So whether it involves videotape machines, vasectomies, or credit cards, the finding that the more educated adopt a new product more readily is not surprising, nor does it necessarily reflect a differential productivity effect of schooling. Higher income which accompanies schooling may determine the observed behavior" (Michaels, 1982, p. 133).

Other possible benefits of education are successful marriages and families, and social ascendancy. Going to school may be a good investment in finding a desirable spouse. It has been estimated, for example, that a wife's schooling raises her husband's earnings by roughly half as much as does his own schooling. Schooling and higher education, moreover, may foster private intergenerational returns by assortative mating by intelligence (Becker, 1981); and more highly educated families are repeatedly found to migrate longer distances when they move, which may lead to better job opportunities.

These findings are consistent with the hypothesis that education increases knowledge of opportunities. But they are also consistent, as Michaels (1982) points out, with other hypotheses: In addition to education, heredity, early family life, and parental socioeconomic status there may be prior or mutual determinants of education, knowledge, and opportunities; and the causal directions and weightings remain controversial.

Long-Term Effects of Education

One of the few longitudinal studies that yields stringent estimates of the long-term effects of education, with social background and early intelligence statistically controlled, was conducted in Sweden (see related research discussed in Schooler, chapter 2 of this volume.) In 1961, Harnqvist (1984) surveyed about 12,000, or 10% of the Swedes born in 1948, and followed up random samples of them with mail and interview surveys in 1980. Education, as compared with parental social class and measured intelligence, showed pervasive effects on adult characteristics of men and women. Those with greater amounts of education liked school more than others; but even early school-leavers saw the need for more education for the present generation of children. Those with more education more often described their job as providing opportunities for new knowledge, and they reported they had more influence on their own working conditions than did others.

Cultural activities such as reading literature and going to the theater and concerts were more frequent among the more educated. By contrast, entertainment activities such as reading weekly magazines and viewing television and sports events were more frequent among the less educated.

The more educated had more frequent contacts with coworkers; the less educated more often saw family and relatives. Highly educated men reported higher skills in cooking and lower skills in car repair, and having more information about how to appeal decisions and less about seeking economic support from society. In hour-long interviews, the more educated men used more words and proportionately more different and longer words. To finish the interviews, the less educated required far more prompts and interventions to complete the answers. Such pervasive education effects on life activities and verbal competence seem likely to be found in other countries.

SOCIOECONOMIC STATUS AND OTHER ATTAINMENTS

A vast literature bears on the inter-generational question of the effects of parents' socioeconomic status (SES) on their children's academic development and life success. Many ambitious surveys and secondary analyses by economists and sociologists such as Featherman, Griliches,

Hauser, Jencks, Lazear, Taubman, and others bear upon this question (see recent reviews by the economist Michaels, 1982, and the sociologist Sewell, 1981). Other studies have examined the influences of parents' education on the cognitive development and health status of their children.

Current reviews conclude that student learning is consistently associated with levels of parent education. But it may prove difficult to synthesize quantitatively the unique effects of parental SES in the context of rival causes as revealed in multivariate analyses because the constructs and their measures vary widely among investigations, thereby reducing the comparability of the causal weightings. These differences are attributable to differences in operationalization and in a priori theory (taken implicitly as a set of untested assumptions rather than hypotheses) on which investigators have achieved little consensus.

The SES influences on academic learning, moreover, may operate in several ways that are difficult to separate: Taking, for example, parental education as an index of SES, knowledge of child rearing, as well as higher income—conferred in part by more parental education— may contribute to parenting capacity and effects on children's learning. More highly educated parents, for example, may themselves provide superior direct services to their children as a result of their knowledge; but they may also purchase, as a consequence of their higher income, superior child-rearing goods and services.

One question, however, that can now be answered concerns the simple association of parental SES and children's learning. White (1976) collected 636 correlation coefficients of parental education, occupation, and income indexes of SES with ability and academic achievement from 101 published and unpublished studies. In White's synthesis, the average correlation of learning with parental income, occupation level, and education, respectively, is .31, .20, and .19. (The correlations may be overestimated or underestimated because of restriction of range in sampling, unreliability of measures, and other reasons.)

That income correlates the highest of the three may suggest that wealthy parents may confer more decisive advantages than highly educated parents by purchasing time-saving household goods such as dishwashers and thereby being able to spend more time with their children; buying intellectually enhancing toys and books for them; or hiring parent-surrogate services, such as day care and tutors, to nurture them. Little should be made of these speculations, however, since the SES correlations are all small and differ only slightly from one another.

Both the mean and standard deviation of all SES-learning correlations are .25; so that, on average, SES accounts for 6% of the variance in learning. Thus, contrary to great importance given to parental SES by some educational sociologists, its association with learning is surpris-

ingly weak; and SES may constrain learning and social ascendancy far
less than many believe.

Family Mobility

Indeed, Duncan's (1984) rare longitudinal analysis of about 5,000 American families showed substantial social mobility. For example, of families in the top or bottom 20% of income in 1971, only about half
remained in these classifications in 1978. Between 1969 and 1978, 25%
of the families fell below official poverty lines in at least 1 year, but
less than 3% remained below in 8 of the 10 years. Even these persistently
poor belied stereotypes: two thirds lived in the South; one third were
elderly; and only a fifth lived in large cities.

Education seemed a minor influence in determining changes in wealth
or poverty. Most decisive were changes in family structure—marriage
or divorce, a birth, or a child leaving home. Job-related changes such
as layoffs and physical disabilities were second in importance.

If education by itself does not decisively influence adult success as
measured by various indexes, neither do SES and other aspects of
social background. Walberg and Weinstein (1984) analyzed the statistical
dependencies of adult outcomes on 25 indexes of social background
(including age and sex of the respondent and parental characteristics),
diplomas and degrees, and a vocabulary test obtained on about 2,000
men and women in the General Social Survey.

All independent variables in combination accounted for only small
amounts of estimated variance in adult outcomes ranging from 3% of
the variance in happiness to 43% in occupational prestige. Family
background, diplomas and degrees, and verbal competence together
accounted for less than 13% of the variance in self-reported income,
health, and happiness. Among the combinations of predictors and
outcomes, diplomas and degrees uniquely accounted for the largest
amount of variance in occupational prestige; but this amount was a
trivial 2.3%.

These findings seem typical of recent associations of educational and
other measured formative effects on various adult outcomes. Only one
of these, however, has been quantitatively synthesized. Witter, Okun,
Stock, and Haring's (1984) collection of 176 zero-order correlations of
self-rated well-being from 90 studies showed that amount and quality
of education accounted for only about 1-3% of the variance in indexes
of life satisfaction and happiness. When the association was controlled
for occupational prestige, the variance estimates were even smaller; and
the association has apparently remained constant for the past half
century.

It appears at best that social background, education, and verbal competence in combination give adults slight to moderate advantages on indicators of adult success. Their separate influences, however, are weak—perhaps nil—and difficult to detect. Although they remain systematically and statistically undocumented, many other factors, such as accidental opportunities and personal initiative and perserverance, may play far larger roles.

NATIONAL ECONOMIC VITALITY

Educational effects, however, cannot be completely dismissed since they may operate more strongly in the macroeconomic aggregate. Economists such as Edward Denison and John Kendrick, who have conducted the largest studies, agree that about 67% of the U.S. economic productivity growth in recent times is attributable to advances in applied knowledge, technology, and in the education and experience of the labor force (see the review in Walberg, 1983).

The only international study of the association of mental test scores and macroeconomic indicators supports this human-capital contention. In the sample of eight countries that participated in the International Studies of Educational Achievement (for which complete data are available), the average test scores of 14-year-olds, in 1970, in the culturally universal subject of science strongly correlated +.77 with national income growth a decade later (1977–1982) and −.74 with unemployment rates in 1982 (and accounted for 55% and 59% of the respective variances). Japan, with by far the highest scores, had a growth rate of 4.4% and an unemployment rate of 2.4%. Britain, Italy, Sweden, and the United States, with the lowest achievement scores, had growth rates of 2% or below, and unemployment rates averaging 9% (Walberg, 1984b).

That education may not confer strong, certain benefits to the individual but possibly to the nation seems paradoxical. But the sum of statistical aggregates may produce a stronger association than random, micropsychological phenomena. Knowing the quadratic formula, three causes of the Civil War, the source of the Nile, the name of the lead guitarist of Culture Club, or the chemical symbol for iron may not be of much use to an individual; but the sum of such minutiae in the social aggregate may contribute to national welfare in several ways.

The division of labor in acquiring knowledge can produce specialized experts whom others may call upon. General knowledge, particularly of how to communicate with others by verbal, numerical, and graphic symbols, can enhance such exchange of information. The acquisition of either general or special knowledge may be worthwhile in itself; and it may also contribute to skill and confidence in acquiring new knowledge. Social sensitivity and cooperative skills acquired in homes and schools may contribute further to the value of knowledge acquisition and enhance the nation's cultural and social capital.

CONCLUSIONS AND POLICY IMPLICATIONS

If education is purely a consummatory good, then what pleases teachers, parents, and students should be taught. But the prevailing conception is that education is both a public and private investment of time and effort that confers future benefits both to the nation and individuals. Abraham Lincoln, who rose from poverty to the presidency, is an outstanding example of the American ideal of education for social and individual good; other exemplary people could also be cited. Yet large-scale surveys and compilations of study results suggest that the independent effects of education on adult accomplishment are difficult to detect.

In response to national reports on the need for excellence in U.S. education, educational psychologists are synthesizing a large body of evidence that suggests how to increase cognitive learning dramatically. Meanwhile, compilations of results of sociological and economic surveys cast doubt or paradoxical evidence on the value of such an increase. Some balance and reconciliation seem in order: To begin, it may be asked: How much can be learned? What is it worth?

Learning as Investment in Productivity?

Cognitive psychologists find an inexhaustible storage capacity in the mind; but perhaps roughly 5 s is "required to store a single new item semi-permanently with a minimum of indexing for later access to it" (Simon, 1983, p. 167). Perhaps 200 million meaningful items might be stored if a lifetime were devoted to it. So people must carefully allocate "very limited processing capacity among the several functions of noticing, storing, and indexing, on the input side, and retrieving, reorganizing, and controlling effectors on the output side" (p.167).

Simon estimates that 50,000 "chunks" or ensembles of meaningfully related items, about the same magnitude as the recognition vocabulary of college-educated readers, may be required for the expert mastery of a special field. The highest achievements in various disciplines, however, may require a memory store of a million chunks, which may take the devoted, say, national ranked chess or cello players about 50 h a week for a decade to acquire. Should nations, families, and schools produce such experts? What are the trade-offs?

Elementary levels of schooling tend to emphasize skills useful for further learning, whereas later levels or terminal programs, whether vocational high schools or professional schools, concentrate more on skills that influence occupational productivity (Michaels, 1982). Thus, one educational choice is general learning with transfer value against specialized learning for immediate application.

Another educational choice involves when learning should occur. "In most societies, human learning capacities are utilized heavily in the child's progress to adulthood, but very much under-utilized in adult life. Learning programs atrophy rather slowly, if at all. In other words, there exists in the adult population a huge reservoir of 'standby' learning capacity that can be called upon, by proper organization, to meet rapid or cataclysmic changes in the environment" (Simon, 1983, p. 96).

Simon attributes the astonishing mobilization of Western countries and Japan during World War II to such underused human capital. Schultz (1981) further attributes the equally astonishing recovery of Japan and the Federal Republic of Germany to relatively undiminished human capital (compared to the devastation of industrial plants, railroads, and the rest of the physical infrastructure).

Of still greater importance to current policies is the dependence of national productivity growth on the mental skills of the labor force, with which the largest studies and most economists agree (Walberg, 1983). "In our society, then, the bulk of the productive wealth consists of programs, corresponding to skills, stored in human minds. Many of these programs are quite specific in application, and hence are intimately interwoven with the structure of the physical technology. Other programs provide rather general capacities for problem solving in domains that are new, and provide learning capacity" (Simon, 1983, p. 95).

Yet, "we must be careful not to equate improvement in the quality of labor with formal education or training. . . . The schools have assumed some of the training burden that was formerly the responsibility of apprenticeship systems, or even of the home (e.g., training in cooking). But the vast bulk of the skill acquisition takes place almost automatically through direct contact with the productive equipment itself" (Simon, 1983, p. 91). For some purposes, it may not be necessary to keep investing increasing national resources in education and human skills. As Simon points out, intellectual skills of new technology may be substituted for human mental skills formerly required. Who can say that a manufactured violin requires greater skill to make than one that is handcrafted?

High technology, moreover, may not be as economically significant or cognitively demanding as some may think. It accounted for only 3% of the 22 million jobs added to the U.S. labor force since 1970. Much of the growth in jobs came in fast food, "lowbrow" entertainment, transportation, and other service industries ("Fast Fries or High Tech?" 1984) that may not demand academic sophistication.

As Levin and Rumberger (1983) point out, even jobs in the computer industry may be "deskilled"; today's "user friendliness" makes computers easier to use than before; and "canned programs" and "artificial intelligence" that can adapt standard operations for a variety of purposes may make skilled workers, including those with white collar jobs and college degrees, obsolescent, or so efficient that fewer may be required.

Thus, "it is easy to exaggerate the vocational or professional value of what is taught in schools, and especially in universities, except possibly in some very specific professional curricula. . . . Diplomas provide the employer with a cheap and relatively efficient device for singling out those who, on the average, have a little more drive and are a little brighter than the usual run of job applicants" (Simon, 1983, p. 129); and much of what is learned in formal education may have little productive significance, except in the cultural and social aggregate.

Learning as Consumption, Resource, and Risk

Homework, diplomas and degrees, and the acquisition of the verbal competence that is measured on tests may be worth something as an investment, possibly even as consumption. Semipermanent assets of knowledge and cognitive skills acquired in formal education may depreciate slowly if they are regularly practiced. But such knowledge and skills may also pay uncertain monetary or psychological returns to individuals. Consistent, convincing evidence has yet to appear.

In addition, recent studies and analyses continue to suggest that economic success may be attributable to a mixture of environmental incentives and skills acquired both before and during the years of work. Weiss (1984), for example, finds that the astounding increases in Japanese manufacturing productivity are due to both school-induced and workplace factors; more engineers per worker, selective hiring of skilled and highly recommended graduates, substantial pay differences based on accomplishments, lifelong training, and the pervasive solicitation of employee suggestions.

In a crisis, nations can call on slack mental capital; but too much of such capital, acquired at some risk, cost, and pain, may also cause boredom in workday jobs that will continue to occupy most people. During periods of technological transformation or an unanticipated crisis, such slack human capital may be more useful to a nation as a whole than to the individuals who acquired it.

Such social utility to a nation may justify public and private subsidies for education. The individual risk, cost, and trouble to acquire it may deserve the monetary and psychological returns to individuals it may confer. Education might be made more psychologically rewarding in itself; but it may never compete with such youth and adult interests as television, cars, dating, clothes, and jobs in the real world. In view of the uncertainites and the differences in prices and values among people, free societies might best leave educational decisions largely in the hands of the individuals and families concerned.

Neither nations nor individuals can fully assess the costs of learning, and its present and future values. But that is a reason for making life an array not of certainties but of interesting possibilities and hopes, perhaps better in anticipation than their realization.

REFERENCES

Averch, H.A., Carroll, S.J., Donaldson, T.S., Kiesling, H.J., & Pincus, J. (1972). *How effective is schooling? A critical review and synthesis of research findings.* Santa Monica, CA: Rand Corporation, Prepared for the President's Commission on School Finance.

Becker, G. (1981). *A treatise on the family.* Cambridge, MA: Harvard University Press.

Borger, J., Oh, S., Low, C., & Walberg, H.J. (1984). *Effective schools: A review of reviews.* Chicago: University of Illinois Office of Evaluation Research.

Bormuth, J.R. (1978). Value and volume of literacy. *Visible Language, 12,* 118–161.

Bridge, R.G., Judd, C.M., & Moock, P.R. (1979). *The determinants of educational outcomes: The impact of families, peers, teachers, and schools.* Cambridge, MA: Ballinger.

Coleman, J.S., Campbell, E., Hobson, C., McPartland, J., Mood, A., Weinfeld, F., & York, R. (1966). *Equality of educational opportunity.* Washington, DC: U.S. Government Printing Office.

Conference Board. (1984). *The role of business in pre-college education* (Research Bulletin RB 160). New York: Author.

Crain, R.L. (1984). *The quality of American high school graduates: What personnel officers say and do about it.* Baltimore, MD: Johns Hopkins Center for Social Organization of Schools.

Diehl, W.A., & Mikulecky, L. (1980). The nature of reading at work. *Journal of Reading, 24,* 227–247.

Duncan, G.J. (1984). *Years of poverty, years of plenty.* Ann Arbor, MI: Institute for Social Research.

Edmonds, R.R. (1979). Effective schools for the urban poor. *Educational Leadership, 37,* 15–23.

Fast fries or high tech? 1984, (June 16). *The Economist.*

Frederick, W.C., & Walberg, H.J. (1980). Learning as a function of time. *Journal of Educational Research, 73,* 183–194.

Freeman, R. (1976). *The over-educated American..* New York: Academic Press.

Gagne, R.M. (1970). Policy implications and future research. *Do teachers make a difference?* Washington, DC: U.S. Government Printing Office.

Hanushek, E.A. (1981). Throwing money at schools. *Journal of Policy Analysis and Management, 1,* 19–41.

Harnqvist, K. (1984). An empirical study of long-term effects of education. Tel Aviv, Israel: First International Conference on Education in the '90s.

Heyneman, S.P., & Loxley, W.A. (1983). The effect of primary-school quality on academic achievement across twenty-nine high- and low-income countries. *The American Journal of Sociology, 88,* 1162–1194.

Horn, E., & Walberg, H.J. (1984). Achievement and interest as functions of quantity and quality of instruction. *Journal of Educational Research, 77,* 227–232.

Hunter, J.E., & Hunter, R.F. (1984). Validity and utility of alternative predictors of job performance. *Psychological Bulletin, 96,* 72–98.

Kohn, M.L., & Schooler, C. (Eds.), (1983). *Work and personality: An inquiry into the impact of social stratification.* Norwood, NJ: Ablex.

Levin, H., & Rumberger, R. (1983). The low-skill future of high tech. *Technology Review, 86*(6), 18–22.

Lucas, R.E.B. (1977). Hedonic wage equations and psychic wages in the returns to schooling. *American Economic Review, 67,* 549–558.

Marshall, T.O., & Lohones, P.R. (1965). Redundancy in student records. *American Educational Research Journal, 2,* 19–23.

McMahon, W.W., & Wagner, A.P. (1982). The monetary returns to education as partial social efficiency criteria. In W.W. McMahon & T.G. Gestke (Eds.), *Financing education* (pp.156–172). Urbana: University of Illinois Press.

Michaels, R.T. (1982). Measuring non-monetary benefits of education: A survey. In W.W. McMahon & T.G. Gestke (Eds.), *Financing education* (pp. 83–102). Urbana: University of Illinois Press.

Mikulecky, L. (1982). Job literacy: The relationship between school preparation and workplace actuality. *Reading Research Quarterly, 12,* 400–419.

Postlethwaite, T.N. (1975). The surveys of the International Association for the Evaluation of Educational Achievement: Implications of the IEA surveys of achievement. In A.C. Purves & D.U. Levine (Eds.), *Educational policy and international assessment* (pp. 173–203). Berkeley, CA: McCutchan.

Psacharopoulos, G. (1983). *Education and national development.* Washington, DC: World Bank.

Purkey, S.C., & Smith, M.S. (1983). Effective schools: A review. *Elementary School Journal, 83,* 427–453.

Raven, J. (1981). The most important problem in education is to come to term with values. *Oxford Review of Education, 7*(3), 253–272.

Riley, M.W., Hess, B.B., & Bond, K. (1983) *Aging in society: Selected reviews of recent research.* Hillsdale, NJ: Erlbaum.

Samson, G.E., Graue, M.E., Weinstein, T., & Walberg, H.J. (1984). Academic and occupational performance: A quantitative synthesis. *American Educational Research Journal, 21,* 311–321.

Schultz, T.W. (1963). *The economic value of education.* New York: Columbia University Press.

Schultz, T.W. (1981). *Investing in people.* Berkeley: University of California Press.

Scott, R., & Walberg, H.J. (1979). Schools alone are insufficient. *Educational Leadership, 37,* 24–25.

Sewell, W.H. (1981). Notes on educational, occupational, and economic achievement in American society. *Phi Delta Kappan, 77,* 322–325.

Simon, H.A. (1983). *Models of bounded rationality: Vol. 2.* Cambridge, MA: MIT Press.

Stigler, G.J. (1961). The economics of information. *Journal of Political Economy, 69,* 213–235.

Tyack, D.B. (1972). The one best system: A historical analysis. In H.J. Walberg (Ed.), *Rethinking urban education.* (pp. 43–61). San Francisco: Jossey-Bass.

Walberg, H.J. (1974). *Evaluating educational performance.* Berkeley, CA: McCutchan.

Walberg, H.J. (1983). Scientific literacy and economic productivity in international perspective. *Daedalus, 112*(2), 1–28.

Walberg, H.J. (1984a). Improving the productivity of America's schools. *Educational Leadership, 41*(3), 19–26.

Walberg, H.J. (1984b). *National abilities and economic growth.* Chicago: University of Illinois Office of Evaluation Research.

Walberg, H.J., & Shanahan, T. (1983). High school effects on individual students. *Educational Researcher, 7,* 4–9.

Walberg, H.J., & Sigler, J. (1975). Business views education in Chicago. *Phi Delta Kappan, 56,* 610–612.

Walberg, H.J., & Tsai, S.L. (1983). Matthew effects in education. *American Educational Research Journal, 20,* 359–374.

Walberg, H.J., & Weinstein, T. (1984). Adults outcomes of connections, certification, and verbal competence. *Journal of Educational Research, 77,* 207–212.

Walker, D.F. (1976). Toward comprehension of curricular realities. In L.S. Shulman (Ed.), *Review of research in education.* (pp.   ). Itasca, IL: F.E. Peacock.

Walker, D.F., & Schaffarzick, J. (1974). Comparing curricula. *Review of Educational Research, 44,* 83–111.

Weinstein, T., Boulanger, F.D., & Walberg, H.J. (1982). Science curriculum effects in high school: A quantitative synthesis. *Journal of Research in Science Teaching, 19,* 511–522.

Weiss, A. (1984). Simple truths of Japanese manufacturing. *Harvard Business Review, 62*(4), 119–125.

White, K.R. (1976). *The relationship between socioeconomic status and academic achievement.* Unpublished dissertation, University of Colorado, Boulder.

Witter, R.A., Okun, M.A., Stock, W.A., & Haring, M.J. (1984). Education and subjective well being: A meta-analysis. *Educational Evaluation and Policy Analysis, 6,* 165–173.

Chapter Twelve

A DEVELOPMENTAL EPIDEMIOLOGICAL PERSPECTIVE ON SOCIAL ADAPTATION AND COGNITIVE FUNCTION

Sheppard G. Kellam

There are important cognitive functions in the performance of social tasks. The focus of this chapter is on those cognitive functions involved in responding to the specific tasks required of each individual in the main social fields of each stage of life. The orientation for this discussion will be community epidemiological and life course developmental. We will consider social fields in the community in which individuals at each stage are confronted by social task demands and must make adaptive behavioral responses. We will call attention to evolving social task demands, conditions, and behavioral response patterns over the life cycle as context for studying cognitive functions.

With a community epidemiological orientation we hold constant the macro characteristics of the population of a defined neighborhood, industrial plant, or other type of fairly small population. We examine the distribution of rates of social adaptive or maladaptive task performance and aspects of health or illness including cognitive functioning. The relationship of variation in rates to variations in social and physical external environments and/or variations in the biopsychology of individuals can be examined and causal models generated and tested. Indeed, field trials of a preventive or treatment nature can be done on the hypothesized external and/or internal antecedent conditions leading to the condition. These trials may have important theory-building functions if targeted at theoretically important aspects of the causal model one has in mind.

The life course developmental perspective integrated with a community epidemiological orientation implies periodic assessment of community-defined age-specific cohorts of individuals in specific social fields over portions of their life course. Social task demands and other characteristics of the specific social field, aspects of biological and psychological status including cognitive function, and the character of behavioral responses can be assessed periodically. This community epidemiological orientation requires both direct and systematic replication in similar and dissimilar communities in order to determine generalizations or specific limitations to the inferences drawn in any one type of community. Both the demands and the behavioral responses may be quite different in different socio-ethnic communities, a point we will elaborate later.

"Social adaptation," a phrase coined by the Woodlawn research group more than 20 years ago, derives from the intimate relationship of each stage of the life course with one or a few main social fields. In each field there are *natural raters* defining social tasks and rating the adequacy of the behavioral responses of individuals. Parents in the home, teachers in the classroom, supervisors on the job, significant others in the peer group, mates or spouses in the intimate social field—all have in common the role of defining social tasks required of individuals within those social fields. Also, each natural rater rates formally or informally the adequacy of performance of individuals within each social field. Teachers provide grades and pass or fail children in the classroom; supervisors in the workplace promote, offer salary increases to, or fire employees; parents make equally powerful but less formal judgments as to "good" or "bad" behavior of their children; spouses get divorced or stay with their mates.

Social adaptation is the interactive process of task demand/behavioral response. The consequent ratings by the natural rater of adequacy of performance we have termed social adaptational status (SAS). Social adaptation is the interface between the individual and the immediate, small environment and is an important focus for studying both the environmental demands in specific social fields and such matters as the individual's cognitive functions as they mediate the responses of the individual to social task demands.

In the Woodlawn studies we have considered it centrally important to distinguish between (SAS) and psychological status or well-being (PWB). Although the two are often empirically related (see e.g., Kellam, Brown, Rubin, & Ensminger, 1983), they are nevertheless conceptually quite different, and the relationships we have found are by no means simple. The difference between them, for example, is a student's failing, according to the teacher, in contrast to how the student is feeling or what he or she is thinking about the grade. The first is a social-status issue; the second is one of psychological status. More Woodlawn first-grade children were thought by their teachers to be maladapting at specific tasks than were considered distressed, that is, symptomatic, by observing clinicians. Also, the short- and long-term courses of SAS and PWB were strikingly different as well. Other investigators (Loney, 1980; Robins, 1966, 1978; Watt, 1978) have reported similar findings.

In considering this two-dimensional view, and in particular the social task demand/behavioral response aspect, the chart in Figure 1 may help. We have called it the Life Course—Social Field Concept (Kellam, Branch, Agrawal, & Ensminger, 1975). It is based on the theoretical development of Havighurst (1952), Erikson (1959, 1963), Neugarten (1968), and many others over the last several decades.

SAS, the adequacy of performance as rated by the natural rater in a specific social field, is a societal judgment of the individual's performance and is a social-status measure of success or failure. Stages of life as defined by Havighurst (1952) are shown in Figure 1 combined with a series of major life events, which often occur at times of transition from one stage to the next. This chart demonstrates how the stages of life and major life events intersect with specific social fields, such as the family, the classroom, or the workplace. The chart also notes the natural rater ("n.r.") in each social field.

Figure 1 presents a generalized interpretation of an individual life course. For many individuals in Woodlawn and in different communities or societies, variations from this prototypical pattern will be frequent (Neugarten, 1979). Variations in the width of the horizontal bars in Figure 1 representing each social field are intended to suggest the relative importance of each field at different stages, and this, too, will vary among individuals, communities, and societies. Not everyone is involved in rearing young children in early adulthood, nor is every adult involved in a work context. Still, the concept illustrates the relationship between an individual's stage of life and important aspects of societal structure and function.

In contrast to SAS stands the question of how the individuals think or feel, that is, their PWB. By PWB we mean the cognitive processes, affective status, self-esteem, and other aspects of individual psychological status.

Cognitive functions are required for the performance of social tasks. They include:

1. the perception of the tasks demanded by the natural rater;
2. the weighing of appropriate behavioral responses;
3. the perception of the natural rater's reaction to the initial behavioral response;
4. the correction of behavioral response in accord with the individual's social adaptive capacities and interests.

We note, however, that social tasks will vary in different social fields

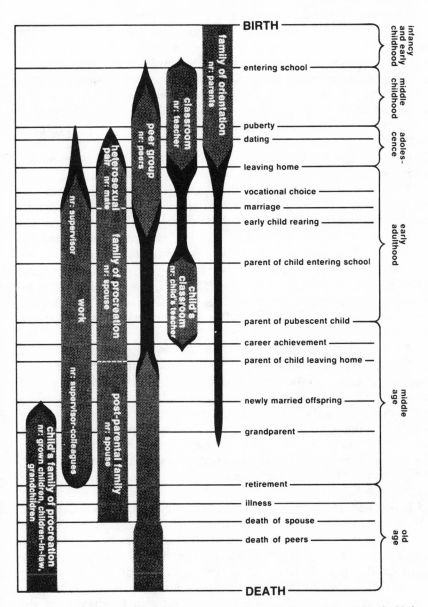

Figure 1. Life course–social field concept. (From Kellam et al., 1975, © University of Chicago Press)

233

at different stages of life and in different communities and societies. Such variation in task demands may be coupled with variation in the perception of tasks, the weighing of acceptable responses, and other cognitive functions.

The two components—SAS and PWB—represent the two major dimensions of mental health. One represents mental health from the viewpoint of society; the other represents mental health from the viewpoint of the individual. This two-dimensional concept draws on a variety of concepts from social and behavioral sciences. Charles Horton Cooley and George Herbert Mead were both concerned with people's perception of how others see them and its effects on their sense of self (Cooley, 1922; Mead, 1934). In fact, the cognitive functions listed above are possibly related to what Cooley meant by the "looking glass," in the sense of observing the effects of our behavior on important other people.

The concepts of family, classroom, peer group, workplace, and the intimate social field are all relevant to specific stages of life in which developing individuals are confronted with particular social task demands and in which, prior to responding, they must recognize the tasks, judge the acceptability of various behavioral responses, weigh their self-interest in being seen as adequately responding. All of these functions can be viewed as cognitive. They are amenable to developmental epidemiological study of total age and social field specific community populations or of smaller, representative samples for laboratory study.

From an epidemiological standpoint, the social fields represent the locations within the community where the individuals at a particular stage of life can be found. Equally important, within each social field can also be found the natural rater. In defining social tasks and rating individuals within the social fields, the natural raters are the sources of social adaptational measures for the epidemiological investigator. In child epidemiology, for example, the family and the classroom are the two earliest major social fields in which young children can be found, and parents in the home and teachers in the classroom are the natural raters.

Chance and idiosyncracy play a large role in SAS. In most social fields natural raters carry great authority, and another person's opinion, no matter how expert, often does not carry the authority of the natural rater. There are harsh teachers and lenient teachers, and likewise parents. Whatever the natural rater's rating tendencies, his or her ratings have a considerable degree of face validity, particularly in regard to children. The relationships of the SAS ratings to the actual behavior of the responding individual can be studied, however, by independent observers in the same social field.

Mental health investigators and clinicians alike have often viewed these two perspectives, SAS and PWB, as opposite sides of the same coin. Psychological status is often considered the antecedent, with social maladaptation the consequence. SAS in the American Psychiatric Association *Diagnostic and Statistical Manual of Mental Disorders* (APA, 1980) is often used as the criterion of illness or its severity. Educators, including classroom teachers of young children, have tended to do the opposite, viewing the social adaptation of the child as antecedent and the psychological status or presence of psychiatric symptoms as a measure of severity. They, too, assume that these two perspectives are opposite sides of the same coin, but it is a different coin from that seen by the mental health professional.

The conceptual distinction between SAS and PWB clarifies at least one of the core problems investigators have confronted for many years over the definition and measurement of mental health and illness. The SAS measure is based on coding social tasks demanded by natural raters and then obtaining assessments by the natural raters of the performance of the individual. In contrast, PWB measures are inferred by indirect evidence based on coding categories of symptoms or other aspects of psychological status of interest. Cognitive function is one of these domains of psychological status. In real life the language of SAS makes use of such words as "pass" or "fail," "promoted" or "fired," "continuing to be married" or "divorced." The language of PWB includes words such as "paranoid," "anxious," "depressed," or "distressed." However, other psychological domains include the person's recognition of the demands by natural raters and the weighing of responses and the like.

By separating the two dimensions, we can investigate their interrelation over time and discover the long-term outcomes of each. We can study cognitive function as a domain within psychological status along with other aspects such as psychiatric symptoms, as long as we distinguish these from the actual social task demands by the natural rater and from the ratings of adequacy of performance by the natural rater of our behavioral responses.

We will use the Woodlawn studies to illustrate some of the long-term importance of this distinction between SAS and PWB. We did not examine the kinds of cognitive functions we point to in this chapter, but we did examine at length the importance of early social maladaptive ratings by teachers and others in regard to such long-term outcomes as drug use, delinquency, and psychiatric symptoms. In parallel with these early studies of SAS over time, we also examined PWB both in relation to social adaptational measures and in its own right as a predictor of long-term outcomes.

Both SAS and PWB in first-grade children in Woodlawn proved to have very important long-term predictive and possibly developmental significance at least as far as late adolescence. These results have been replicated in part by many other investigators, and it is because of these results that we must now turn to improving our understanding of the cognitive processes that have made these results occur. How were the natural rater's demands perceived; what were the processes leading to behavioral responses; how was the natural rater's approval or disapproval of the first responses perceived; and how did the individual then weigh the responses of the natural rater and other interests in determining the next stage of behavioral response?

We point to merely a few salient references here. Robins (1966), for example, reported on the long-term importance of early truancy, breaking rules, and fighting. This kind of behavioral response is frequent and is, of course, rated maladaptive by teachers. This often replicated SAS predictor is a particularly important antecedent to heavy substance use and delinquency. Watt (1978) also has reported the long-term importance of aggressiveness in young males as an antecedent of schizophrenia in adulthood. Loney (1980) has shown evidence that early aggressiveness is the key prognostic component of the hyperactivity syndrome.

In Woodlawn, the general relationship of various categories of PWB to SAS early in the first grade was relatively modest but replicated in several cohorts in several periods during first grade and as far as third grade. The longitudinal relationships between PWB and SAS, however, were strong and marked by major sex differences, with males showing strong prediction from early SAS to later SAS, while females showed stronger prediction from early PWB to later PWB. Thus, as we will illustrate later, the behavior of young first-grade boys was strongly predictive of their behavior 10 years later, while the PWB of first-grade girls was more predictive of their PWB later. The area in which both genders were predictable in regard to early SAS and later PWB was that of learning itself. We will describe these results next.

ILLUSTRATIONS FROM LONGITUDINAL ANALYSES ON WOODLAWN DATA

To further our discussion of cognitive function and its importance in understanding the relationship between SAS and PWB, we will describe briefly some of the central results of analyses based on longitudinal, prospective community-epidemiological data from Woodlawn, a black urban ghetto community in Chicago. Four total cohorts of first graders were followed over time in the 12 elementary schools, the longest being the 1966–67 total population, which was followed-up in 1976 when the former first graders were 16 or 17 years old.

In order to obtain SAS measures in the first grade, we obtained from 57 first-grade teachers in the 12 elementary schools in Woodlawn lists of tasks they expected first-grade children to perform (see Kellam et al., 1975). We then inferred five main social tasks suggested by these:

1. socializing with other children, speaking up, and not sitting alone too much;
2. obeying rules and not fighting, not being truant;
3. demonstrating sufficient independence so as not to be too clinging to the teacher;
4. learning up to ability as the teacher sees it;
5. paying attention and being able to concentrate on tasks.

Scales were constructed to measure SAS on these tasks, and standardized interviews were carried out with each of the first-grade teachers three times in first grade and again in third grade, on four consecutive cohorts of total first-grade populations, each about 1,800 children.

Teacher ratings of SAS were obtained in the early years, as were measures of PWB, particularly psychiatric symptoms. Pairs of clinicians observed stratified random samples of children drawn from first-grade classrooms, and we also used symptom inventories to record reports by mothers on their child's psychiatric symptoms. Third graders rated themselves on their tension and sadness. From all of these ratings we were able to examine the relationships of early SAS and PWB together and separately on a variety of teenage outcomes. The PWB categories of psychiatric symptoms included anxiety, depression, bizarre behavior, obsessive/compulsive behavior, and other traditional symptom domains.

At the time of the 10-year follow-up of 1966–67 Woodlawn first graders, they provided us with self-reports of psychiatric symptoms, self-esteem, and other aspects of their PWB. In addition, information regarding drugs, alcohol, and cigarette use was obtained from both mothers and teenagers, along with school records including achievement and attendance. Reports by mothers and teenagers of delinquency and criminal behavior were also obtained.

During the 10-year follow-up we located and reinterviewed 939 (75%) of the mothers or mother surrogates of the 1,242 families in the 1966–67 cohort. Following the reinterviews of the 939 mothers, and with their permission, 705 teenagers participated fully in the reassessments. We compared the early information on the three relevant groups: mothers we reinterviewed, those whose teenagers we did not reinterview, and mothers we did not reinterview. The mothers we could not reinterview were more likely to have been teenagers when they gave birth to their first child; they were more mobile before and during their child's first-grade year; and their children were somewhat more likely to have been in parochial schools in first grade, where the record-keeping systems were more primitive. We found no differences among the three groups of mothers as far as their own PWB, early family income, welfare status, or the variety of combinations of adults at home. There were no differences as well in the children's SAS or PWB among the three groups. For all of these results the reader can examine methods in more detail in Kellam et al. (1983) and Agrawal, Kellam, Klein, and Turner (1978). Log linear analyses including three of the SAS and/or PWB variables in first grade and drugs, alcohol, or cigarette use, psychiatric symptoms, or delinquency 10 years later are summarized here.

Figure 2 shows reports by the teenagers in regard to their substance use 10 years later as a function of whether they had been rated by their first-grade teacher as shy or aggressive or both. Heavy substance use as shown in Figure 2 was defined as use 20 times or more by the time of follow-up at age 16 or 17. Cigarette use refers to regular daily smoking. Learning problems did not predict drug use but instead strongly predicted psychiatric symptoms. In contrast, the analyses revealed strong relationships between shyness and aggression in first grade and heavy substance use 10 years later. Only 5% of the shy first graders reported regular cigarette use 10 years later, whereas a much greater percentage of the aggressive and an even greater percentage of shy/aggressive children (loners who fought and broke rules) were regular smokers. The same relations can be seen in the other categories of substance use. Delinquency was similarly predictable from shyness and aggression, and in a paper by Ensminger, Kellam, and Rubin (1983) we showed the same kind of relationships with early shyness and aggression. These two early SAS measures of shy behavior and aggressive behavior show a significant interaction, namely, an enhancement of the aggressive effect in later substance use and delinquency.

Psychiatric symptoms in first grade were not at all predictive for males in regard to long-term PWB or the more behavioral outcomes. Shyness and aggression, in contrast, were very predictive for males but not for females. Psychiatric symptoms in first grade for females were strongly predictive of psychiatric symptoms 10 years later, particularly of depressive symptoms. The psychiatric symptom ratings in first grade were provided both by the clinicians' ratings of the small groups of children drawn from first-grade classrooms and by a symptom inventory filled out by the mothers on their children.

Underachievement (or learning problems) in first grade was clearly predictive of depressive symptoms at age 16 or 17. Figure 3 reveals for males the magnitude of risk to be roughly twice that of children

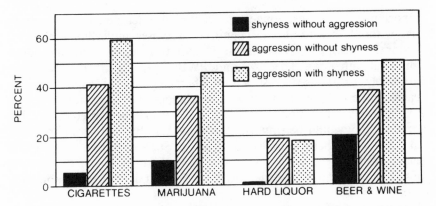

SHYNESS AND AGGRESSION AS RATED BY FIRST-GRADE TEACHERS

Figure 2.   Shyness and aggressiveness in first grade and heavy teenage substance use: Results for the 1966/67 Woodlawn cohort assessed in first grade and 10 years later.

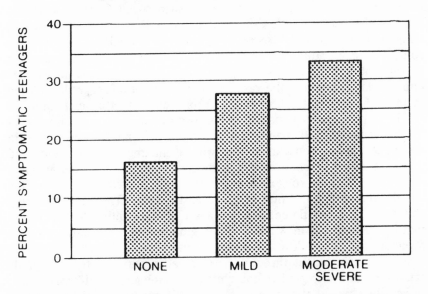

UNDERACHIEVEMENT AS RATED BY FIRST-GRADE TEACHERS

Figure 3.   Underachievement in first grade and depressive symptoms in teenage males: Results for the 1966/67 Woodlawn cohort assessed in first grade and 10 years later.

without underachievement problems at age 6 or 7. Outcome is measured here by self-reports of depressed mood beyond one-half standard deviation compared to the total population of teenagers at follow-up.

The congitive functions we listed earlier must have played a centrally important role in these long-term predictive outcomes. It is our thesis that without measuring the cognitive processes underlying these behavioral developmental paths, we cannot truly understand the developmental outcomes. The SAS and PWB measures are clearly linked intimately to the social structural characteristics of classroom and teacher. The relationships between psychological distress and cognitive functions are dimly understandable, if at all, by these predictions, but together they would be important in understanding and doing research on preventing these long-term outcomes. Such cognitive function research would open many vistas, including the question of the relation of the major mental disorders to these SAS and PWB developmental paths.

We have said that those cognitive functions related to social task performance can be best understood by examining them in specific social fields at specific stages of life. Social fields of importance are shown in Figure 1, but a community epidemiological perspective allows us to go farther in the examination of such social fields. The family is a good illustration. We examined the variation in the child-rearing families in two total cohorts of first graders in Woodlawn. The various combinations of adults in the household raising the first-grade children in 1964–65 and in 1966–67 were examined. Figure 4 contains a taxonomic classification of the varieties of families with first-grade children in the 1966–67 total cohort in this urban black ghetto neighborhood.

The importance of variation in family structure lies in the differences in the social task demands and in the particular natural raters in different kinds of households who will be making these demands and rating behavioral responses. Different combinations of adults at home allow for different role differentiations and indeed often limit the possibilities of specification of child-rearing roles. The mother raising children by herself potentially has a set of roles quite different from that in a household in which mother, grandmother, and father all live together with the children. Different combinations of adults were differentially effective in the child's social adaptation to the first-grade classroom and in regard to the child's psychological well-being.

Family types at the time of first grade were classified in terms of the various combinations of adults at home on the basis of information obtained in interviews with the mothers or mother surrogates of the first-grade children (Kellam, Ensminger, & Turner, 1977). The various combinations of adults present in the households of the 1966–67 population of first graders are shown in Figure 4. We found 10 different constellations of adult relatives present in the families, plus 4 residual categories of male and female relatives and nonrelatives. There were 86 different combinations of these adults in 1966–67, while in 1964–65 there were 79 combinations.

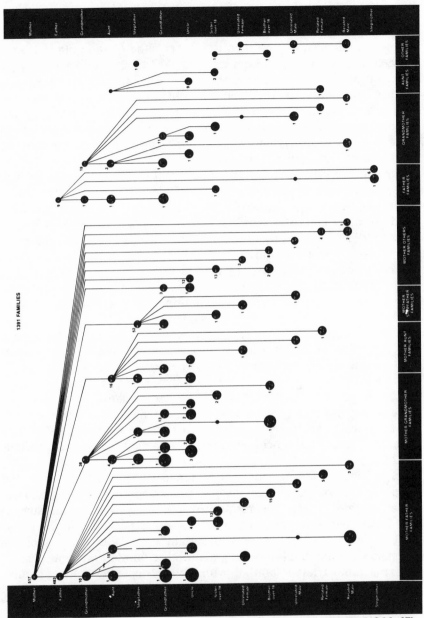

Figure 4. Variation in families of Woodlawn first-grade children (1966–67). (From Kellam et al., 1977)

Figure 4 is cumulative from top to bottom. If one begins, for instance, at the upper left-hand corner with mother alone, and descends directly down to mother/father and then to mother/father/grandmother, it may be seen that mother-alone families occur 517 times, mother/father 483 times, mother/father/grandmother 10 times, mother/father/grandmother/aunt only 1 time. When a combination does not contain the next relative listed in the left and right margins, it is shown by a line moving laterally and downward to the next included relative. Thus there are 38 mother/grandmother alone families, 4 mother/grandmother/aunt families; and so on.

Eight major classes of families plus a residual "other" category may be seen in the conelike clustering of family types. These are named across the bottom of Figure 4. These 9, plus mother-alone families, yield 10 major classes of families raising first-grade children in Woodlawn in 1966–67, which was almost identical to the one derived from the 1964–65 first-grade families.

This taxonomy illustrates the great diversity in households of first-grade children in this community. We have no reason to assume that considerable variation would not be an important characteristic of other kinds of communities. Some of the family types are relatively rare and, though intriguing, are difficult to study because of infrequent occurrence (for example, the father who is raising a first grader with no other adult in the home). Categories can be collapsed for analytic purposes in ways informed by the taxonomy and by the results of other studies. We have studied the developmental course of family structure and have found important relationships to such life-course events as the age at which mothers begin child rearing. These relationships in turn affect long-term child outcomes (Kellam, Adams, Brown, & Ensminger, 1982).

In Woodlawn family type was found to be strongly related to the child's social adaptational status and psychological well-being at least as far as third grade. The results in both study populations suggest that (a) mother-alone families entail the highest risk to the SAS and PWB of the child; (b) the presence of certain second adults has important ameliorative functions—mother/grandmother families are nearly as effective as mother/father families, with mother/stepfather families similar in risk to mother alone; and (c) in terms of risk, the absence of the father was less important than the aloneness of the mother.

From the life-span developmental perspective, these studies were important because they illustrate two of the three main perspectives described by theoreticians in this area (Baltes, Reese, & Lipsitt, 1980; Baltes and Schaie, 1973a, 1973b). First, there was a clear relationship between family structure and the child's social adaptation to school and his or her PWB. Second, while these relationships were found in both the 1964–65 and the 1966–67 first-grade populations, there was at the same time a marked shift in the baseline percentage of maladapting children in these two separate groups. This result is probably a cohort effect which changed the frequencies of social maladaptation and PWB, but their interrelationships remained intact. Cohort effects must be taken into account as potential influences on social task demands, cognitive functions, and behavioral responses.

The advantage of community epidemiologic research is that the concept of community focuses on variation in the familial, educational, political, and economic institutions, along with the physical environment, which might influence both the social task demands and the behavioral responses in particular social fields. Variations in the families, in the classrooms, and in peer groups within a particular kind of community can be studied in regard to their contribution to the child's cognitive functions and behavioral performance.

Community cannot be defined merely by drawing arbitrary lines around areas on a map. Such a process would not be likely to coincide with the local citizens' views or with the existing social and political structure.

Ecological studies (Shaw and McKay, 1969) have long shown that within urban areas there are neighborhoods that have been the entry point to the city for various ethnic groups who bring with them values and expectations. As soon as the entering population has become established within the city, it moves to other, more prestigious and comfortable neighborhoods, making way for later entrants. Or a community may serve as a "bedroom" residential area for a metropolitan area. By recognizing the function different communities serve, the investigator may focus not only on the individual characteristics of the population but also on the social structure and ecological processes going on within that community and their impact on the task demands, cognitive processes, and behavioral responses.

Especially important to those interested in children is the concept of the "community of limited liability" (Janowitz, 1967; Suttles, 1972). This concept recognizes that the local community may not be very relevant for many activities of the urbanized American; however, it may have more importance for certain groups (e.g., the very old and the very young) than for others. The young are limited in their freedom of geographic mobility; the main activities of play and school usually take place within the local neighborhood. Services designed for the young and the aging such as educational, recreational, and medical services are usually provided in local settings. For those researchers and clinicians, then, who focus on these stages of life, the local community may be particularly important.

Our own research illustrates that epidemiologic studies may follow a community population even though they may have "graduated" from the community. As part of the 10-year follow-up, in 1975–76 we reinterviewed the mothers or mother surrogates and the children from the 1966–67 first-grade classes. Though our population originally lived in Woodlawn, by the time of the follow-up about 70% of these children and families lived elsewhere in the Chicago metropolitan area. About 8 of every 10 of the mobile families lived in areas with better housing and higher median incomes.

The concept of community cannot be defined in static terms. While the child is growing and the family evolving, the community may be doing the same. Communities as well must be thought of as evolving, presenting a changing social, political, economic, and even physical environment as background for the life-span development of the individual. For developmental epidemiologic study of social adaptation and cognitive function, this means that relevant aspects of community evolution must be measured. Mobility and social integration are vital aspects of the social context in which to study task demands, behavioral responses, and cognitive functions.

DISCUSSION

Our purpose in this chapter has been to develop a conceptual frame regarding the social context in which cognitive functions can usefully be examined. We can summarize by referring first to the community epidemiological orientation, which defines a population and its environment. Combining this orientation with that of a life-course development allows us to examine specific social fields at particular stages of life which are particularly important arenas for the life-course development of individuals. We can examine variation in these social fields epidemiologically by looking at the varieties of families, for example, that are raising first-grade children and even by studying the evolution of these family types over major portions of the life cycle. The epidemiological perspective allows us to understand what the total universe is from which our sampling of varieties of families derives.

In the last decade long-term developmental studies on total or at least large populations of children have been done that reveal early behavioral responses predictive of important long-term outcomes. The next stage of research requires us to examine the cognitive functions that mediate these behavioral responses. We need to include the perceptions of children regarding what is expected; their evaluations of possible behavioral responses; their own evaluation of the impact of their behavior on the natural rater; and their subsequent weighing of whether or how to modify their behavioral responses. To be successful this stage of research into child development must take into account the nature of the social task demands from the point of view of both the immediate situation and of adjacent or surrounding small social fields and the larger community or even societies as a whole.

We might pose the research question, for example, of whether shy Woodlawn children from mother-alone homes differ qualitatively or quantitatively in cognitive functions from aggressive or adapting children. We can also ask whether cognitive functions such as those we listed differ between shy children in mother-alone households and shy children in mother/father homes or homes characterized as having more child-rearing resources. Comparisons across types of behaving children, across stages of life, across proximal and distal environments are part of what we are suggesting.

We are talking here, of course, about the integration of anthropologic, sociologic, social adaptational, and cognitive as well as other psychological functions in models leading to greater understanding of life-course development including mental health and illness. Many biologists have defined their field as the interaction of organisms with their environments. From a biopsychosocial perspective, cognitive function research can best be done by including within our research models the environment in which the functions occur. Environment is not a homogeneous external condition; it can be systematically measured at different levels of proximity, and indeed the evolution of environments is as characteristic of nature as the evolution of individuals over the life cycle.

REFERENCES

Agrawal, K.C., Kellam, S.G., Klein, Z.E., & Turner, R.J. (1978). The Woodlawn mental health studies: Tracking children and families for long-term follow-up. *American Journal of Public Health, 68*(2), 139–142.

American Psychiatric Association. (1980). *Diagnostic and statistical manual of mental disorders* (3rd ed.). Washington, DC: Author.

Baltes, P.B., Reese, H., & Lipsitt, L. (1980). Life-span developmental psychology. *Annual Review of Psychology, 31,* 65–110.

Baltes, P.B., & Schaie, K.W. (Eds.). (1973a). *Life-span developmental psychology: Personality and socialization.* New York: Academic Press.

Baltes, P.B., & Schaie, K.W. (1973b). On life-span developmental research paradigms: Retrospects and prospects. In P.B. Baltes & K.W. Schaie (Eds.), *Life-span developmental psychology: Personality and socialization* (pp. 366–396). New York: Academic Press.

Cooley, C.H. (1922). *Human nature and the social order.* New York: Schocken.

Ensminger, M.E., Kellam, S.G., & Rubin, B.R. (1983). School and family origins of delinquency: Comparisons by sex. In K.T. Van Dusen & S.A. Mednick (Eds.), *Prospective studies of crime and delinquency* (pp. 73–97). Boston, Kluwer-Nijhoff.

Erikson, E.H. (1959). Identity and the life cycle, selected papers. In G.S. Klein (Ed.), *Psychological issues,* (Vol. 1, No. 1). New York: International Universities Press.

Erikson, E.H. (1963). *Childhood and society* (rev. ed.). New York: Norton.

Faris, R.E., & Dunham, W.H. (1939). *Mental disorders in urban areas.* Chicago: University of Chicago Press.

Havighurst, R.J. (1952). *Developmental tasks and education* (2nd ed.). New York: Longmans Green.

Janowitz, M. (1967). *The community press in an urban setting: The social elements of urbanism* (2nd ed.). Chicago: University of Chicago Press.

Kellam, S.G., Adams, R.G., Brown, C.H., & Ensminger, M.E. (1982). The long-term evolution of the family structure of teenage and older mothers. *Journal of Marriage and the Family, 44,* 539–554.

Kellam, S.G., Branch, J.D., Agrawal, K.C., & Ensminger, M.E. (1975). *Mental health and going to school: The Woodlawn Program of assessment, early intervention and evaluation.* Chicago: University of Chicago Press.

Kellam, S.G., Brown, C.H., Rubin, B.R., & Ensminger, M.E. (1983). Paths leading to teenage psychiatric symptoms and substance use: Developmental epidemiological studies in Woodlawn. In S.B. Guze, F.J. Earls, & J.E. Barrett (Eds.), *Childhood psychopathology and development* (pp. 17–51). New York: Raven Press.

Kellam, S.G., Ensminger, M.E., & Turner, R.J. (1977). Family structure and the mental health of children: Concurrent and longitudinal community-wide studies. *Archives of General Psychiatry, 34,* 1012–1022.

Loney, J. (1980). Hyperkinesis comes of age. What do we know and where should we go? *American Journal of Orthopsychiatry, 50,* 28–42.

Mead, G.H. (1934). *Mind, self and society.* Chicago: University of Chicago Press.

Neugarten, B.L. (1968). The awareness of middle age. In B.L. Neugarten (Ed.), *Middle age and aging: A reader in social psychology* (pp. 93–98). Chicago: University of Chicago Press.

Neugarten, B.L. (1979). Time, age, and the life cycle. *American Journal of Psychiatry, 136,* 887–894.

Robins, L.N. (1966). *Deviant children grown up: A sociological and psychiatric study of sociopathic personality.* Baltimore: Williams & Wilkins.

Robins, L.N. (1978). Sturdy childhood predictors of adult outcomes: Replications from longitudinal studies. In J.E. Barrett, R.M. Rose, & G.L. Klerman (Eds.), *Stress and mental disorders* (pp. 611–622). New York: Raven Press.

Shaw, C.R., & McKay, H.D. (1969). *Juvenile delinquency and urban areas* (rev. ed.). Chicago: University of Chicago Press.

Suttles, G.D. (1972). *The social construction of communities.* Chicago: University of Chicago Press.

Watt, N.F. (1978). Patterns of childhood social development in adult schizophrenics. *Archives of General Psychiatry, 35,* 160–170.

Chapter Thirteen

Sociocultural Determination of Mental Aging

David R. Heise

Psychology has predictable emphases when applied to aging—looking for different profiles of ability at different ages, evaluating these in terms of growth and decrement, and interpreting the variations physiologically. However, at least in part, the aging process is defined culturally, and sociocultural factors are another possible source of age variation in mental activity.

> A person's competencies, interests, and behaviors rise and fall over the life-span roughly in correspondence with the different age phases. Because age is a biosocial variable, it has to be recognized that some of these psychological changes might be due to shifts in the operating genotypes, while other variations between age levels could be due to the different social experiences associated with different age identities. (Heise, 1973, p. 157)

This chapter outlines a framework for understanding how a culture can structure mental aging by imposing expectations for the age-graded identities that are part of the culture.

In brief, the argument is as follows. A trajectory of age-graded identities is defined within a culture in terms of the power and activity appropriate for each age, and the trajectory leads to stereotypes about how mental processing should vary over the life span. The stereotypes shape reality as each person tries to confirm self-identities related to age and as others exert social pressure on a person to conform with the age identity that they attribute to that person. The typical trajectory in Western industrialized nations aligns adulthood with productive mental activity, childhood with impractical thinking, and old age with enfeeblement. However, trajectories in some other societies give more potential to the elderly, suggesting that Western stereotypes are not grounded in human biology.

AGING TRAJECTORY IN THE UNITED STATES

Sociologists study the distributions of social identities or roles on fundamental dimensions. For example, Kemper (1978) has argued that two dimensions—he calls them power and status—are fundamental sociologically and correspond to Potency and Evaluation, dimensions of psychological response to stimuli that Osgood found in people around the world (Osgood, May, & Miron, 1975). With precedent from Sorokin (1937) and Parsons (1951), sensate expressiveness—as opposed to ideational stolidity—can be added as another sociological basis for classifying roles, and this dimension corresponds to Osgood's third response universal, Activity. Age-graded identities vary less on Evaluation than they do on the other two dimensions, so I will focus here only on Potency and Activity.

Potency and activity of roles can be measured subjectively using Osgood's semantic differential (Osgood et al., 1975), and semantic differential ratings for hundreds of role identities have been collected from American respondents by Osgood and by myself. For the sake of continuity later in the chapter I use Osgood's data[1] to show the trajectory of age-graded roles in the United States, bypassing my own data which replicate the results (e.g., Heise, 1979, appendix). Osgood's atlas of semantic differential ratings provides Evaluation-Potency-Activity profiles for 617 concepts rated by youths speaking American English. I use measurements standardized on the basis of all 617 concepts for the sake of comparability in later cross-cultural analyses.

Figure 1 shows the Potency-Activity trajectory of age identities in the U.S.—the kinds of stereotypes held about people when age is an issue. From impotent liveliness in childhood, Americans move up in power as they mature—peaking in adulthood, then declining dramatically in both power and activity as they move on to old age. The trajectory climbs much higher in power for males than for females, reflecting the fact that Americans maintain stereotypes about gender differences as well as age differences. Figure 2 shows that a similar trajectory is obtained when looking at age-graded roles within specific institutions—the family, in this case. In general, whenever age is a facet of role definition in the U.S., the adult roles are more powerful than those of childhood or old age, and the roles of the elderly are seen as less active than the roles that younger people occupy.

---

[1] Osgood's data collection procedures and analytic methodologies are documented in Osgood et al. (1975). The data themselves are unpublished, but Osgood provided me with computer printouts in the mid-1970s. A semantic differential scale has contrasting adjectives at each end (e.g., "good" versus "bad" and a series of check positions in between which are defined adverbially (e.g., "slightly," "quite," "extremely"). A stimulus—like "child" or "adult"—is rated on a set of such scales.

AGE ROLES--U.S.A.

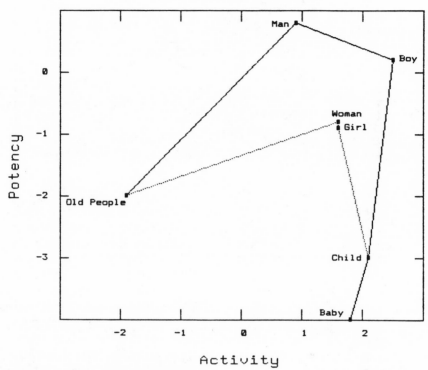

Figure 1. Age roles—United States.

Figures 1 and 2 are specific to the U.S., but numerous contemporary societies show similar features. Osgood provided atlases for 16 different sociocultural groups. I extracted Potency-Activity data on 27 age-related concepts from each atlas and computed similarities among societies. Guttman's (1968) multidimensional scaling procedure applied to the similarities produced a reasonable two-dimensional organization shown in Figure 3. Most of the societies cluster in the middle near the U.S. The typical aging trajectory in all of these cases is a climb in power from childhood to maturity with power peaking higher for males than for females, and a decline in power and activity as a person moves to elderly roles.

SOCIAL IDENTITIES AND MENTAL ACTIVITY

Potency-Activity impressions of age-graded identities are more than stereotypes about what people are like at different ages. They are cultural

FAMILY ROLES-U.S.A.

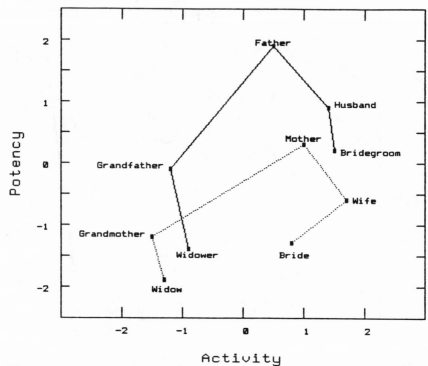

Figure 2.   Family roles—United States.

definitions of the conduct appropriate for people at different ages. As role definitions, these impressions control the kinds of behavior people are likely to produce and the kinds of behavior for which they will receive rewards and punishments from others.

Confirmatory Activity

Substantial evidence (Heise, 1979; Smith-Lovin & Heise, in press) supports the proposition that people anticipate and produce events that confirm their identities. Events are constructed to produce an impression of the actor as a certain kind of person—as one who holds a particular identity.

To a large extent the impression created by an event is a function of the behavior enacted, and confirming an identity is a matter of selecting a behavior that is fitting for the actor. Complicated interactions operate while events generate impressions about a person—for example, bad acts usually create a bad impression of an actor but not when

CULTURAL SIMILARITIES IN MEANINGS OF AGE CONCEPTS

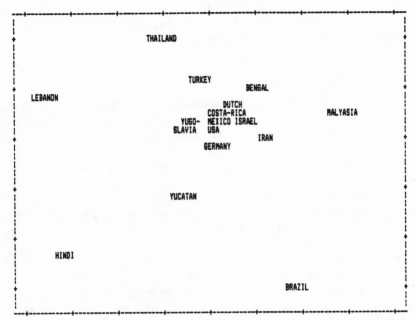

Figure 3. Results of nonmetric scaling of cultures based on similarities
of their Potency-Activity ratings of age-related concepts.

they are directed at evil objects. However, ignoring complications and
speaking roughly, people who are trying to maintain high-status identities by creating good impressions have to engage in valued behaviors,
people who are trying to confirm a powerful identity have to produce
deep, potent acts, and an active identity has to be maintained with
lively conduct.

Research so far has focused on interpersonal behavior, while the
concern here is with behaviors that take nonsocial, even abstract objects—like solving a problem or mulling over an experience. However,
I hypothesize that essentially the same processes are at work in the
nonsocial realm as in the social domain. In particular, when people
are engaged in mental activity, they employ a form of mental processing
that confirms their salient identity. Similarly, when we observe others
engrossed in mental activity, we expect them to be thinking in ways
that correspond to who we think they are and sanction them if they
appear to be deviating.

Accordingly, the trajectory of age stereotypes should lead to variations
in how people are inclined to think when their age-based identities are
salient in a situation. A child's mind should be immature, full of
shallow, lively thoughts. A male adult's mind should be the ideal

problem-solver—a quick powerful computer. As the adult male moves into middle age, he should think slower while retaining his depth—becoming the conservative theoretician. Elderly mental processes should return to the shallowness of childhood, but now in a plodding fashion.

Types of Mental Activity

A key part of the theoretical framework being applied here (Heise, 1979) is that people select activities from culturally defined categories. For example, someone enacting an adult male role does not simply choose a style of activity—to operate in a fast and potent manner—but rather tries to produce particular acts that are fast and potent by cultural definition. Self-confirmation has to be conducted in terms of qualitative units of action that have cultural meaning. This leads to the question: What are lay conceptions of mental activities, and what meanings are attributed to mental activities that allow them to be confirmatory or not?

Not much attention has been given to folk conceptions of mental processing. However, Western cultures do provide a substantial vocabulary for distinguishing between different kinds of subjective activities. I mined two thesauruses of American English in search of verbs that can be substituted without too much awkwardness into the frame: "First he acted, then he went off alone and ——— the consequences," or "First he acted, then he went off alone and ——— the puzzle." The phrase "first he acted" partitions mental activity from overt behavior. The phrase "went off alone" emphasizes the nonsocial aspect of mental processing. The final words—"consequences" or "puzzle"—suggest that mental processing is a transitive activity operating on an object. I found more than 150 verbs relating to mental processing. The list may not be exhaustive for American culture, but it represents a wide variety of mental processes.

These categories of mental processing could be defined in various ways, but the relevant definition with respect to their potential for identity confirmation is connotative—the impression the conduct evokes in terms of the dimensions Evaluation, Potency, Activity, particularly the latter two in the study of aging. A small exploratory study was conducted to obtain some data relating to the connotations of the mental processes.

Respondents—77 Indiana University undergraduates in a sociology course—provided semantic differential ratings of mental activities presented in infinitive form, for instance, "to meditate on something." Each stimulus was followed by three bipolar scales defined with adjectives: "bad-awful" versus "good-nice" for Evaluation; "powerless-little" versus "powerful-big" for Potency; and "slow-quiet-old" versus "fast-noisy-young" for Activity (the same scales used by Smith-Lovin & Heise, in press).[2] Nine rating positions on each scale were defined by "neutral" at the middle and "slightly," "quite," "extremely," "infinitely" going in both directions. Four different forms distributed randomly with 40 stimuli on each form obtained data on 160 stimuli altogether, with 15 or more raters for each stimulus (occasionally fewer when some respondents did not know the meaning of a word). Ratings on each scale were quantified with an assumed-interval metric, and means were computed across all of the respondents who had rated a given stimulus.

Table 1 shows the distribution of mental processes cross-classified in terms of their Activity-Potency connotations.[3] Activity is divided into high and low categories, with high including all mental activities having a mean rating greater than 0 (the value assigned to "neutral" on the rating scale). Potency is represented by three categories: high includes mental activities with a mean rating greater than 1.0 (slightly powerful); medium includes mean scores greater than 0 but less than 1.0; and low is for mean scores less than 0. Evaluations of the processes are indicated by their ranking within each list and by the mean Evaluation score for all mental activities in a category, given at the end of the list.

Age Grading of Mental Activity

The materials in Table 1 permit clearer specification of what is being suggested here. Children might dream and daydream, fantasize, notice, marvel—if they select the nearest positively evaluated mental activities to confirm their good-weak-lively role identities. Low-potency, high-activity mental activities represented by "fret," "stew," "disregard," "fear" are disvalued, but they would be appropriate for children who are in a bad mood. A young adult male might comprehend, attend to, discover, analyze when in a good mood; and mark, scheme, memorize when operating with lowered self-esteem. A middle-aged male might understand, resolve, reason, concentrate, theorize, meditate. The elderly

---

[2] The inclusion of "young" and "old" among the adjectives for the Activity rating scale cues a judgment that is particularly relevant in the current context. Decades of research on the semantic differential suggest that results would be about the same with or without this adjective pair, but future studies might examine the difference.

[3] Since each stimulus was rated by a small sample of respondents, the means are subject to large sampling errors, and classification reflects the precision of the data better than would a table of means. Three stimuli were rated twice by different respondents in order to gauge reliability: In all three cases the replications ended up in different—though adjacent—cells of the cross-classification before the replications were combined to yield overall profiles for these three activities.

Table 1. **Distribution of Lay Categories of Mental Processing in Terms of Activity and Potency Connotations**

Potency	Activity	
	Low	High
High	respect, understand, appreciate, resolve, solve, reason about, have faith in, concentrate on, be concerned about, picture, think over, theorize about, hypothesize about, consider, take inventory of, meditate on, calculate, weigh, contemplate (Evaluation mean: 2.35)	love, learn, comprehend, have insight about, think about, believe in, pay attention to, discover, realize, invent, be passionate about, explore, grasp, analyze, figure out, acknowledge, clarify, hope for, trust in, prove, decide on, envision, question, investigate, recall, perceive, recognize, imagine, plan, study, introspect on, untangle, conceive of, confirm, decipher, remember, test, anticipate, distinguish, ascertain, differentiate, verify, rehearse, account for, unravel, focus on, recollect, forecast, identify, specify, have a hunch about, approve of, attend to, interpret, derive, discern, inspect, compute, reckon, yearn for, define, regard, intuit,[a] take in, watch over, memorize, determine something about, apprehend, classify, gauge, vindicate, scheme over, mark[a] (Evaluation mean: 1.93)
Medium	wonder about, speculate on, deliberate on,[a] acccept, ponder, digest, revere,[a] surmise, search through, probe, heed,[a] process, justify, explicate,[a] scrutinize, forget, agonize over (Evaluation mean: 0.90)	dream about, fantasize about, notice, reflect on, examine, evaluate, marvel over, daydream about, check, elucidate,[a] abstract, contrast, compare, enumerate, predict, estimate, muse about, suspect, pretend, doubt, conjecture about,[a] characterize, fear, plot, judge, ignore, stew over, hate (Evaluation mean: 0.69)
Low	wait for, ruminate about,[a] moon over,[a] pine over,[a] dwell on, worry about, overlook, anguish over, brood over, dread, neglect (Evaluation mean: −1.15)	guess about, count on, gamble on, expect, presume, have contempt for, disregard, fret over, take for granted (Evaluation mean: −0.98)

[a] Rated by 15 or fewer respondents. Other words have been rated by more than 15 respondents.

at their best should wonder, speculate, accept, ponder; and in less positive states they should dread, brood, ruminate, forget.

Limited as these data are, they demonstrate the point being made here. If people think in a manner to confirm their age-graded identities, then they engage in mental processes that are stereotypical for their age. If people suppose that others act in accord with their age identities, then they expect others to think in stereotypical ways and put others under pressure to do so.

It might be noted that the most idealized mental processes in Western civilization belong to adulthood, while the mental activities available to the elderly are few and negatively toned in evaluation. "Decrement" in thought processes of the aged is intrinsic in the way Western lay cultures evaluate powerless, quiet activities.

OTHER CULTURES

One possible response to the correspondence between age roles and stereotypical mental processing is that the lay culture has come to reflect biological reality accurately. Children and the elderly are weak, their thinking and other behavior lacks depth, and their social power is defined in accordance with these realities. Adult males are strong, they behave assertively and vigorously in thought as in other action, and the social power of their roles reflects their capacities. Moreover, lay interpretations of mental processes also might be viewed as accurate: Understanding, discovering, reasoning, and analyzing justifiably are viewed as potent and valuable activities because they are adaptive. Brooding, ruminating, and dreading have to be seen objectively as weak, passive, useless wastes of mind, and this is reflected in the way people rate such activities.

Cross-cultural analysis can help distinguish valid sociobiological arguments from ethnocentric ones. If something is not biologically determined, we are likely to find variations in going from one society to another. Thus I return to Figure 3, which shows similarities among cultures in age-related concepts, this time attending to outlying cultures rather than the central cluster. Do the societies that are different offer evidence against the argument that lay cultures accurately reflect biological realities?

Figures 4 through 7 show trajectories for age roles in the noncentral cultures. Figure 4, for Brazil, shows a pattern largely similar to that of the U.S., but Brazil lacks major gender distinctions and none of its age roles is as powerless as some age roles are in the U.S. Figure 5, for Thailand, also shows a pattern fairly similar to that of the U.S.: However, the elderly do not decline so much in either power or

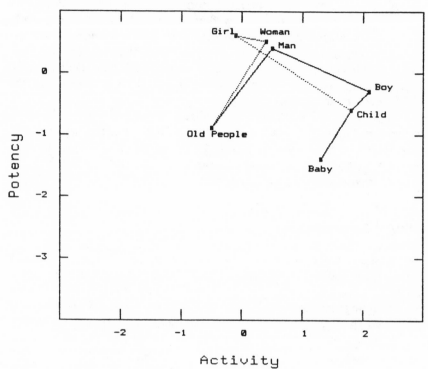

Figure 4.   Age roles—Brazil.

liveliness. In Malaysia (see Figure 6) adult aging corresponds to a decline in liveliness but no loss in power. Figure 7, for New Delhians speaking Hindi, show a small decline in power and a small increase in liveliness with advanced age.[4]

All cultures for which data are available, except New Delhi Hindi, see the aged as slower and quieter than people in other age levels. Slowing down with age could be a biological fact usually reflected in cultural conceptions.[5] Not all cultures see the aged as impotent, however.

---

[4] I do not present the charts for family roles here: They are more complex but reasonably in accord with these summaries.

[5] A striking phenomenon appears on one of the charts—the conception of infants as quiet in Malaysia. This might mean that activity, too, can be culturally determined, and a further search might turn up more cultures like New Delhi Hindi in which the old are seen as lively. However, I prefer to be conservative in interpretation because cross-cultural analyses have many fallibilities. For example, babies might not be any more quiet in Malaysia than elsewhere—instead the rated concept might not have been the translation equivalent of *baby* in English.

AGE ROLES--THAILAND

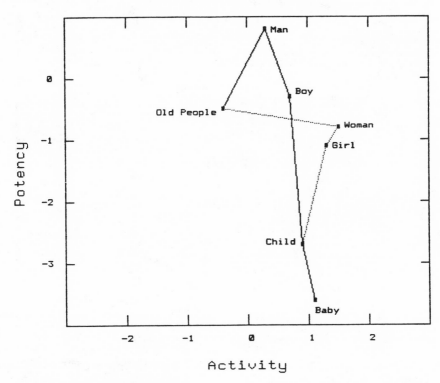

Figure 5. Age roles—Thailand.

Biologizing Western notions of the elderly as frail and weak-minded is ethnocentric.

Osgood's atlases contain data on a few categories of mental processing, permitting a check on whether a particular kind of mental activity has the same significance everywhere. The final chart (Figure 8) shows connotations of "hope" and "thought" in five cultures. Hoping lies within a fairly narrow band of activity connotation, but there are cultural variations in its perceived potency. Thinking connotes quite different things in different cultures in terms of both liveliness and potency.[6]

Thus, different cultures not only have different aging trajectories defining what it means to be of a certain age. Additionally, different

---

[6] The differences for "thinking" are so great that they beg anthropological interpretation (which I am not qualified to give). They also suggest a ripe area for cross-cultural research by psychologists who want to transcend Western notions of mental ability.

AGE ROLES--MALAYSIA

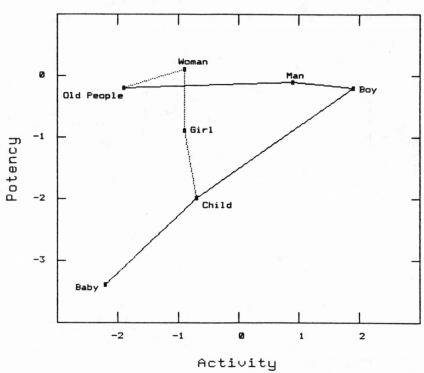

Figure 6. Age roles—Malaysia.

cultures interpret mental acts in different ways so, for example, "thinking" may connote mental depth in one culture, shallowness in another.

I have glossed over the many difficulties and ambiguities in cross-cultural research, expecting general patterns to overwhelm doubts about any one case. I believe the results are supportive. Certainly the cross-cultural analyses shatter a simplistic sociobiological argument that the elderly always behave in a certain fashion and therefore they invariably are viewed as weak and passive.

CONCLUSION

I have shown empirically that age-graded roles in Western society vary in terms of levels of potency and activity attributed to them. Different kinds of mental processing also vary in their presumed potency and activity. I argued theoretically for a connection between these two facts, that people at different ages engage in mental activities that express

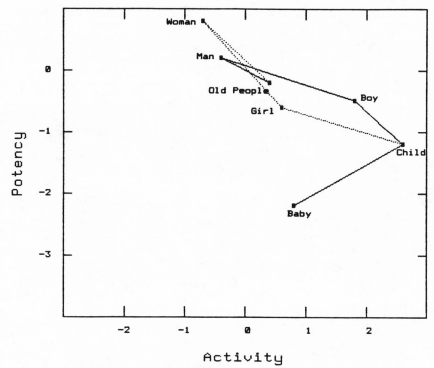

Figure 7.   Age roles—New Delhi Hindi.

their age roles. Indeed, matching the Potency-Activity of thought processes to the Potency-Activity of age roles does reproduce common expectations about how people at different ages think.

An alternative argument would be that biological factors determine the potency and activity of action (including mental action) and stereotypes about age roles evolve to fit the biological facts. However, an examination of data from some non-Western societies indicated that stereotypes about age, and about kinds of mental processing, vary widely across cultures. The cross-cultural materials indicate that even if particular activities are characteristic of a specific age everywhere, the inferences drawn from those activities in terms of power and activity are culturally variable. Thus stereotypes about age roles are not *objective* derivations from the capacities of people at different ages.

This is what I have tried to do in this chapter: outline the hypothesis that people engage in mental activities to express their age roles; and deal with one extreme counterclaim, that people's age roles objectively

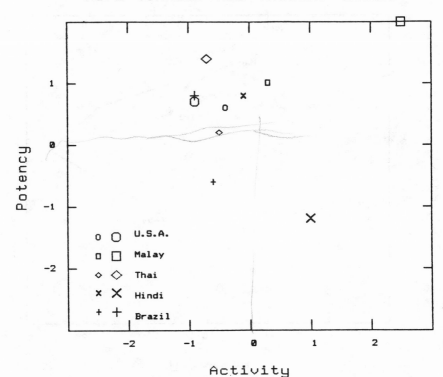

Figure 8. Potency-Activity connotations of "hope" (small marks) and "thought" (large marks) for several cultures.

reflect biological capacities. For a conclusion, I will presume my overall argument is correct.

Psychological decrement among the aged is a problem produced by culture as much as it is an outcome of biology. Western societies force the elderly into powerless roles that encourage them to give up potent thought. In the U.S. problem-solving abilities are glorified and defined outside the province of the elderly, while the few intellectual processes that are stereotypically assigned to the old are disvalued.

The social power of the aged probably will increase as the proportion of elderly in Western populations moves to unprecedented levels. Perceptions of elderly mental competence may rise with the power of the aged; slow, methodical mental activities may be valued more; and conceptions of some productive activities may be reformulated so they are fitting for the aged. Indeed, the National Institute on Aging workshop that generated this chapter may be one instrument stimulating such social change.

REFERENCES

Guttman, L. (1968). "A general nonmetric technique for finding the smallest coordinate space for a configuration of points." *Psychometrika, 33,* 469–506.

Heise, D.R. (1973). *Personality: Biosocial bases.* Chicago: Rand McNally.

Heise, D.R. (1979). *Understanding events: Affect and the construction of social action.* New York: Cambridge University Press.

Kemper, T.D. (1978). *A social interactional theory of emotions.* New York: Wiley Interscience.

Osgood, C.E., May, W.H., & Miron, M.S. (1975). *Cross-cultural universals of affective meaning.* Urbana: University of Illinois Press.

Parsons, T. (1951). *The social system.* New York: Free Press.

Smith-Lovin, L., & Heise, D.R. (Eds.). (1985). Special issue of *Journal of Mathematical Sociology.*

Sorokin, P. (1937). *Social and cultural dynamics.* New York: American Book.

Chapter Fourteen

AFTERWORD

Carmi Schooler
K. Warner Schaie

This book is an attempt to examine how, as individuals pass through the various stages of their lives, their ways of thinking are affected by their position in the social structure. Among those researchers whose work comes closest to dealing with this problem, the life-span psychologists have generally focused on how thinking processes have been affected by age. The social psychologists (of either the sociological or psychological persuasion) have been concerned with whether or not environmental conditions determined by social structures affect levels of intellectual functioning, and the cognitive psychologists have focused on developing models of thinking processes, most especially the thinking processes of those who are experts in solving limited domains of problems (e.g., the microworlds of chess, dinosaur classification, or the memorization of long strings of numbers).

These disparate approaches have indeed been fruitful. The social psychologists have succeeded in showing that social-structurally determined conditions, such as occupational self-direction, can affect intellectual flexibility. The life-span psychologists have demonstrated that there is a near universal slowing-down of response time with age, and that many—but not all—individuals undergo not only quantitative but also qualitative changes in their cognitive functioning as they grow older. The cognitive psychologists have developed models that successfully mimic the individual's acquisition and use of expertise in delimited areas.

In this book we have taken the additional step of trying to interrelate social structural, life span, and cognitive approaches and findings. We have done this both by identifying those researchers whose work comes closest to bridging the gap between social structure and cognitive processes and by inviting some of the best researchers in each of these fields who had not yet considered these issues, to apply themselves to the problem in both theoretical and empirical terms. We believe we have been successful in this effort. We hope that the contributions to this volume will provide firm evidence that will serve as a foundation for future research. We have found that:

1. Social structural conditions seem to affect cognitive functioning throughout the life span (Miller, Slomczynski, & Kohn; chapter 10; Schooler, chapter 2). Cultural conditions probably do so as well (Heise, chapter 13).

2. Although the biological aging process constrains the speed of individuals' cognitive functioning and, possibly, also their ability to cope with maximally demanding situations, individuals can and do develop mechanisms to deal with this decrement. They may, as Salthouse (chapter 8) has demonstrated, adjust their mode of functioning to take into account their loss of speed or they may, as Schaie (chapter 3) has found, increase their efficiency or accuracy as their speed diminishes.

One possible factor contributing to the maintenance, or even increase, of performance levels with age is the increase in expertise gained through experience in the various domains. Cognitive researchers have demonstrated that such expertise results in a decrease in the amount of conscious processing involved and an increase in automaticized responses—responses that seem to be least affected by aging (Hoyer, chapter 7).

Other mechanisms that maintain cognitive functioning may be developed through the intervention of society. There are many examples of planned ameliorations that have been successful. Several are reviewed by Abeles and Riley (chapter 9). On the other hand, there are also hints that much of the cognitive decrement in individuals is the result of societally imposed restrictions on the complexity of older individuals' environments (see, e.g., Miller et al., chapter 10). However, given the probable necessity, brought about by the demographic cycle of baby boom and baby bust (Abeles & Riley, chapter 9), that people continue to be socially productive till later and later ages, it may be incumbent on our society, if it is to survive, to insure that the elderly continue to function at as high a level as possible.

If we are to increase the likelihood that high levels of cognitive functioning will last to the end of the life span, we need to learn much more about the central concerns of this book—the interrelationships among social structural conditions, individuals' life courses, and cognitive functioning. Here the chapters by Loftus, Truax, and Nelson (chapter 4), Kliegl and Baltes (chapter 6), and Salthouse (chapter 8)—all describe experimental approaches to the interrelationships between cognitive functioning and extended life span. These studies, however, are unconcerned about how their subjects' positions in the socioeconomic structure might affect their performance.

On the other hand, the chapters by Schooler (chapter 2), Abeles and Riley (chapter 9), Miller et al. (chapter 10), Walberg (chapter 11), Kellam (chapter 12), and Heise (chapter 13), do deal with the effects of social structural position on cognitive functioning, and as such are generally based on representative samples of individuals from a broad range of social statuses. They also deal with the effects of life course. They do not, however, contain any models of cognitive functioning, nor do they come close to specifying exactly which social structural, or even more proximal environmental conditions, experimental cognitive psychologists should include in their experiments.

A third group of chapters, those by Sternberg and Berg (chapter 1), Glaser (chapter 5), and Hoyer (chapter 7) all discuss models of cognitive functioning. These models tend to be concerned with the development of expertise and its importance in the individual's functioning. They link such development to the individual's life course. With the exception of the one by Sternberg and Berg, these chapters do not concern themselves with possible effects of social structure. Nor do the theories presented provide ready models for either social-structurally oriented social psychologists or experimental cognitive psychologists to include in their work. Thus, in terms of our broadest goal, our book has been only partially successful. We have gotten the workers in the different disciplines to look beyond their own fields, but we have not gotten them to look far enough.

Problems other than interdisciplinary ones also remain. One matter of serious concern is sampling. The subjects in research done by cognitive psychologists are frequently either college sophomores or experts in various fields, chosen primarily on the basis of their availability. Much of the work on the elderly is, again, based on samples of convenience, gathered in senior citizens' centers. These procedural problems, however, reflect real difficulties in designing appropriate samples. In developing their samples, researchers in these areas are frequently faced with two seemingly incompatible concerns. On the one hand, the individuals who may be the most appropriate for studying a researcher's substantive problems may be statistically rare, for example, chess experts, or children with extensive knowledge of dinosaurs. On the other hand, if such statistically rare individuals are the sole focus of study, it remains unclear to which populations the results can be generalized. The problem is not insoluble, but care has to be exercised that it is approached in a scientifically meaningful and rigorous way.

Another problem to be dealt with is the applicability of models of cognitive behavior based on expert functioning to problems facing normal individuals in their occupational and daily lives. Much of the relevant evidence suggests a relatively low level of generalizability from one domain of expertise to another. Yet people must function in many domains and the results of the occupational studies suggest some level of generalizability. Such generalizability may come about in various ways. One source may be that certain combinations and permutations of ability components may be essential in a variety of situations having different attributes. Thus there is not necessarily a far transfer effect but, rather, the development of expert knowledge in one field may lead directly to superior performance in an apparently unrelated field. What is needed to test such a hypothesis is an appropriate taxonomy of situational demands that individuals face across their life spans. Both of our chapters (Schooler, chapter 2; Schaie, chapter 3) represent the beginnings of such an attempt, but obviously much more has to be done. Discovering the relevant demand characteristics of environments also lies at the heart of what we regard as a basic problem in linking the three approaches we have considered—extracting from the work of social psychologists the environmental factors that cognitive and life-span psychologists should include in their research designs. If we can also extract from the work of the cognitive psychologists models of cognitive functioning that can be used by the life-span and social psychologists in their research, we will have gone a long way toward intellectually solving the problem of how people's thinking is affected by their social environment over the life span. This is a problem whose answer we must know if we are to develop ways of keeping people productive and fulfilled throughout their lives.

Author Index

Wechsler, D., 6, *23,* 52, *58*
Weinert, F.E., 100, *119*
Wernfeld, F., *227*
Weinman, C., 36, *47*
Weinstein, T., 214, 222, *228, 229*
Weintraub, M., 52, *57*
Weiss, A., 226, *229*
Wenger, L., 70, 76, *77*
White, K.R., 221, *229*
Wiedl, K.H., 98, *119*
Wilensky, H.L., 179, *202*
Williams, D.M., 8, 12, *21*
Williams, M.L., 32, *48,* 60, 61, *77*
Williams, T., 33, *49*
Willis, S.L., 5, 12, *21, 23,* 36, *45, 48, 49,*
    52, 53, 55, 56, *57, 58,* 97, 102,
    117, 119, 123, *136, 141,* 163, 166,
    167, 172, *173, 175*

Windley, P.G., *140*
Wise, L.L., 167, *173*
Witkin, H.A., 27, *49,* 182, *202*
Witter, R.A., 222, *229*
Wyatt, R., 42, *47*

Y
Yarrow, L.J., 32, *49*
Yates, F.A., 105, *119*
Yeates, K.G., 34, *48*
York, R., *227*

Z
Zacks, R., 127, *137*
Zahn, T., 41, 42, *48*
Zuckerman, M., 42, *49*

Subject Index